MESQUITE COUNTRY

Tastes & Traditions from the Tip of Texas

HIDALGO COUNTY
HISTORICAL
MUSEUM

RIO GRANDE VALLEY OF TEXAS

Cover and Section Divider Design:
Erren Seale

Photographs and memorabilia from
Hidalgo County Historical Museum
Archives & Collections

ISBN: 1-888594-00-4

For additional information regarding this cookbook,
or the museum, write or call:

Hidalgo County Historical Museum
121 East McIntyre
Edinburg, Texas 78539
210 383-6911

Printed in the USA by

WIMMER

C O O K B O O K S

Memphis
1-800-548-2537

PREFACE

Deep in the southernmost part of Texas, where the state dips its toe into the warm waters of the Gulf, and exchanges daily greetings across the Rio Grande River with neighboring Mexico, is a place called the Rio Grande Valley. A feast of cultures, customs and flavors, this border region has so many alluring facets, it is difficult to describe. There is the excitement of living on an international border, the balmy year-round climate, the beautiful beaches of South Padre Island, the expanses of ranch lands and farms, and of course, the warmth of the people who live here. Indeed, the Valley has so much to offer that thousands of northerners have made it a second home, flocking south every winter and departing each spring to homes as far away as Wisconsin, Nebraska, and Canada.

In addition to the wonderful attributes enjoyed by these "Winter Texans" and natives, alike, the Valley is blessed with a rich and powerful history. This is a region where fates of nations have been decided, where wars have begun and ended, and where the roots of the American cattle industry can be traced. In the late 1960s, Margaret H. McAllen and a group of Valley residents decided it was imperative that this remarkable history be preserved, and in 1970, they opened the Hidalgo County Historical Museum to the public. Located in Edinburg, Texas in the Old County Jail building, its mission was to "increase and diffuse knowledge and appreciation of history..." and to "...bring about a better understanding and appreciation by children and adults of the history of the Rio Grande Valley and northern Mexico area."

This cookbook was created in keeping with that mission. All proceeds go to the Hidalgo County Historical Museum so that it may continue to preserve the regional heritage that is so precious to our community and its future generations.

From the Board of Trustees
Hidalgo County Historical Museum

Mesquite Country
is dedicated to
Mrs. Margaret H. McAllen
(1914-1995)
Chairman Emeritus and Founder
Hidalgo County Historical Museum

THE COOKBOOK COMMITTEE

Chairman
Monica Zárate Burdette

Note from the Chairman: Because of the dedicated efforts of many concerned people, this unique cookbook is finally a reality! I extend my heartfelt gratitude to all of you who helped create this special book, whether you served on a committee, submitted a recipe, or tested recipes (see the "Special Thanks" list on page 267 for a complete listing). Very special thanks to Kathryn Kaplan who persistently kept me going in the right direction, and Sandra Thomas who selflessly helped me complete the project.

Theme Development
Alice East, Chairman
Joe Edmonson
Juanita Garza
Mara Lessa Holand
Joan Jones
Kathryn Kaplan, Staff
Margaret H. McAllen
Mary Cozad-Schach

Copywriting & Editing
Bonnie Brown, Chairman
Nancy Boultinghouse
Tom Fort, Staff
Oliver Franklin, Staff
Margaret H. McAllen
Loreita McCormick
David Mycue, Staff
Jackie Nirenberg, Staff
Erren Seale

Proofreading
Sandra Thomas, Chairman
Bonnie Brown
Shannon Brown
Monica Burdette
Gilda de la Garza
Debby Dyer
Julie Flores
Amy Frase
Kathy Hook
Carol Hudsonpillar
Hilda Lewin

Design & Artwork
Joan Jones, Co-Chairman
Madelaine McLelland, Co-Chairman
Kathryn Kaplan, Staff
Margaret H. McAllen
Jackie Nirenberg, Staff

Recipe Collection
Julie Flores, Chairman
Nancy Boultinghouse
Alice East
Melissa McAllen Guerra
Colleen Hook
Carol Hudsonpillar
Madelaine McLelland
Barbara Steidinger
Victoria Shawn Stephen
Benito Treviño
Toni Treviño
Karen Valdez

Recipe Testing
Sandra Thomas, Co-Chairman
Jennifer Wright, Co-Chairman
(See "Special Thanks" on page 266 for complete list of testers)

Marketing & Public Relations
Carol Hudsonpillar, Chairman
Kathryn Kaplan, Staff
Jackie Nirenberg, Staff
Barbara Steidinger

TABLE OF CONTENTS

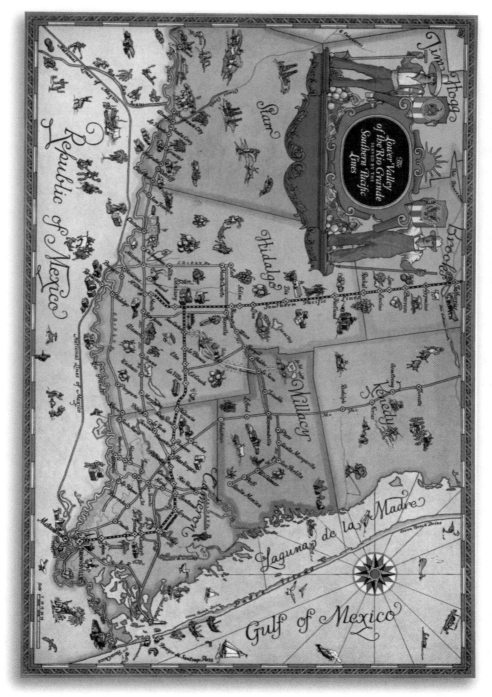

This page: *This ornate and colorful map was produced in the 1920s by Southern Pacific Railroad to help entice people to visit and settle in the Rio Grande Valley. Courtesy Union Pacific Railroad.*

INTRODUCTION

This unique cookbook is the result of months of hard work and dedication, both by the volunteers and staff of the Hidalgo County Historical Museum, and by those who worked on the Museum's first cookbook, the *Heritage Cookbook*, published in 1983. *Mesquite Country*, our newest collection of regional recipes and lore, includes many of the original recipes found in the *Heritage Cookbook*. Look for the HCHM logo 🏛 designating these recipes.

The vision of that first cookbook committee was to compile a collection of recipes that could express the unique blend of cultures that make up this border region, as well as instill a sense of pride in the people who lived here. Indeed, the *Heritage Cookbook* became a local classic and a virtual staple in the kitchens of many Rio Grande Valley residents. It is our hope that *Mesquite Country* will reach out to people all over the country, and the world, to let them in on the secret of this wonderful place we have known about all our lives.

Mesquite Country is not your run-of-the-mill cookbook. It is an album of the Valley experience, put together by individuals eager to share their love of this unique culture that is, itself, a recipe—a recipe comprised of the multitude of cultural ingredients that have blended together over the years. Each chapter begins with an exploration of a unique aspect of life in these borderlands. Historical photographs and fascinating trivia provide a backdrop for the wonderful recipes that follow. A "Gringo Glossary" at the end of the book provides additional information regarding terminology, ingredients, equipment and procedures listed in these recipes.

Each page of *Mesquite Country* offers a glimpse into this very unique little corner of the world; each recipe, a taste of the way life is lived here. *Mesquite Country* is an invitation to a place where folks still smile at each other on the street and wish each other good morning; a place where some business deals are still made over a strong cup of coffee and a steaming flour tortilla; and a place where even newcomers can feel they are always among friends.

We invite you to taste the good life in a magical place on a legendary river—a place we call *Mesquite Country*. Enjoy!

Cooking with native plants

SPANISH DAGGER
RIO GRANDE VALLEY
ESKILDSEN
PHTO

Nature's
Bounty

 Cover page: *The graceful bloom of the yucca plant sports a plume of tender white petals.*
Right: *Aztec stories, told to Spanish conquerors, spoke of salt gathering expeditions far north—suggesting that some of that salt may have come from Valley salt lakes, like Sal del Rey. From HCHM's José Cisneros collection.*
Below: *Sometimes nuisance, sometimes nutrition, the venerable prickly pear cactus once covered the Valley. Shown here in the early years being cleared by workers, the unstoppable, drought-resistant plant is sometimes used by ranchers to feed cattle (after the spines are burned off) during dry spells.*

Nature's Bounty

Mesquite

There is something uniquely beautiful about the landscape of South Texas. It is a canvas of aesthetic contradiction, monochromatic yet colorful, prickly yet soft, tropical yet desert-like, lush yet rugged. Indeed, South Texas boasts its very own eco-system—one in which the flora and fauna of both tropics and desert blend seamlessly.

The result is a wondrous alchemy of native trees, cacti and plants for which the ancient indigenous cultures of the region found many uses. These uses, both culinary and medicinal, were passed down from generation to generation and continue to thrive in South Texas culture today. Among them are a multitude of recipes and concoctions that feature the ever-present mesquite tree that characterizes this fascinating landscape. The sweet seed pods of the mesquite are used to make cakes and candies and are even eaten in their natural form when golden and ripe.

Pitaya
STRAWBERRY CACTUS

Other trees common to the area produce edible seeds and fruit. These include the Texas Ebony, or *ebano*, and the Mexican Olive Tree, or *anacahuita*. The wide variety of cacti that grow wild also provide sustenance in various forms. The prickly pear cactus, or *nopal*, produces tender baby pads that are considered a local delicacy. They are harvested in the spring, and when properly prepared, make a savory vegetable dish. The *nopal* also produces a sweet fruit, called *tuna*, that is used in many recipes. And the Spanish dagger, or *yucca*, produces white edible flowers which can be prepared a number of delicious ways.

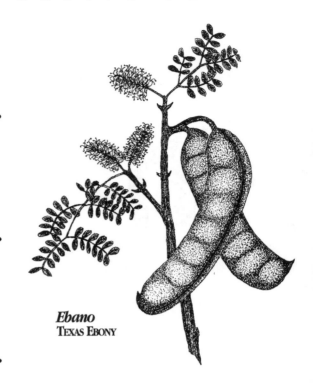

Ebano
TEXAS EBONY

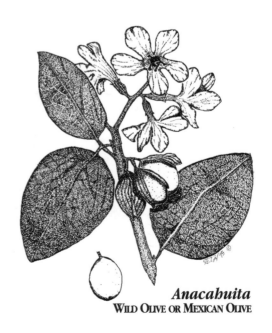

Anacahuita
WILD OLIVE OR MEXICAN OLIVE

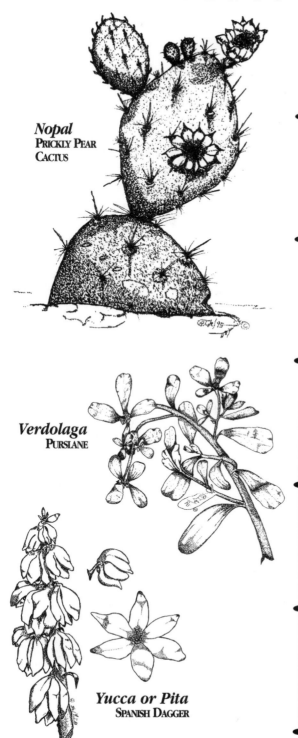

Nopal
PRICKLY PEAR
CACTUS

Verdolaga
PURSLANE

Yucca or Pita
SPANISH DAGGER

The wide variety of herbs and grasses that grow in South Texas are used not only for the wonderful flavors they add to regional dishes, but also for their many medicinal purposes. These herbs, or *yerbas*, are harvested, dried, packaged and made available even in the largest supermarkets in the area's metropolitan cities. But for the best selection, local residents go to *yerberías*, or herb shops. *Curandéras*, or medicine women, who are often the proprietors of such shops, "prescribe" specific herbs as remedies, offer healing advice, and even give spiritual guidance to their clientele.

The native plants found in the homes of

both healers and cooks are evidence of the undeniable role that nature plays in the cultural and spiritual life of these border-lands. And just as the native bounty provides for the unique tastes and delicious aromas that waft so gracefully from local kitchens, so does it flavor the lives of the people who cook and eat in those kitchens. Indeed, nature and culture share many magical secrets in Mesquite Country.

The following chapter is based on recipes originally compiled for the *Heritage Cookbook*, the Hidalgo County Historical Museum's first cookbook, published in 1983. Local botanist and chemist Benito Treviño has elaborated with his own recipes, background information, and beautifully rendered botanical drawings. Treviño has made the use and study of native plants his life's work.

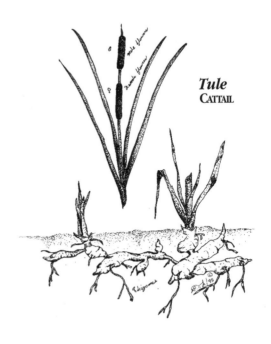

Tule
CATTAIL

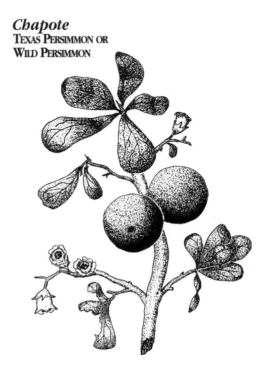

Chapote
TEXAS PERSIMMON OR
WILD PERSIMMON

M E S Q U I T E

In Season: April through July

The mesquite seed pods are similar to string beans. They are reddish-yellow when ripe and still on the tree. Later, when dry, they turn light gold-yellow and fall off the tree. The ripe seed pods are the sweetest and contain about 30 percent sugar. Both ripe and dry seed pods were a very important food source for the indigenous people and wildlife. The seed pods were ground into flour, rolled into balls, and sun dried. These mesquite balls were used like granola bars or trail mix. The flour can also be used to make mesquite bread and cookies. The juice is used to make atole (hot cereal) and jelly.

MESQUITE FLOUR

Making mesquite flour requires use of a flour mill, which can be purchased at Broadway Hardware Store in McAllen. Collect and inspect the dry mesquite beans. If you see small holes or discolorations, break off that part of the pod and discard. Place the clean, dry pods in the flour mill and pass through the mill about 5 times. After the third pass, begin to remove the larger pieces which do not appear to be pulverizing. After 5 passes, the resulting flour will be finer than cornmeal, but coarser than wheat flour.

MESQUITE SPICE CAKE

1 cup all-purpose flour
¼ cup mesquite flour
¼ teaspoon salt
½ cup packed brown sugar
1 teaspoon baking powder
¼ teaspoon baking soda
½ teaspoon cinnamon
¼ teaspoon nutmeg
⅓ cup vegetable oil
½ cup milk
1 egg, beaten

Combine all-purpose flour and next 7 ingredients. Mix thoroughly. Stir in oil, milk, and egg. Mix well. Pour into a greased 8- or 9-inch round or square cake pan. Bake at 375° for 25 to 30 minutes.

Yield: 1 cake

Toni Treviño
Rancho Lomitas

MESQUITE CHOCOLATE CHIP COOKIES

2 sticks butter or margarine
1½ cups packed brown sugar
3 eggs
1 teaspoon vanilla
1 teaspoon salt

1½ cups all-purpose flour
½ cup mesquite flour
1½ cups chocolate chips
1 cup chopped nuts

Cream butter and sugar. Mix in eggs, vanilla, and salt. Combine flours and gradually add to butter mixture, mixing well between additions. Stir in chocolate chips and nuts. Drop by tablespoonfuls onto a greased baking sheet. Bake at 350° for 12 to 15 minutes or until browned around the edges.

Yield: 36 cookies

Toni Treviño
Rancho Lomitas

MESQUITE JELLY

MESQUITE INFUSION
4 cups ripe mesquite seed pods

JELLY
1¾ cups prepared mesquite
  infusion
3½ cups sugar

1 (3-ounce) pouch liquid fruit
  pectin
2 tablespoons lemon juice

To prepare infusion, inspect each pod and remove any parts that appear discolored. Wash remaining pods thoroughly and place in a saucepan. Add water to cover. Bring to a boil and cook 60 minutes or until pods soften and fall apart. Mash with a potato masher occasionally and add more water as needed while cooking. Strain liquid through about 4 layers of cheesecloth. If liquid is not clear, strain through a coffee filter. To make jelly, follow the directions for Mint Jelly in the fruit pectin package, substituting mesquite infusion for the mint.

Note: This delicious, amber-colored jelly is delightful on biscuits or bread.

Mary Morris

🏛 ATOLE DE MESQUITE

mesquite infusion (page 18)　　**sugar**
all-purpose flour or masa harina　**cinnamon**

Place infusion in a medium saucepan. Add enough flour to thicken. Bring to a boil. Reduce heat and simmer until done. Add sugar and cinnamon as desired.

Luz Jimenez

CHAHUITE

Chahuite is a gum secreted from the mesquite tree. It is found on the trunk and on the branches. It is a common practice among local people to collect the *chahuite* and mix it with water to make a cool drink. It is also eaten like hard candy when hiking or working in the woods.

E	B	A	N	O

TEXAS EBONY

In Season: May through December

One of the most beautiful trees in South Texas, an evergreen with emerald green leaflets and edible seed pods. The Ebony seed pods, called *Maguacatas*, are 4 to 8 inches long and about 1 inch wide. They are collected when green and full, during the summer and fall. They are cracked open by twisting with both hands to expose seeds, which can be eaten raw, boiled, roasted on a grill, or roasted in a skillet. The dry roasted brown seed coat can also be used as a coffee substitute.

GREEN *MAGUACATAS*, EATEN RAW

The green seed pods can be opened and the seeds inside removed and eaten raw. The seeds are covered with a soft white seed coat when green, and a hard brown seed coat when dry. The whole seed, white seed coat and the green seed inside, can be eaten raw. Or the white seed coat can be removed and the green seed eaten by itself. The seeds are high in protein and taste like a sweet pea when green and like a peanut when dry and roasted.

GREEN *MAGUACATAS*, BOILED

The seed pods are collected while green and full. Rinse in clean water, place in a 4- to 5-quart pot, and cover with water. Boil 20 to 30 minutes or until the pods crack open. Drain and allow pods to cool to room temperature. Open pods by twisting with both hands. Seeds are ready to eat.

GREEN *MAGUACATAS*, ROASTED

Collect green, full seed pods. Rinse in clean water and pat dry. Place on a grill over hot coals and roast until lightly browned. Roast on both sides, about 15 minutes total. Allow to cool. Open pods by twisting with both hands and remove seeds, which are ready to eat.

DRY *MAGUACATA* SEEDS, RAW

Collect dry *Maguacatas* from tree or dry seeds from ground, selecting seeds not damaged by insects. Rinse in clean water and pat dry. Crack open with a small hammer over a cutting board. Separate the hard brown seed coat from the peanut-like seed inside. Discard the hard seed coat; the peanut-like seed is ready to eat.

DRY *MAGUACATA* SEEDS, ROASTED

Collect dry *Maguacatas* from tree or dry seeds from ground, selecting seeds not damaged by insects. Rinse in clean water and pat dry. Place clean, dry seeds in a heavy iron skillet; heat over medium heat, stirring constantly. When most have roasted and cracked open, remove from heat and allow to cool. With a small hammer, gently hit seed and separate the hard roasted seed coat from the roasted seed inside. The roasted seed is ready to eat. The hard roasted seed coat can be broken into small pieces and used as a coffee substitute.

A N A C A H U I T A

WILD OLIVE OR MEXICAN OLIVE

In Season: January through December

The *Anacahuita* is a small round-topped tree usually less than 30 feet high. It can be identified by its large velvet green leaves and its showy white flowers. The fruit is olive shaped and whitish-yellow when ripe. The fruit will usually fall to the ground when ripe.

WILD OLIVE PRESERVES

2 pounds wild olives   **2 pounds sugar**

Cut olives and remove seeds. Place olives in a saucepan. Add sugar. Cover with water. Bring to a boil and cook until pulp is transparent. Add extra sugar or water as needed. Place in a bowl and serve hot or cold.

Margaret Rohde McAllen

C H A P O T E

TEXAS PERSIMMON OR WILD PERSIMMON

In Season: May through August

The persimmon is a small thornless bush of 12 to 15 feet. Some trees have grown to 40 feet, but this is unusual. It can be identified by its smooth ash to gray or brownish paper-like bark. The bark peels back in some parts along the trunk. The fruit looks like a green grape, it turns dark brown to almost black when ripe.

COLD PERSIMMON PUDDING

ripe persimmon fruit, washed
½ cup light honey
1 teaspoon fresh lemon juice
2 tablespoons fresh orange juice

⅔ cup whipping cream, whipped
1 teaspoon freshly ground ginger

Mash persimmon fruit pulp through a large metal strainer into a bowl. Discard skin and seeds remaining in the strainer. Collect 2 cups pulp. Combine pulp, honey, juices, and cream. Pour into a serving bowl and chill. Sprinkle with ginger just before serving.

Persimmon Bread and Muffins

Simply use your favorite banana bread or muffin recipe and substitute persimmon pulp for the bananas.

Y U C C A   O R   P I T A
SPANISH DAGGER

In Season: February through April (flowers and stalk)
May through July (green and ripe seeds)
January through December (roots and leaves)

"Spanish Dagger" is an apt name for this plant because of the dangerously sharp spine-tipped leaves. The many varieties of the interesting yucca plant are all related to the lily family.

The Spanish settlers gave the plant the name "Our Lord's Candle" because of the creamy white, fragrant blossoms that appear on a large stalk in the spring. The blossoms are considered a great delicacy and are used in soups, salads, and with eggs. They have a flavor similar to fresh asparagus. Indians ate the buds, the flowers, the fruits, and the young stalks, and made a fermented drink from the fruit. They also extracted the fiber from the leaves and used it to make fishing nets, sandals, and rope. The roots were used as soap.

The best flowers are the older, mature ones at the base of the stalk. The young flowers and unopened buds are slightly bitter.

Steamed Spanish Dagger Bloom

fully blooming Spanish Dagger   **butter or margarine to taste**
½ cup water   **salt and pepper to taste**

When all blooms are open on the Spanish Dagger, cut the stalk at the base of the flower. Remove and wash blooms. Remove the centers and discard. Place blooms in a saucepan. Add water and steam for a few minutes. Transfer to a serving bowl and add butter. Season with salt and pepper.
Yield: 8 servings

Evelyn East
Santa Fe Ranch

FLORES DE PITA
SPANISH DAGGER FLOWERS

1½ cups mature, white yucca
  flowers
¼ cup vegetable oil
1 tomato, diced

½ onion, diced
1 clove garlic, minced
2 green chili peppers, preferably
  hot, seeded and diced

Remove petals from flowers, discarding remaining parts. Slice petals into small pieces. Heat oil in a skillet over medium heat. Stir in tomato and remaining 3 ingredients. Cook 5 minutes, stirring constantly. Stir in flower petals and cook until tender.

Variation: Cook petals in a small amount of boiling water for about 10 minutes. Drain well. Beat 6 egg whites. Beat 6 egg yolks. Combine white and yolk. Add petals and fry lightly in butter until brown. Add salt and pepper. Sprinkle with paprika.

Chonita Rodriguez

SPANISH DAGGER BLOOM "GUISADO"

fully blooming Spanish Dagger
2 tablespoons vegetable oil
2 cloves garlic
1 teaspoon salt
1 tablespoon black pepper

1 teaspoon cumin seed
½ cup water
1 (10-ounce) can Rotel diced
  tomatoes with green chiles

When all blooms are open on the Spanish Dagger, cut the stalk at the base of the flower. Remove and wash blooms. Remove the centers and discard. Place blooms in a saucepan and add oil. Grind garlic and next 3 ingredients in a *molcajete* or mortar. Mix in water. Add mixture to saucepan. Stir in Rotel tomatoes. Cover and cook for about 7 minutes over medium heat. Serve hot.

Yield: 8 servings

Note: If desired, substitute 3 medium diced tomatoes and 1 minced serrano or jalapeño chili pepper for the canned Rotel tomatoes.

Evelyn East
Santa Fe Ranch

M A G U E Y

CENTURY PLANT

In Season: January through December

The century plant grows low to the ground with long, broad leaves and vicious, jagged spines on the edges. It blooms only once in its lifetime of 10 to 75 years. The flower stalk will grow until it is 15 to 30 feet high. After blooming, the plant shrivels and dies. The pale yellow flowers form clusters on short stems branching from the stalk. The bud of the flower-stalk is considered a delicacy when roasted. The large leaves of the *maguey* are used to line the pit in which *barbacoa* is cooked.

Maguey Candy

Remove the center leaves or top of the plant with a sharp tool, like a small ax. Remove the pulp from the center, leaving a bowl-like depression. Overnight, this depression will fill with a liquid called "*agua miel*" or honey water. Collect this liquid and serve it hot or cold, or place in a pan and simmer over low heat until it cooks down. When thick and dark in color, spoon onto wax paper. The result is a delicious candy.

Maria Gonzalez

N O P A L

PRICKLY PEAR CACTUS

In Season: March through April (pads)
May through August (tunas)

The pads (*nopalitos*) and fruit (*tunas*) of the prickly pear cactus have been table fare for man in the Americas since before there were tables. The prickly pear fruit was especially popular with the Indians of Texas and Mexico long before the Spanish arrived.

The Coahuiltecan Indians, a tribe that inhabited the Texas coast and all of South Texas until they were decimated by Spanish-introduced diseases, preserved cactus *tunas* by squeezing out the juice and sun-drying them. Even the skins and seeds were dried and pounded into flour.

Spanish explorer Cabeza de Vaca said that the dried fruit was placed in "hampers like figs". Because of this widespread use of cactus *tunas* by the Indians, they became known as Indian figs.

Gathering cactus *tunas* must have been a tough assignment. They had no butane burners to burn off the stickers. If that wasn't bad enough, Apache legend has it that all cacti with edible fruit were covered with sharp spines that made it nearly impossible to pick the fruit. One of the Apache demigods, called "Killer of Enemies", took pity on the people and by magic, caused most of the stickers to disappear. One wonders why he didn't finish the job.

Prickly pear cacti have two types of stickers, regular spines about ¾ to 2½ inches long, and glochids (glo' kids). Glochids are nefarious little stickers that this genus of cactus produces especially to bedevil unsuspecting human beings. They are from ⅛ to as much as ⅝ of an inch long. Individually, they are nearly invisible, but when embedded in the sensitive flesh on the inside of the fingers, they feel like fence posts.

Despite the spines and glochids, modern folks follow the Indian's example and harvest prickly pears for a variety of uses. Sometime in the spring, the new pads, *nopalitos*, are picked. These *nopalitos* can be breaded with cornmeal and fried, or they can be boiled, cut into chunks, and included in omelets.

Fresh *nopalitos* can be found in season for sale at markets in South Texas and they are even available in cans on some supermarket shelves. Campers in cactus country might like to try young cactus pads roasted on the coals of an open campfire in early spring.

The *tunas* are probably more popular for human gourmandizing than *nopalitos*. The *tunas*, which ripen between July and September, can be peeled, cut up, sugared, and eaten like berries, with or without cream. They can even be made into a pie. The juice can be cooked out of the *tunas* and used to make wine or jelly, or in combination with the pulp to make jam or marmalade.

Before rushing out to the nearest cactus patch to get your share of the barbed bounty, you should review a few precautions. Never try to handle the fruit barehanded or even with gloves. Gloves soon become loaded with glochids, which work through to your hands. So take along a pair of kitchen tongs, and pick only the dark purple *tunas*. They are fully ripe and will be filled with juice.

Frank Beesley
Texas Highways, May, 1982

CONCENTRATED *TUNA* JUICE

The best way to collect *tunas* is to use tongs to twist the *tunas* from the cactus pad. Place *tunas* in a large bowl. Clean *tunas* under running water, using latex gloves and a plastic vegetable brush to rub or scrub the spines off. Cut the cleaned *tunas* into thirds or quarters and place in a 4- to 5-quart pot. Add water to just cover. Bring to a boil for about 20 to 30 minutes. Use a potato masher to mash *tunas* as they cook. Strain juice through four layers of cheesecloth.

SPARKLING *TUNA* COOLER

½ cup concentrated *tuna* juice
 (above)
⅓ cup sugar

3 tablespoons lemon juice
sparkling water

Combine *tuna* juice and sugar in a small saucepan. Cook over low heat until sugar dissolves. Remove from heat and stir in lemon juice. Allow to cool. When ready to serve, dilute mixture with three parts sparkling water. Serve over ice.

Toni Treviño
Rancho Lomitas

TUNA PINEAPPLE PIE

1 (3-ounce) package lemon jello
2 cups concentrated *tuna* juice,
 boiling (above)
1 (15-ounce) can crushed
 pineapple, drained

½ cup chopped nuts
1 cup whipped topping
1 graham cracker pie crust

Dissolve jello in boiling juice. Chill until thickened, but not set. Carefully stir in pineapple and nuts. Fold in whipped topping. Pour into pie crust and chill 3 hours or until firm.

Yield: 8 servings

Toni Treviño
Rancho Lomitas

MOLDED *TUNA* CREAM CHEESE DELIGHT

1 (6-ounce) package lemon jello
1¾ cup water, boiling
8 medium *tunas*, cleaned

1-1½ cups concentrated *tuna* juice (page 26)
½ (8-ounce) package cream cheese, softened

Dissolve jello in boiling water. Chill until thickened, but not set. Cut *tunas* in half. Use a teaspoon to scoop out seeds. Remove pulp and puree. Combine pulp and enough juice to make 2 cups. Combine *tuna* mixture and cream cheese. Add to jello and blend well. Pour into a mold and chill until set.
Yield: 8 servings

Toni Treviño
Rancho Lomitas

TUNA JELLY

2½ cups concentrated *tuna* juice (page 26)
1 (1¾-ounce) package powdered fruit pectin

¼ cup lemon juice
3½ cups sugar

Combine *tuna* juice and pectin in a saucepan. Bring to a fast boil. Add lemon juice and sugar. Boil 4 minutes. Remove from heat and skim juice. Pour into sterilized jelly jars and seal.

Toni Treviño
Rancho Lomitas

FROZEN *TUNA* POPS

16-20 *tunas*
½-1 cup water

½ cup sugar
3 tablespoons lemon juice

Wash *tunas* under running water to remove thorns. Cut into quarters and place in a blender or food processor. It may be necessary to do this in 2 batches. Add ½ cup water to each batch. Puree. Strain juice through 4 layers of cheesecloth. Add water as needed to juice to equal 3 cups. Mix in sugar and lemon juice. Freeze in plastic ice cube or pop molds, placing a stick in the center of each.

Toni Treviño
Rancho Lomitas

NOPALITOS CON HUEVO
PRICKLY PEAR PADS WITH EGG

small, tender, new *nopalitos*
mesquite leaves (optional)
salt to taste
½ small onion
6 cloves garlic
1 stalk fresh cilantro

2 tablespoons vegetable oil or
    bacon drippings
¼ cup diced onion
½ cup chopped cilantro
3 teaspoons chili powder
4 eggs, lightly beaten
black pepper to taste

Collect *nopalitos* and place in a bucket. Use mesquite leaves to separate pads, or place in a bucket containing water. To prepare, cut away the entire outer edge and remove remaining spines with a sharp knife. Wash pads and cut into short, thin strips or cubes. Prepare enough to equal about 7 cups. Place in a deep saucepan. Cover with water. Add salt and next 3 ingredients. Bring to a boil. Cook 20 minutes or until tender.

Discard onion, garlic, and cilantro. Drain nopalitos in a colander. In a skillet, heat oil. Add diced onion and chopped cilantro and sauté. Mix in *nopalitos*. Add chili powder. Simmer until ready to serve. Add egg and season with salt and pepper. Stir gently until eggs are cooked.

Yield: 4 servings

Variations: Omit egg and chili powder and serve as a vegetable side dish.

Omit egg and chili powder and add diced, boiled potato.

Add chopped fresh tomato to recipe or any of its variations.

Soak dried shrimp in water for a few minutes and drain. Add shrimp to nopalitos in a saucepan and simmer until ready to serve. Omit egg.

Luz Jimenez

NOPALITOS RELLENOS
STUFFED PRICKLY PEAR PADS

small (2- to 3-inch) *nopalitos*
mesquite leaves (optional)
salt to taste
1 small onion, quartered
6 cloves garlic
1 sprig fresh cilantro
cheddar cheese slices

Swiss cheese slices
chopped onion (optional)
eggs, beaten
all-purpose flour
black pepper to taste
vegetable oil for frying

Collect *nopalitos* and place in a bucket. Use mesquite leaves to separate pads, or place in a bucket containing water. To prepare, cut away the entire outer edge and remove remaining spines with a sharp knife. Wash pads and place in a saucepan. Add water to cover. Bring to a boil. Add salt and next 3 ingredients. Boil until tender. Discard onion, garlic, and cilantro. Drain pads and cool slightly. Place a slice of each cheese and chopped onion on a pad and top with another pad. Repeat with remaining pads. Prepare a batter using egg, flour, salt, and pepper. Dip each pad sandwich in batter, then fry in about 1 inch of hot oil in a skillet until nicely browned. Serve with a tomato sauce with chilies.

Margaret H. McAllen
McAllen Ranch

ENSALADA DE NOPALITOS
CACTUS SALAD

This is at its best when very young, tender cactus pads are used. The pads are small and delicate, and it is said that one should only use those that come out after the first spring rains.

2 cups cubed fresh *nopalitos*
3 medium tomatoes, peeled and chopped
3 tablespoons olive oil
4 teaspoons red wine vinegar
¼ teaspoon dried oregano
⅓ onion, finely chopped
½ teaspoon salt, or to taste
6 sprigs fresh cilantro
freshly ground black pepper

jalapeños en escabeche (marinated canned jalapeños), seeded and cut into strips, for garnish
1 small onion, sliced, for garnish
1 medium tomato, sliced, for garnish
1 avocado, sliced, for garnish

Combine *nopalitos* and next 8 ingredients in a large bowl. Let stand for about 60 minutes to allow flavors to blend. Place in a lettuce-lined serving dish and garnish with jalapeños and remaining 3 ingredients.

Fran Alger

ENSALADA DE NOPALITOS CON QUESO
PRICKLY PEAR SALAD WITH CHEESE

2 cups diced cooked *nopalitos*
1-2 tomatoes, diced
1 cup cubed white cheese
fresh cilantro, chopped
onion, chopped

serrano chili peppers, finely chopped, to taste
salt and pepper to taste
dried oregano to taste
olive oil
lime juice

Combine *nopalitos* and next 5 ingredients in a bowl. Season with salt, pepper, and oregano. When ready to serve, add oil and lime juice.

Yield: 4 servings

Carmen Guerra

🏠 *NOPALITO* AND CRABMEAT SALAD

1 (32-ounce) jar sliced *nopalitos*,
   drained and slices halved
3 medium-size red potatoes,
   boiled, peeled, and cubed
2 stalks celery, finely diced
2 carrots, finely diced
20 small pimiento-stuffed olives,
   sliced in thirds
1 bunch fresh cilantro, stemmed
   and chopped
3 fresh or canned jalapeño
   peppers, finely chopped

1 hard-cooked egg, chopped
1 pound cooked crabmeat
½ cup mayonnaise
salt and pepper to taste
1 head romaine lettuce
1 (2-ounce) jar red pimiento, cut
   into strips
3 avocados, halved lengthwise,
   sliced, and peeled
1 orange, cut into 12 slices

Combine *nopalitos* and next 7 ingredients in a large salad bowl. Carefully mix in crabmeat. Add mayonnaise, salt, and pepper. Separate lettuce leaves and divide among 6 serving plates. Top each with crabmeat mixture. Garnish with pimiento, avocado, and orange.

Yield: 6 servings

Note: Sliced nopalitos can be found in the Mexican food section of the grocery store.

McAllen Monitor

NOPALITO PIZZA

I came up with this recipe while trying to get our children to eat nopalitos. Since they love pizza, I thought it would be good.

3½ cups tender cactus leaves,
   thorns removed and diced
1 pizza crust
1½ cups pizza sauce

2 cups grated mozzarella,
   Monterey Jack, or American
   cheese

Place diced cactus in a saucepan and cover with water. Boil until tender. Drain, cover with paper towels, and set aside. Place crust on a 10-inch pizza pan. Spread sauce over crust. Sprinkle with cactus and cheese. Bake at 325° for 30 minutes or until crust browns and cheese melts.

Yield: 10 slices

Aurora Garcia

NOPALITOS CON CAMARON
NOPALITOS WITH SHRIMP

12 *nopalitos*, cleaned, washed, and chopped
1 teaspoon cumin seed
⅛ teaspoon black peppercorns
6 cloves garlic
2 tablespoons vegetable oil
¼ cup chopped onion
salt to taste
3 tablespoons chili powder
1 pound raw shrimp, peeled and deveined

Place *nopalitos* in a 3-quart saucepan. Add water to cover and boil about 30 minutes. Drain and rinse well. Grind cumin seed, peppercorns, and garlic in a *molcajete* (mortar). Heat oil in a skillet. Add nopalitos, cumin mixture, onion, salt, and chili powder. Cook over low heat for about 15 minutes. Add shrimp and cook 5 minutes.

Variation: If desired, add 3 beaten eggs at the end and cook until done.

To make a soup, add 4 cups water when shrimp are cooked. Heat and serve.

Mary Lou Medina

P I T A Y A
STRAWBERRY CACTUS

In Season: May through June

This cactus grows in clumps near the ground. Each individual branch is 5 to 12 inches in length and about 3 inches in diameter. Its flowers are numerous and of a brilliant pinkish-red to reddish-purple color. The fruits are round, about 1½ inches in diameter, and covered with clusters of thorns. The fruit is greenish-brown to light pinkish-purple when ripe. The thorn clusters easily rub off when the fruit is ripe.

The delicious fruit has a strawberry flavor and is used in making preserves. The fruit can be peeled, chilled, and served fresh or with whipped cream.

V I Z N A G A

HORSE CRIPPLER

In Season: March through April

This is a cactus more popularly known as the "Devil's Pin Cushion" or the "Devil's Head". The thorns are very strong and sit star-fashioned in groups of 6, usually down the ridges of the plant. Candy is a popular food made from the cactus plant.

Marcelino Aldape was a bone-picker. During the 1930's, he traveled around the ranch country and was a well-known figure with his covered wagon and team of mules. He always wore *huaraches* (sandals) made of old tires and tied on with rawhide. He collected the bones from livestock that had died on the ranches, loaded them on his wagon, and then sold them. He always camped out in the brush and often made a small shelter with rawhide and the bones he had found, or he slept in his wagon with the bones, which had been bleached white by the sun. While camping and searching for the bones, he also collected *viznaga* cactus which he made into candy. He peddled this candy around to the various ranches he visited while searching for bones. In view of the fact that he took only one bath a year, in the spring, it is easy to see why some people were reluctant to buy his candy, but I must admit, he did not lack for buyers and sold all of the *viznaga* candy that he made. He refused to have his picture taken. On seeing a camera, he would duck his head, whip up the mules, and off they would go in a cloud of dust.

Margaret H. McAllen

🏠 VIZNAGA CANDY

Peel the *viznaga* skin and remove spines. Cut the plant into large slices and boil in water for 20 minutes or until barely tender. Do not overcook. Drain. In a 4- to 5-quart saucepan, place 3½ pounds sugar. Add water to cover. Bring to boil over medium-high heat, stirring constantly. Reduce heat and add *viznaga*. Stir gently and simmer until *viznaga* becomes candied and the liquid evaporates. Add food coloring, if desired, to vary the candy's color.

Maria Gonzalez

CABUCHES
FLOWER OF VIZNAGA

1 tablespoon vegetable oil
8 ounces *cabuches*
½ onion, diced
½ tomato, diced

2 cloves garlic, mashed
fresh jalapeño pepper, chopped, to taste
salt and pepper to taste

Heat oil in a skillet. Add *cabuches* and cook and stir until almost done. Add onion, tomato, and garlic. Sauté until softened. Add jalapeño pepper and cook over low heat until liquid is almost evaporated. Season with salt and pepper.

C H I L I P I Q U I N

In Season: April through December (in the wild)

Chilipiquin or *chili del monte* (chili from the woods) offers a special treat for those who enjoy a hot pepper with their meal, but do not have a grocery store nearby. If the little pepper is oblong, it is called *pequin*. If it is round, it is called *chiltecpin*.

The hottest *pequins* are those that are heat and water stressed. The hotness in peppers is measured in Scoville Heat Units, on a scale from 0 (mild) to 300,000 (very hot). A serrano chili pepper has a rating of 10,000 to 20,000 Scoville Units. The little *chilipiquin* has a rating of 50,000 to 100,000 Scoville Units!

SALSA DE CHILIPIQUIN

4 cloves garlic
few black peppercorns
½ - ¾ cup water
3 tablespoons olive oil

1 cup diced wild green *chilipiquin*
⅓ cup lime juice
1½ teaspoons salt
chopped fresh cilantro to taste

Grind garlic and peppercorns in a *molcajete*. Add water. Place in a blender and puree. Add oil and blend. Combine garlic mixture, *chilipiquin*, and remaining 3 ingredients.
Yield: about 1 cup

Luz Jimenez

P E P P E R G R A S S

In Season: April through December

Also called Birdpepper, Peppercress, and Poor Man's Pepper.

Each tiny seed pod has a pungent peppery taste and adds a distinctive flavor to raw salads. It is rich in Vitamin C, Vitamin A, and iron. Stems grow from a few inches to over 2 feet high. Flowers are tiny, with 4 petals. Do not cook peppergrass as it destroys the vitamins. Add it chopped to soups and stews just before serving. Sprinkle on top of scrambled eggs and broiled fish.

Chop peppergrass and blend with butter or margarine. Use on toast or hot biscuits. For a flavored vinegar, add 1 tablespoon chopped peppergrass to 1 cup cider vinegar. Allow to age 1 week before using.

D I E N T E D E L E Ó N

DANDELIONS

In Season: March through May (most tender)

Dandelions usually grow in fields and pastures and sometimes in yards and gardens. The plant is a rosette of oblong, toothy leaves attached to a tap root. Yellow, silky, ball flower heads identify this plant. Seeds become wind-borne, attached to a streamer of silk thread. Although the dandelion is reputed to have medicinal value, it is well known as an early spring, green vegetable, rich in Vitamin A. Unless the leaves are gathered at a tender stage and properly prepared, they can be very bitter. When cooking, be sure to change the water at least twice. When the flower stems appear, it is usually too late for the leaves to be any good.

Dig the root 2 to 3 inches below the ground level. Cut off the top and any white leaves. These can be sliced in a salad or boiled and seasoned as a vegetable. The roots may also be roasted over low heat or in an oven until completely dry and dark brown. Grind and make coffee. Use about 1 teaspoon per cup of hot water; this is somewhat stronger than coffee, but it has a good flavor.

Ivy Holzem

🏠 DANDELION WINE

1 gallon dandelion blossoms, washed	4 lemons, quartered
1 gallon water, boiling	4 pounds sugar
4 oranges, quartered	1 (.06-ounce) cake yeast

Combine blossoms and boiling water. Let stand 24 to 48 hours. Strain liquid, discarding blossoms. Add oranges and remaining 3 ingredients to liquid. Let stand 4 to 6 weeks. Strain liquid, bottle, and seal tightly.
Yield: about 2 gallons

Bessie Yeary

E P A Z O T E

In Season: January through December

(Not a native plant, but much used and easy to grow.)

When this plant is referred to as *epazote de comer*, it is used as a seasoning. When the word *epazote* is used by itself, it is used for tea, and this bush is more purple in color. The odor of the plant is very strong until it is cooked.

The plant can be about 3½ feet tall, if it gets enough water. The leaves are long, green, and serrated, with stiff and woody stems. The flowers grow in loose spikes. Dried *epazote* can be used, but the fresh leaves are much better. It is considered one of the best seasonings in Mexico.

Take a piece of the dried stem with leaves, cut or gash the stem in several places, and drop into whatever you are cooking in the way of vegetables, dried beans, seafoods, or meats. It is especially good in crab dishes, and beans should always be cooked with *epazote*. It is especially good in *menudo*. *Epazote* allegedly takes the gas out of beans.

T U L E

CATTAIL

Tule has been a very useful plant. The Indians used the fluffy down as a diaper filler. Pioneers used the down as blanket and pillow filler, and they used the leaves to weave floor mats and baskets. During the Civil War, the down was used as a wound dressing. During World War I, the down was used as a filler for life preservers, and during World War II, it was used as a substitute for cotton and silk parachutes. The rhizome (the tips), which are high in starch, can be eaten in many different ways. They are sweet and delicious raw in salads, boiled, baked, roasted in the campfire, or cooked in soups and stews. Before use, the tender rhizome need to be washed in clean water, scrubbed, and peeled.

CATTAIL STEW

salt and pepper to taste
2 pounds stew beef
1 bay leaf
½ cup dry red wine
2 pounds tender cattail rhizome
  tips, scrubbed and peeled

4-6 medium onions
1 (28-ounce) can tomatoes,
  undrained
2 cups water

Combine salt, pepper, and next 3 ingredients and marinate in the refrigerator overnight. Chop rhizome tips and onions into ¼-inch pieces. Place beef mixture in a skillet over low heat. Add rhizome tips, onion, tomato, and water. Season with salt and pepper. Simmer 2 to 3 hours.
Yield: 6 servings

V E R D O L A G A
PURSLANE

In Season: March through December

This wild plant is a ground creeper, with many small, oval, succulent, green leaves, found in moist areas. It can be purchased in many Mexican markets. It has an unusual flavor, something like *nopalitos*. *Verdolaga* has a long central root with many runners extending from it. It is similar to domestic purslane. Each fleshy stem contains a multitude of light green succulent leaves. The tender stems and leaves can be eaten raw in salads, or cooked in stew or in casseroles. The thick stems can also be pickled in vinegar and pickling spices.

VERDOLAGA

verdolaga
2 tablespoons bacon drippings
1 clove garlic, mashed
1 tomato, diced

½ cup diced onion
salt and pepper to taste
½ cup grated cheddar cheese

Separate verdolaga leaves and stems, collecting leaves and tender stems to measure about 3 cups. Place in a saucepan and cover with water. Cook for about 10 minutes. Drain in a colander. Heat bacon drippings in a skillet. Stir in garlic, tomato, and onion and sauté until onion is transparent. Add verdolaga and cook 15 to 20 minutes. Season with salt and pepper. Sprinkle cheese over top and allow to melt before serving.

Yield: about 2 to 3 cups

Maria Gonzalez

LEBANESE FATTOUCH SALAD WITH PURSLANE

3 ripe tomatoes, cut into large chunks
1 large bell pepper, chopped into medium-size pieces
1 large yellow bell pepper, chopped into medium-size pieces
1 large red bell pepper, chopped into medium-size pieces
1 large red onion, thinly sliced
3 green onions, diagonally sliced
2 cucumbers, thinly sliced

salt and pepper to taste
1 cup chopped fresh parsley
1 bunch fresh mint, finely chopped
1 cup snipped verdolaga leaves
1 teaspoon ground sumac
1 clove garlic, minced
juice of 3 or 4 lemons
¼ cup extra virgin olive oil
2 pitas, crisply toasted and crumbled

Combine tomato and next 6 ingredients in a large bowl. In a small bowl, mix together salt, pepper, and next 7 ingredients. Pour over vegetable mixture and toss. Add pita and toss.

Yield: 6 to 8 servings

Note: Ground sumac can be found in Middle Eastern markets.

Appetizers & beverages

The Great Outdoors

BIG GAME IN THE VALLEY

DID YOU KNOW?

THE RIO GRANDE VALLEY IS CONSIDERED TO BE ONE OF THE TOP BIRD WATCHING AREAS IN THE COUNTRY. THERE HAVE BEEN 389 SPECIES OF BIRDS OBSERVED HERE. WITH ROUGHLY 650 SPECIES OF BIRDS NESTING IN NORTH AMERICA, THE VALLEY IS HOME TO 60% OF THESE THROUGHOUT THE YEAR. THIS INCREDIBLE STATISTIC IS WHAT BRINGS BIRD WATCHERS FROM ALL OVER THE COUNTRY TO THE VALLEY EVERY YEAR.

Above: Early Valley hunters took game of incredible variety. This cougar was shot in the ranch lands circa 1919.
Cover page: "Grab yer pole and let's go fishin'," the weekend battle cry of many generations of Valleyites!
At right: Catfish of enormous size used to be commonplace in Valley canals and inlets.
Opposite: Paleo Indians hunted buffalo with rocks and spears. From HCHM's José Cisneros collection.

The Great Outdoors

Long before Europeans arrived in the area now known as the Rio Grande Valley of South Texas, the land belonged to the Coahuiltecan (ko-ah-WEEL-tay-can) Indians, a hardy native people who lived by hunting animals and gathering herbs and plants. They were comprised of several groups that inhabited different areas of this vast region. In the area that is now Mercedes, Texas, a group known as the Tampacuas once thrived. Another group, the Karankawas, lived near the sparkling waters of the Gulf of Mexico, on Padre Island.

For thousands of years, all the Coahuiltecan people managed to thrive in this rugged environment, braving the scorching heat and strong winds that still typify the area's climate. Using tools and weapons of stone, wood, and bone they hunted for food. Deer, turkey, and rabbit were among the most common prey that fell to their flint-tipped arrows and darts. Knives and scrapers of the same flint were used to prepare the kill for eating.

When larger game was lacking, they would eat almost anything that crawled or slithered—snakes, worms, insects, even snails. Their ability to adapt to environmental changes and to live in harmony with nature provided a blueprint for survival from which others would learn.

Although the arrival of the Spanish in around 1749 brought about the virtual disappearance of the Coahuiltecan way of life, the Indians left behind a great legacy to the land and its future inhabitants. The Spaniards used this legacy to survive. By adopting Coahuiltecan food gathering techniques, they discovered the great bounty that existed in a land they once thought was barren. And they developed a love for the hunt— a love that would eventually be passed on to future generations of South Texans.

Today, despite urban growth, the natural environment of the Rio Grande Valley is still as rugged as when the Indians

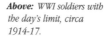

Above: WWI soldiers with the day's limit, circa 1914-17.
Below left: *Though still good, bird hunting at the turn of the century was phenomenal, as quail, whitewing dove, and migrating ducks (shown here) blackened the sky.*

knew it and is renowned as a sportsman's paradise. People from all over the country come to the Valley to enjoy unparalleled hunting and fishing. Whitewing dove, deer, javelina, and other game are plentiful, and the unique hospitality of these borderlands lures the hunters back year after year. For many local residents, hunting is an important part of cultural life and is still one of the most revered rites of passage between father and son. Fishing, too,

Above: Nothing beats a day fishing with your buddies, as these 1920s gents can attest.
Right:
Like most of Texas, the Valley has an ample supply of deer. c. 1909.
Below:
For many South Texans, the hunting tradition is passed down from father to son.

plays an important role in local life, as the warm waters of the Gulf are just a sea breeze away. Fishing enthusiasts enjoy casting their lines into the

hyper-saline Laguna Madre—the bountiful shallow bay between the mainland and Padre Island—where they catch plenty of redfish and speckled trout, or embarking on a deep-sea adventure to catch a prize red snapper or kingfish. Each season brings new bounty and the opportunity to celebrate it with others. A weekend of hunting or fishing is usually followed by a wonderful feast, whether it be a backyard barbecue or an elegant seated dinner.

Clearly, the ancient connection between man and his environment still exists in South Texas.

And although much has changed since the Coahuiltecans roamed this rugged land, today's Mesquite Country natives still relish their natural surroundings as much as their indigenous predecessors did some 3,500 years ago.

Left: Drawn by year 'round flowering plants, many varieties of hummingbirds frequent Valley ranches, backyards and wild areas. **Below:** *The rugged and dense chapparal north of Edinburg in 1912 provided ideal hunting conditions for Dr. McMillan, Jim Fox and R.B. Curry.*

ARMADILLO EGGS

1 (7-ounce) can jalapeño
peppers, drained and seeded
1 pound mozzarella cheese,
sliced
1 pound mozzarella cheese,
grated

1 pound lean ground sausage
1 cup biscuit baking mix
2 eggs, beaten
1 (6-ounce) box Shake and Bake
coating mix

Stuff the peppers with sliced cheese. Combine grated cheese, sausage, and baking mix. Enclose the peppers by pressing the mixture around the outside. Dip in egg and roll in coating mix. Bake at 350° for 45 minutes.

Yield: about 20 peppers

Note: Peppers can be prepared ahead of time, frozen, and baked as needed. Leftovers also freeze well.

Elizabeth Ballard

AVOCADO CRAB MORNAY

1 stick butter, divided
¼ cup all-purpose flour
1 cup half-and-half
¾ cup chicken broth
¼ cup sherry
¼ cup Parmesan cheese, plus
extra for topping

2 tablespoons grated Gruyère
cheese
dash of cayenne pepper
salt to taste
6 green onions, minced
1½ pounds crabmeat
3 avocados, peeled and diced

Melt 4 tablespoons butter in a saucepan. Whisk in flour. Add half-and-half and broth and stir until smooth. Blend in sherry, cheeses, cayenne pepper, and salt. Remove from heat. In a large skillet, gently sauté green onions in remaining 4 tablespoons butter until softened. Add crabmeat and avocado. Stir until heated through. Add cheese sauce and heat. Mound mixture in scallop shells or individual ramekins. Sprinkle with Parmesan cheese. Bake at 500° for 5 minutes. Serve immediately.

Mary Vance Jones

SOUTH TEXAS CEVICHE

1½ pounds raw red snapper
fillets, diced
10-15 limes
6 large tomatoes, diced
2 medium onions, diced

1 handful fresh cilantro,
chopped
2 serrano chili peppers, seeded
and diced (optional)
salt to taste
crackers or tortilla chips

Place snapper in a large bowl. Squeeze lime juice over fish to cover. Mix in tomato and next 3 ingredients. Season with salt and refrigerate at least 1 hour, 30 minutes, or overnight. Eat on crackers or chips.

Yield: 8 to 10 servings

Note: The acid from the lime juice "cooks" the fish.

Any mild white-meat fish can be substituted, such as speckled trout, redfish, or cod.

Ruby dela Garza Krautkremmer

SPINACH QUESADILLAS

2 tablespoons chopped green
onions
1 tablespoon chopped bell
pepper
salt and pepper to taste
6 cups grated Monterey Jack
cheese

2 (10-ounce) packages frozen
chopped spinach (thawed and
squeezed dry)
1 teaspoon finely minced garlic
1 teaspoon ground cumin
48 flour tortillas

Sauté onions and bell pepper in a double boiler. Mix in salt, pepper, and next 4 ingredients. Place a tortilla on a lightly greased griddle. Spread about ¼ cup spinach mixture over tortilla. Cover with another tortilla. Cook about 1 minute on each side, or until spinach mixture melts. Cut into wedges and serve.

Yield: 24 quesadillas or 96 wedges

Note: This recipe can be halved for smaller parties.

Sergio Rodriguez
Executive Chef
Catering by Don Strange
San Antonio, Texas

BRIE AND PAPAYA QUESADILLAS

½ yellow onion
½ cup water
10 flour tortillas
1 pound Brie or Camembert
   cheese, cut into¼-inch strips

2 poblano chili peppers,
   roasted, peeled, and diced
1 ripe papaya or mango, peeled,
   seeded, and diced
4 tablespoons butter, melted
¼ cup vegetable oil

Cut onion into thin slices, then cut slices in half. Bring water to a boil in a medium skillet. Add onion and remove from heat. Let stand 12 minutes or until softened. Drain and set aside. Heat a nonstick or well-seasoned skillet over medium heat for several minutes. When hot, place tortillas, one at a time, in skillet to soften for about 15 seconds on each side. To assemble quesadillas, place a few strips of cheese on half of each tortilla. Top with onion and 1 tablespoon each of pepper and papaya. Combine butter and oil. Fold tortillas in half and brush with butter mixture. Brown quesadillas on both sides in a heated skillet over medium heat. Keep warm in a 200° oven on a baking sheet while remaining quesadillas brown. Cut each into 3 wedges.

Yield: 10 to 20 servings

Note: Serve with Jícama And Orange Salad (page 119). If preparing ahead, cover and refrigerate after assembling quesadillas. Bring to room temperature before browning.

Colleen Curran Hook

TORTILLA ROLL-UPS WITH *TOMATILLO SALSA*

TORTILLA ROLL-UPS

2 (8-ounce) packages cream
   cheese, softened
½ cup chopped black olives
2 teaspoons ground cumin
1 teaspoon garlic salt

½ cup chopped jalapeño
   peppers
½ pound ground venison,
   cooked (optional)
8-10 flour tortillas

TOMATILLO SALSA

3 cups water
2½ teaspoons salt
3 cloves garlic
4 serrano chili peppers

1 pound tomatillos, husks
   removed
½ cup fresh cilantro
¼ cup finely chopped onion

Combine cream cheese and next 5 ingredients. Mix well. Divide evenly among tortillas and spread. Roll tortillas in jelly-roll fashion. Wrap in wax paper and place in an air-tight container or plastic bag. Refrigerate several hours. When ready to serve, cut each tortilla into 1-inch slices and arrange on a serving platter. Serve with salsa.

To make salsa, bring water and salt to a boil in a large saucepan. Add garlic, peppers, and tomatillos. Cook, uncovered, for 8 to 10 minutes or until tomatillos are softened. Drain, reserving ½ cup liquid. When cool, remove pepper and tomatillo stems. Place garlic, peppers, tomatillos, cilantro, and reserved liquid in a blender or food processor. Puree. Stir in onion.

Yield: 10 to 12 servings

Note: May be doubled and frozen.

Salsa will keep up to 1 week in the refrigerator.

Kathryn Kaplan

JÍCAMA

A turnip-like tuberous white root plant with a sweet, astringent taste. Peel and cut in strips or slices. Dust with salt, paprika, and lime juice and serve as an appetizer. A bit of chili powder can also be sprinkled over it. Small strips of jícama are good in a tossed green salad.

HONGOS EN ESCABECHE
MARINATED MUSHROOMS

8 ounces fresh mushrooms
¼ cup red wine vinegar
⅓ cup vegetable oil
½ teaspoon dried tarragon
¼ teaspoon salt

1½ teaspoons lemon juice
½ clove garlic, mashed
sliced or chopped pimiento or
  chopped parsley (optional)

Discard mushroom stems, if desired, and place mushrooms in a bowl. Combine vinegar and next 5 ingredients in a jar. Shake well and pour over mushrooms. Refrigerate several hours, stirring occasionally. Add pimiento or parsley for color.

Yield: 4 to 6 servings

Leslie Stephen Renzi

SPINACH STUFFED MUSHROOMS

1 (10-ounce) package frozen
  creamed spinach, thawed
¼ teaspoon lemon pepper
½ teaspoon garlic powder
¼ teaspoon salt
1 stick butter, divided

12-18 large fresh mushrooms,
  stems removed and reserved
1 tablespoon chopped green
  onions
Parmesan cheese

Combine spinach and next 3 ingredients in a bowl. Melt 5 tablespoons butter in a small saucepan. Dip mushroom caps in butter and place on a baking sheet, stem-side up. Mince mushroom stems. Melt remaining 3 tablespoons butter in a small skillet over medium heat. Add mushroom stems and onions and sauté until softened. Add to spinach mixture and mix well. Fill mushroom caps with spinach mixture. Sprinkle with cheese. Bake in a preheated 375° oven for 12 to 15 minutes. Serve immediately with crisp white wine.

Yield: 6 servings

Kathryn Kaplan

MARINATED MUSHROOMS

1 pound whole or sliced fresh
mushrooms
1 small to medium onion, thinly
sliced
¼ cup red wine or tarragon
vinegar
2 teaspoons salt
1 teaspoon black pepper
½ cup extra virgin olive oil
1 clove garlic, crushed
dash of hot pepper sauce
2 teaspoons dried basil
2 teaspoons dried parsley

Place mushrooms and onion in a large jar, such as a mayonnaise jar. Combine vinegar, salt, and pepper in a food processor. Blend until salt dissolves. Add oil and blend until well mixed. Add garlic and remaining 3 ingredients. Mix well. Pour into jar. Cover with a lid and shake to distribute marinade. Let stand 24 hours. Serve as an hors d'oeuvre or in a recipe calling for marinated mushrooms.

Yield: 1½ cups

Monica Burdette
The Inn at El Canelo
Raymondville, Texas

SPINACH BALLS

2 (10-ounce) packages frozen
leaf spinach
3 cups herb stuffing mix
1 medium to large onion, finely
chopped
1½ sticks margarine, melted
½ cup Parmesan cheese
1 tablespoon black pepper
1½ teaspoons garlic salt
½ teaspoon dried thyme
6 eggs, well beaten

Cook and drain spinach. Squeeze dry and chop. Combine spinach and remaining 8 ingredients. Shape into balls and place on a lightly greased baking sheet. Bake at 325° for 15 to 20 minutes.

Yield: 6 dozen balls

Note: If making ahead, shape balls and freeze on a baking sheet. When frozen, transfer to a plastic bag. Baking time may increase for frozen balls.

Joan Moldt

CHEESE BALL

1 pound colby or sharp cheddar cheese, grated
2 (8-ounce) packages cream cheese, softened
4 teaspoons chopped pimiento
4 teaspoons finely chopped bell pepper
4 teaspoons finely chopped onion
1 stick butter, softened
dash of hot pepper sauce or cayenne pepper
dash of salt
dash of garlic powder
1 cup finely chopped pecans

Combine cheese and next 8 ingredients. Mix well and form into a ball. Roll in pecans.
Yield: 1 ball

Mary Ashley

AVOCADO DIP

2 avocados, peeled, pitted, and mashed
1 tablespoon grated onion
1 tablespoon lemon juice
1 teaspoon salt
¼ teaspoon chili powder
⅓ cup mayonnaise

Combine avocado and next 4 ingredients in a bowl. Cover completely by spreading mayonnaise over top. Chill. When ready to serve, stir in mayonnaise until well blended.
Yield: about 1 to 2 cups

Lica Pinkston
Santa Fe Ranch

BROCCOLI DIP

1 small onion, finely chopped
2 tablespoons butter
1 (8-ounce) can mushroom pieces, drained
1 (10¾-ounce) can condensed cream of mushroom soup
1 (6-ounce) garlic cheese roll
1 (10-ounce) package chopped broccoli, cooked
2 drops hot pepper sauce
½ cup almonds (optional)

Sauté onion in butter until translucent. Add mushroom pieces and sauté 1 to 2 minutes. Stir in soup and cheese roll. Heat until cheese melts. Mix in broccoli, hot pepper sauce, and almonds. Serve in a chafing dish.
Yield: 6 to 8 servings

Mariella Gorena

CREAMY PICANTE DIP

1 (16-ounce) container sour
cream or light sour cream
½ cup picante sauce

¼ teaspoon cayenne pepper, or
to taste

Combine all ingredients in a bowl. Mix with a wire whip. Let stand at least 60 minutes to allow flavors to blend.

Yield: 2 cups

Note: *Serve with tortilla chips, as a dressing for a taco salad, or as a baked potato topping.*

Monica Burdette
The Inn at El Canelo
Raymondville, Texas

VEGETABLE SANDWICHES

½ teaspoon salt
2 tablespoons packed brown
sugar
dash of black pepper
2 tablespoons olive oil
2 tablespoons lemon juice
4 bell peppers, chopped
3 stalks celery, chopped
1 medium onion, chopped

3 carrots, grated and chopped
1 (8-ounce) package cream
cheese, softened
1 tablespoon mayonnaise
1 loaf white sandwich bread,
crusts removed
1 loaf wheat sandwich bread,
crusts removed

Combine salt and next 4 ingredients to make a marinade. Place bell pepper and next 3 ingredients in a large bowl. Pour marinade over vegetables and refrigerate overnight. Drain vegetables through 2 or 3 layers of cheesecloth, reserving a small amount of marinade. Squeeze vegetables in cheesecloth to remove excess liquid. Combine vegetables and cream cheese in a bowl. Blend in mayonnaise. If mixture is too thick, use some of reserved marinade to thin. Spread mixture on slices of white bread. Cover with wheat bread. Cut into quarters or finger sandwiches.

Yield: about 30 finger sandwiches

Sue Wilson

HOT SPINACH DIP

2 (10-ounce) packages frozen chopped spinach
4 tablespoons butter or margarine, melted
2 tablespoons chopped onion
3 tablespoons all-purpose flour
½ cup evaporated milk

1 (6-ounce) jalapeño cheese roll, softened
½ teaspoon black pepper
¾ teaspoon celery salt
¾ teaspoon garlic salt
1 tablespoon Worcestershire sauce
dash of cayenne pepper

Cook spinach according to package directions. Drain well, reserving ½ cup liquid. Combine butter, onion, and flour in a saucepan. Cook and stir about 1 minute. Gradually add reserved spinach liquid and evaporated milk. Cook until slightly thickened, stirring constantly. Add cheese roll and remaining 5 ingredients. Mix in spinach. Serve hot with crackers.

Yield: 1¾ cups

Linda Y. Thompson

ROASTED RED PEPPER DIP

1 (14-ounce) jar roasted red bell peppers
8 large cloves garlic
2 medium plum tomatoes
1 cup whole almonds
2 teaspoons cumin seed
1 tablespoon lime juice

½ teaspoon salt
¼-½ teaspoon crushed red pepper flakes, or to taste
¼ teaspoon freshly ground black pepper
3 tablespoons olive oil
¼ cup hot water

Place bell peppers and next 8 ingredients in a food processor. Puree until smooth. With machine running, add oil and hot water through the tube. Store in refrigerator up to 3 days. Serve at room temperature.

Yield: about 2 cups

Note: Serve with a platter of raw vegetables. For an interesting presentation, serve in a hollowed out round loaf of coarse bread. Use the bread chunks removed from the center for dipping.

Margaret H. McAllen
McAllen Ranch

🏠 TURKEY DIP

Use leftover turkey for Thanksgiving weekend football get togethers!

1 hard-cooked egg, finely
  chopped
1 cup mayonnaise
1 teaspoon fresh ginger
½ teaspoon ground ginger
1 clove garlic, crushed
1 green onion, minced

1 stalk celery, minced
1 teaspoon curry powder
1 teaspoon salt
1 teaspoon lemon juice
2 cups shredded turkey
white wine (optional)

Combine egg and mayonnaise. Mix in fresh ginger and next 4 ingredients. Add curry powder and next 3 ingredients. If dip is too thick, thin with white wine.

Yield: about 3 cups

Dorothy Martin

ICED TEA COOLER

Excellent for luncheons or when you don't want too sweet a punch — if in a hurry, make the day before.

1 cup sugar
6 cups strong hot tea
2 cups pineapple juice

1 (6-ounce) can frozen
  concentrate lemonade or
  limeade
3 cups water
fresh mint sprigs for garnish

Dissolve sugar in tea. Cool. Mix in pineapple juice, lemonade, and water. Chill. Serve as a punch or over ice in tall glasses. Garnish with mint.

Yield: 15 to 20 servings

Mariella Gorena

MINT ICED TEA

A good brunch beverage.

3 family-size tea bags
2 stalks fresh mint
3 quarts plus 1 cup water
1½ cups orange juice

⅓ cup fresh lemon juice
1 cup sugar (optional)
fresh mint sprigs or orange
    slices for garnish

Brew tea and mint stalks in water in a sun tea jar for 3 to 4 hours. Remove tea bags and mint stalks. Add juices and sugar. Chill. Serve over ice and garnish.

Yield: 15 servings

Variation: For a richer mint flavor, boil 1 cup of brewed tea with juices, sugar, and mint stalks. Discard mint stalks, add liquid to tea, and chill.

Carol Lynn Looney

RUSSIAN TEA

A wonderful treat for the holidays or the next time a Norther blows into the Valley.

2 (7-ounce) jars powdered
    orange-flavored drink mix
2 (.17-ounce) packages
    powdered unsweetened
    limeade or lemonade

1 teaspoon ground cloves
½ cup instant tea
1½ teaspoons cinnamon
1½ cups sugar

Combine all ingredients in a bowl. Store in a glass jar. To serve, add 2 teaspoons mix to 1 cup boiling water.

Yield: 20 ounces dry mix

Sue Peterson

SUN TEA

2 family-size tea bags
2 cups sugar, or to taste

juice of 3 large Valley lemons

Fill a 1 gallon glass container with water, allowing room for the addition of sugar and lemon juice. Place tea bags in water and set in the sun until water turns dark brown. Stir in sugar until dissolved. Add lemon juice and chill.

Yield: 8 servings

Note: Valley lemons, a Rio Grande Valley specialty, are larger, juicier, and a bit sweeter than regular lemons. If unavailable, substitute regular lemons to taste.

For a stronger tea, use more tea bags. An empty pickle jar works well for the container.

Irma Valdez-Laurel

REAL OLD-FASHIONED LEMONADE

A healthy choice over sodas.

1 cup fresh Valley lemon juice
¾ cup sugar, or to taste

1 quart cold water
1 lemon, unpeeled and sliced

Combine lemon juice and sugar in a large pitcher. Stir until dissolved. Mix in cold water, lemon slices, and ice.

Yield: 6 (8-ounce) servings

Barbara Steidinger
Texas Agri-Women, Inc.

BETTIE'S PUNCH FOR A CROWD

Substitute other gelatin flavors such as strawberry-banana or raspberry for the orange-pineapple, depending on the color and flavor desired.

4 cups sugar	1 (16-ounce) bottle lemon juice
1 quart water	concentrate
2 (3-ounce) packages lemon-	2 (46-ounce) cans pineapple
flavored gelatin	juice
1 (3-ounce) package orange-	2 quarts plus 1 cup hot water
pineapple-flavored gelatin	6 (1-liter) bottles ginger ale,
	chilled

Combine sugar and water in a saucepan and bring to a boil. Combine gelatins in a large bowl. Pour boiling sugar water over gelatin. Stir until dissolved. Add juices and hot water. Place in large containers and freeze. Remove from freezer 3 to 4 hours before serving. To serve, pour ginger ale over gelatin mixture and mash with a wooden spoon. Serve immediately.
Yield: 75 servings

Bonnie Brown

ORANGEADE

Mix it by the pitcher and serve as a non-alcoholic cocktail.

3 cups orange juice	3 packets NutraSweet sugar
3 cups club soda	substitute

Combine all ingredients and stir well. Serve over ice.
Yield: 5 servings

Maxine McClendon

CINNAMON COFFEE WITH KAHLÚA

1½ cups whipping cream, chilled
¼ cup sugar

ground coffee to make 24 brewed cups
1½ teaspoons cinnamon
Kahlúa to taste

Whip cream and sugar in a large bowl with an electric mixer until soft peaks form. Cover and chill until ready to use, up to 6 hours in advance. Brew coffee with cinnamon per label instructions. Serve brewed coffee in mugs with Kahlúa and cream on the side.

Yield: 12 to 14 servings

Colleen Curran Hook

WATERMELON SLUSH

Tastes as fresh as summer. Will keep for weeks in freezer.

2 cups water
¼ cup sugar
1 (12-ounce) can frozen fruit punch concentrate
5 cups cubed and seeded watermelon, divided

1 tablespoon lemon juice
1 (1-liter) bottle lemon-lime carbonated drink, chilled
watermelon wedges, lemon twists, or fresh mint leaves for garnish

Combine water and sugar in a saucepan. Bring to a boil, stirring until sugar dissolves. Boil gently, uncovered, for 3 minutes. Remove from heat. Stir in punch concentrate until dissolved. In a blender or food processor, combine 2½ cups watermelon and lemon juice. Process until smooth. Stir into punch mixture. Process remaining 2½ cups watermelon and add to punch mixture. Place in a plastic container and cover. Freeze at least 8 hours or overnight until firm. To serve, scrape the top of frozen mixture with a spoon to form a slush. Spoon about 1 cup of slush into a 12-ounce tumbler. Slowly pour in about ½ cup carbonated drink. Garnish as desired.

Yield: 8 servings

Gilda dela Garza

CAFÉ MEXICANO

1½ (1-ounce) squares semi-sweet
chocolate, broken into pieces
1 cup milk
1 tablespoon sugar
¼ teaspoon almond extract

¼ teaspoon cinnamon
1 cup hot, strong coffee
¼ cup brandy
2 cinnamon sticks (optional)

Combine chocolate and milk in a small saucepan. Cook and stir over low heat just until chocolate melts and milk is hot. Do not boil. Transfer to a blender or food processor. Add sugar, almond extract, and cinnamon. Process 15 seconds. Divide mixture between 2 large mugs. Add enough coffee to almost fill mugs. Add brandy to each and garnish with cinnamon sticks.
Yield: 2 servings

Mariella Gorena

JOHNNY'S BLOODY MARY MIX

Johnny Santiago worked at McAllen Country Club for 30 years, then went to The Patio at Jones & Jones when the store opened in 1976. He worked there for about 10 years - until he retired. He knew all of his customers by name and their favorite drinks. He was always making special "drinks" - even for kids.

2 (40-ounce) cans tomato juice
2 (10-ounce) cans beef broth
⅔ cup lemon juice
⅔ cup Worcestershire sauce

1 quart orange juice
2 dashes Tabasco sauce
¼ cup salt
vodka

Combine tomato juice and next 6 ingredients. When ready to serve, fill glasses with ice. Add desired amount of vodka. Fill glass with mix and serve.
Yield: 1 gallon mix

Mary Vance Jones
The Patio at Jones & Jones

QUICK MARGARITAS

1 (6-ounce) can frozen limeade
concentrate
¾ cup tequila

¾ cup beer
juice of ½ lime

Combine all ingredients in a blender. Fill to the top with ice. Blend until smooth.

Yield: 4 to 6 servings.

Note: Serve in chilled salt-rimmed glasses.

Madelaine McLelland

PIÑA COLADAS

½ cup coconut cream
1 cup pineapple juice
½ cup light rum

fresh pineapple slices for
garnish

Combine cream, juice, and rum in a blender. Fill to the top with ice. Blend until smooth and thick. Garnish with pineapple slices.

Yield: 6 servings

Madelaine McLelland

Breads & sweets

Home on
the Range

Cover page:
Early ranchers
Judge Lamar Gill,
Charles Kennedy and
George Edwards took to
horseback in 1904 to survey
their lands and check the
herds at the La Coma Ranch
near San Manuel.
Above: *George Edwards and*
his wife, Susie Hatch, whom he
taught to ride a horse and
shoot a rifle.

TEXAS' LEGENDARY KING RANCH

ORIGINALLY MOST OF THE KING RANCH HAD BEEN PART OF THE LARGEST LAND GRANT THAT SPAIN HAD AWARDED A FAMILY NORTH OF THE RIO GRANDE (TO THE CAVAZOS CLAN). RICHARD KING BUILT HIS RANCHING EMPIRE BY ACQUIRING ABOUT 300,000 ACRES OF THE NEARLY 600,000 ACRES FROM THE CAVAZOS' HEIRS. NAMED **EL AGOSTADERO DE SAN JUAN DE CARRICITOS** (ST. JOHN OF THE LITTLE CANE PASTURE), IT WOULD TODAY COVER MUCH OF CAMERON AND WILLACY COUNTIES, AS WELL AS EXTENDING INTO KENEDY, BROOKS AND HIDALGO COUNTIES.

Home on the Range

Above: A man and his prize steer in Starr County, c. 1920.
Below: La Coma Ranch headquarters as it looked in 1909. The house was made from brick salvaged from the home of assassinated Hidalgo County Judge Max Stein.

F or over 150 years, ranching was the dominant way of life on the lower Rio Grande. The sun-baked prairies and the dense, thorny brush were home to tough Spanish and Mexican stockmen long before Texans arrived. Ranching was brought to the area by José de Escandón and the first Spanish colonists in 1749. They surveyed and portioned off the lands along the river into long, narrow strips called *porciónes,* guaranteeing equal access to precious water. On these lands, the settlers grazed their cattle, horses and sheep, and founded small villages, or *ranchos.*

Drawing upon the Spaniards' long experience with stock-raising from horseback, these colonial "cow-men," or *vaqueros,* adapted their methods and tools to this raw, new frontier. Wearing wide-brimmed *sombreros* for shade, they caught horses and cattle with a rope, or *riata,* made into a loop, or *lazo.* Each year they collected their stock in a round-up, or *rodeo,* and marked them with a brand, or *fiero.*

Below right: A delivery receipt for 28 head of cattle shipped via the St. Louis, Brownsville & Mexico Railway.

Below: Water, a commodity as precious and rare as it is today, was pumped out of wells and stored in ponds on those ranches that were too far from the Rio Grande to siphon it directly.

Early ranch life was simple, but hard, with routine work to do for everyone. On small ranches, the owner and his family did the chores, while on larger ones there were many workers.

The men's labors centered on livestock and crops. Horses, cattle, sheep, goats, hogs, and chickens all required constant attention. Water for the animals and the people living on the ranches was vital. Those ranches near the Rio Grande could rely on the river for their water. Ranches far from the river had to rely on wells. Pulling water up from those wells was, in itself, a full-time job. Men's labors also included tending

DID YOU KNOW?

THE LONGHORN BREED OF CATTLE ACTUALLY CAME TO BE IN THE WILD. THEY WERE BORN FROM THE INTERBREEDING OF CATTLE THAT STRAYED FROM THE ENORMOUS HERDS BROUGHT TO THE SOUTH TEXAS REGION IN THE 18TH CENTURY BY SPANISH SETTLERS. CONDITIONS WERE GOOD FOR THESE STRAYS TO SURVIVE AND PROPAGATE—FEW LARGE CARNIVOROUS ANIMALS EXISTED IN THE AREA AND FOOD WAS PLENTIFUL. THE RESULTING LONGHORN BREED HAS BECOME A TEXAS ICON.

crops such as corn, beans, chili peppers, pumpkins, garlic, onions, and potatoes.

Cooking was usually done by women. They ground corn on a *metate,* a stone slab, to be made into *tortillas* and *tamales.* Dried chiles were ground up for seasoning in a stone bowl called a *molcajete,* as were garlic and cocoa. They prepared meat dishes

Right: Tough breeds like Herefords thrived on the grassy chaparral.
Below: Life was no day at the beach—here an early Valley family eats out of the back of a chuck wagon possibly near Boca Chica beach, c. 1920s.

from beef and *cabrito,* or goat meat, along with wild game such as deer and turkey. Dried beef, called *machacado,* was prepared for the *vaqueros* to carry in their saddle bags and on trail drives. Special feast days throughout the year called for special foods. At Christmas, there were savory *tamales,* sugary *buñuelos* at New Year's, and delicate *pan de polvo* cookies at weddings and baptisms. By the 1900s, pre-packaged foods were more common, but the local ranch meals still relied on the age-old staples of corn, beans, and chiles.

Women's chores also included making and laundering clothes, tending to the sick, and minding the ranch when the men were off on trail drives—sometimes for several months. Dangers often threatened them. Indian attacks, outlaw raids, droughts, floods, rattlesnakes, and diseases were all part of the difficult life on a ranch. But the ranch families held on and survived. The legacy of their hard work and perseverance gave way to the birth of the American cattle industry. And their rugged independence and resourcefulness are the rulers by which true character is still measured in today's Mesquite Country.

Below: **Cattle Coming Into Texas, c. 1690,** *from HCHM's José Cisneros collection.*

SHORTY'S BISCUITS

This recipe is so large because Shorty, the cook for the Santa Fe Ranch, makes biscuits for the cowboys when they round-up. The recipe can easily be cut in half or a third for family-size portions.

10 cups all-purpose flour	2 sticks margarine or 1 cup
3½ tablespoons baking powder	vegetable shortening
2 tablespoons salt	2 cups milk
1 cup sugar	melted butter

Combine flour and next 3 ingredients in a large bowl. Cut in margarine. Mix in just enough milk for dough to leave sides of bowl. With floured hands, form dough into a ball. Place on a floured smooth surface and roll out to about ½-inch thick. Cut with a biscuit cutter and place on a greased baking sheet. Bake at 400° for about 15 minutes. Remove from oven and brush with butter.

Yield: 60 biscuits

Weneslado Perez
Sante Fe Ranch

PECAN FRUIT MUFFINS

This recipe looks as if it won't work with only 3 tablespoons flour, but don't be fooled - they're awesome!

¾ cup sugar	1 cup chopped pecans
3 tablespoons all-purpose flour	3 eggs, lightly beaten
1 cup chopped dates	1 teaspoon vanilla
½ cup raisins	

Combine sugar and flour in a bowl. Fold in dates, raisins, and pecans. Combine egg and vanilla and fold into sugar mixture. Spoon into greased and floured small muffin tins. Bake at 275° for 40 minutes.

Yield: 24 muffins

Mariella Gorena

RAISIN BRAN MUFFINS

5 cups all-purpose flour
5 teaspoons baking soda
1 (15-ounce) box raisin bran
  cereal
2½ cups sugar
2 teaspoons salt

4 eggs
1 cup vegetable oil
1 quart buttermilk
1 cup raisins (optional)
2 cups pecans (optional)

Combine flour and next 4 ingredients in a large paper bag or a bowl. Mix well. In a large bowl, beat together eggs, oil, and buttermilk. Stir in dry ingredients and mix well. Add raisins and pecans. Spoon into greased muffin tins, filling about two-thirds full. Bake at 400° for 15 to 20 minutes or until browned.

Note: This recipe makes a lot of muffins. The muffins can be frozen, or the recipe can be cut in half.

Nancy Boultinghouse

BANANA NUT BREAD

Great as a snack or for breakfast. Spread cream cheese on thinly cut slices.

2 cups sugar
2¼ cups all-purpose flour
½ teaspoon salt
¾ cup vegetable oil
3 eggs
½ teaspoon vanilla

1½ teaspoons baking soda
  dissolved in ¼ cup sour milk*
4 large ripe bananas, mashed
1 cup chopped pecans
  (optional)

Combine ingredients in order listed. Pour into two 5X9 inch loaf pans. Bake at 350° for 45 to 50 minutes.

Yield: 12 to 16 servings per loaf

Note: This recipe freezes well.

*To make sour milk, place 1 tablespoon vinegar in a measuring cup. Add milk to ¼ cup.

Loreita McCormick

CARROT BREAD

Delicious bread to take to a new neighbor or for breakfast.

2 cups all-purpose flour	4 eggs
1½ cups sugar	½-1 cup nuts
2 teaspoons baking soda	3 cups grated carrot
2 teaspoons cinnamon	½ cup raisins (optional)
1½ cups vegetable oil	½ cup golden raisins (optional)

Sift together flour and next 3 ingredients. Add oil and eggs. Stir in nuts and remaining 3 ingredients. Pour into three (7½X3½ inch) loaf pans. Bake at 350° for 45 to 50 minutes.

Yield: 3 small loaves

Ruth Penn

ORANGE BREAD

CANDIED ORANGE PEEL

2 teaspoons baking soda	1½ cups sugar
8 oranges	1 cup water

BREAD

2 eggs	1 cup milk
1 cup sugar	3 tablespoons butter, melted
2½ cups all-purpose flour	chopped candied orange peel
1 tablespoon baking powder	1 cup finely chopped pecans, or
½ teaspoon salt	more to taste

Fill a saucepan with running water and heat. Add baking soda. Remove peel of oranges and add peel to water. Bring to a boil and cook until tender. Drain, rinse peel under cold running water, and drain again. Return peel to saucepan. Add sugar and 1 cup water. Cook over low heat, stirring occasionally, for 30 minutes or until mixture is very moist, but not watery. Cool and chop. To make bread, cream eggs and sugar. Combine flour, baking powder, and salt. Mix in dry ingredients and milk, alternately. Stir in butter. Beat with an electric mixer on medium speed. Stir in orange peel and pecans. Pour into greased and floured small loaf pans or molds, filling two-thirds full. Bake at 350° for 60 minutes or until a toothpick inserted in the center comes out clean. Cool and wrap tightly. Chill or freeze, cut into thin slices, and serve.

Yield: three (7½ X 3½ inch) loaves

Barbara Savage

NONNIE'S CINNAMON ROLLS

These are the kind of soft cinnamon rolls that make you feel pampered and cozy.

1 cup skim milk
¼ cup canola oil
½ cup granulated sugar
¼ teaspoon salt
2 packages dry yeast
¼ cup warm water
1 egg
2 egg whites

5½ cups all-purpose flour
1 cup packed light brown sugar
1½ tablespoons cinnamon
½ cup golden raisins
1 cup frozen concentrated apple
  juice, thawed
¼ cup chopped walnuts

Scald milk in a saucepan. Add oil, granulated sugar, and salt. Stir until dissolved and cool to lukewarm. In a small bowl, combine yeast and water. Let stand 5 minutes or until dissolved. In a large bowl, beat eggs and egg whites well. Add flour, milk mixture, and yeast mixture. Beat until a soft dough forms. Turn onto a lightly floured board and knead 5 minutes or until smooth and elastic. Cover with plastic wrap and let rise 1 hour, 30 minutes or until doubled in bulk. Divide dough in half and form into 2 balls. Cover with plastic wrap and let rest 10 minutes. Combine brown sugar, cinnamon, and raisins in a small bowl and set aside. Roll each ball of dough into an 8X16 inch rectangle. Spray or brush dough with vegetable oil. Sprinkle cinnamon mixture over top of each rectangle. Starting at the long end, roll dough tightly. Slice each roll into sixteen (1-inch) pieces. Place on a lightly greased 11X14 inch baking sheet. Cover and let rise 1 hour, 30 minutes or until doubled in bulk. In a saucepan, reduce apple juice to a syrup consistency. Brush each roll with juice and sprinkle with walnuts. Bake at 350° for 15 minutes or until golden brown. Serve warm.

Yield: 32 rolls

Norma Cardenas

Easy Coffee Cake

Quick and easy.

4 tablespoons butter	2 teaspoons baking powder
1 egg	½ teaspoon salt
milk	1 cup sugar
1 cup all-purpose flour	2 teaspoons cinnamon

Place butter in a 11X9 inch pan. Place in oven until melted. Tip pan to coat with butter. Pour butter out of pan and set aside. Break egg into a measuring cup. Add milk to equal 1 cup liquid. Sift together flour, baking powder, and salt. Pour milk mixture into dry ingredients. Stir lightly and pour into pan. In a bowl, combine sugar and cinnamon. Sprinkle over batter. Drizzle melted butter over top. Bake at 350° for 20 minutes or until a knife inserted in the center comes out clean.

Yield: 6 to 8 servings

Note: May be frozen.

Joan Jones

French Bread

2¼ cups warm water, divided	2 tablespoons sugar
1 package dry yeast	6 cups sifted flour
1 teaspoon salt	

Combine ¼ cup water and yeast in a large bowl and let stand until frothy. Stir in remaining 2 cups water. Combine salt, sugar, and flour and mix into water mixture. Knead until smooth and elastic. Cover and place in a warm place to rise for 60 minutes. Shape into a loaf and place on a greased pan. Let rise 40 minutes or until doubled. Place in a 450° oven. Immediately reduce heat to 400° and bake until lightly browned.

Yield: 1 large loaf

Chon Cantu

MULTI-GRAIN BREAD

"My favorite way of serving this is buttering a slice, drizzling it with wild honey from the ranch, and placing it under the broiler until well toasted."

4 cups all-purpose flour, divided
2 tablespoons sugar
1 cup unprocessed wheat bran
1 cup untoasted wheat germ
1 cup oatmeal
1 cup rye flour
2 tablespoons salt
6 tablespoons vegetable oil
¾ cup honey
4¾ cups warm water (110-115°), divided
3 packages dry yeast
4 cups whole wheat flour

Combine 2 cups all-purpose flour and next 8 ingredients in a large mixing bowl. Combine ¾ cup warm water and yeast and stir until dissolved. Add yeast mixture and remaining 4 cups water to bowl and mix well. Place in a warm, dry, draft-free area (a closed oven or microwave works well) and let stand 30 minutes or until bubbly. Beat in remaining 2 cups all-purpose flour and whole wheat flour with an electric mixer. Knead with a dough hook for 10 minutes. Let rise until doubled in bulk. Punch down and divide into thirds. Place in greased standard loaf pans and let rise until doubled in bulk. Bake at 350° for 45 minutes or until loaf sounds hollow when tapped. Cool overnight before slicing to prevent crumbling.

Yield: 3 loaves

Melissa McAllen Guerra
Santillana Ranch
Linn, Texas

PARMESAN HERB BREAD

1 large loaf French bread, halved horizontally
1 stick butter or margarine, melted
garlic powder
dried oregano
Parmesan cheese

Place bread halves on a baking sheet, cut-side up. Spread most of butter over cut surfaces of bread. Sprinkle sparingly with garlic powder and oregano. Top with Parmesan cheese. Spread remaining butter over top with the back of a spoon to moisten the cheese. Slice into 1-inch wide sticks. Bake at 400° for 10 minutes or until golden. Serve immediately.

Yield: 10 to 12 servings

Monica Burdette
The Inn at El Canelo
Raymondville, Texas

TEXAS CORN BREAD

1 cup yellow cornmeal
½ cup all-purpose flour
1 teaspoon salt
1 cup buttermilk or sour milk (½ cup sour cream and ½ cup milk)
1 egg
1 tablespoon baking powder
1 teaspoon baking soda
¼ cup vegetable shortening, melted

Combine cornmeal, flour, and salt. Mix thoroughly. Add, without mixing, buttermilk and remaining 4 ingredients. Stir thoroughly and pour into well-greased and heated muffin tins. Bake at 450° for about 15 minutes.

Yield: 6 to 8 servings

Lynn Wright Parker

CORNBREAD WITH FRESH CORN

Such a tasty cornbread that you will surely want to double it.

1½ cups yellow cornmeal
1 cup unbleached all-purpose flour
¼ cup sugar
1 teaspoon baking soda
1 teaspoon baking powder
¼ teaspoon salt
½ cup vegetable oil
2 eggs, lightly beaten
1 (16-ounce) carton sour cream
½ cup fresh corn, or frozen, thawed
¼ cup minced red bell pepper

Sift cornmeal and next 5 ingredients into a large bowl. Make a well in the center. Pour oil, egg, and sour cream into well. Stir quickly until just blended. Fold in corn and bell pepper. Pour into a greased 9X13 inch baking pan. Let stand at room temperature 4 minutes. Bake at 375° for 25 minutes or until top is golden brown and springs back when lightly touched. Cool in pan on a rack for 10 minutes. Cut into squares and serve warm.

Yield: 18 to 24 servings

Patricia Chapa

APPLE CAKE WITH CAJETA FROSTING

Undoubtedly, the Rio Grande Valley's most successful and entertaining fund-raising event is the Hidalgo County Historical Museum's Heritage Ranch Gala. Each spring, a picturesque site on a local ranch is selected as the setting for this festive evening under the stars. Right in the middle of this rustic Mesquite Country, guests sit at beautifully set tables, dine on gourmet food, and dance under the moonlit Texas sky. After several years of providing the sophisticated ranch cuisine for this one-of-a-kind event, Don Strange Catering of Texas, Inc. has become a Ranch Gala tradition. Sergio Rodriguez, Executive Chef, has generously shared the recipes for some of his most memorable dishes. Look for more of Sergio's recipes throughout this cookbook.

CAKE

1½ cups vegetable oil	2 teaspoons cinnamon
2 cups sugar	3 cups peeled and diced apple
4 eggs	1 cup pecans
1 teaspoon baking soda	2 teaspoons vanilla
3 cups all-purpose flour	

CAJETA FROSTING

1 (14-ounce) can sweetened condensed milk	1 tablespoon corn syrup
	1 teaspoon lemon juice

Blend oil and sugar. Beat in eggs. Add baking soda, flour, and cinnamon. Fold in apple, pecans, and vanilla. Pour into a Bundt pan and bake at 325° for 45 to 60 minutes, or until a toothpick inserted in the center comes out clean. Cool about 25 minutes and frost. To make frosting, combine milk, syrup, and juice in a saucepan. Cook and stir over low heat until thickened.

Yield: 12 to 16 servings

Variations: Substitute other fruits such as mangoes, peaches, or pears for the apple.

Sergio Rodriguez
Executive Chef
Catering by Don Strange
San Antonio, Texas

AUNT POKEY'S COCONUT CAKE

Great for coconut lovers.

1 (18-ounce) box white cake mix
1¼ cup water
⅓ cup oil
3 eggs

½ cup flaked coconut, plus extra
  for topping
1 (16-ounce) can coconut cream
1 (12-ounce) container frozen
  whipped topping, thawed

Combine cake mix and next 3 ingredients. Beat with an electric mixer on low for 30 seconds or until moistened. Increase to medium speed and beat 2 minutes. Mix in coconut. Pour into a greased and floured 9X13 inch baking pan. Bake at 350° for 25 minutes or until a toothpick inserted in the center comes out clean. While still hot, pierce all over with a fork. Pour coconut cream over cake. Cool. Spread whipped topping on top. Sprinkle liberally with coconut.

Note: Cake can also be made in two 9-inch round layer pans.

Shan Rankin

CARROT CAKE

CAKE

2 cups all-purpose flour
2 cups sugar
2 teaspoons baking powder
2 teaspoons baking soda
½ teaspoon cinnamon

1 teaspoon salt
4 eggs, beaten
1½ cups vegetable oil
3 cups grated carrot
½ cup chopped nuts

FROSTING

4 tablespoons butter, softened
1 (8-ounce) package cream
  cheese, softened

1 (16-ounce) package powdered
  sugar

Combine flour and next 5 ingredients in a bowl. Combine egg and oil and mix into dry ingredients. Add carrot and nuts. Divide among 3 greased and lightly floured 9-inch round pans. Bake at 300° for 45 minutes or at 350° for 25 to 30 minutes. Cool in pans 10 minutes. Invert onto a rack, remove pans, and cool. To make frosting, cream butter and cream cheese. Add sugar and beat well. Spread lightly between layers and then on sides and top.

Jennifer Wright

Fresh Rio Red Grapefruit Cake

Citrus is our business in the Rio Grande Valley. We grow it, we eat it, we promote it. It is the State Fruit of Texas. You can really taste the Rio Red grapefruit in this cake and frosting. You can smell it, too.

Cake

1⅓ sticks butter or margarine, softened
1¾ cups sugar
2 eggs
3 cups sifted cake flour
2½ teaspoons baking powder
½ teaspoon salt

½ cup fresh Rio Red grapefruit juice
¾ cup milk
1 teaspoon Rio Red grapefruit zest
1½ teaspoons colorless vanilla extract

Rio Red Grapefruit Frosting

1½ cups sugar
2 egg whites
1 tablespoon light corn syrup
⅛ teaspoon salt
⅓ cup fresh Rio Red grapefruit juice

1 tablespoon Rio Red grapefruit zest
2 teaspoons colorless vanilla extract

Cream butter. Gradually beat in sugar. Add eggs, one at a time, beating well after each addition. Combine flour, baking powder, and salt. Add dry ingredients and juice, alternately, to butter mixture. Slowly add milk. Stir in zest and vanilla. Mix well. Pour into 2 greased and floured 9-inch round pans. Bake at 350° for 25 minutes or until a toothpick inserted in the center comes out clean. Cool in pans 10 minutes. Invert onto a rack, remove pans, and cool completely. To make frosting, combine sugar and next 4 ingredients in the top of a double boiler. Beat with an electric mixer on low speed for 30 seconds or until moistened. Place over boiling water. Beat constantly on high speed for 7 minutes or until stiff peaks form. Remove from heat and add zest and vanilla. Beat 1 to 2 minutes or until thick enough to spread. Immediately spread between cake layers and then on sides and top.

Yield: one (2-layer) cake, 3¾ cups frosting

Barbara Steidinger
Texas Agri-Women, Inc.

KAHLÚA PECAN CAKE

CAKE

1 (18-ounce) package butter cake
mix
4 eggs
1 cup sour cream
1 (3-ounce) package instant
French vanilla pudding

¾ cup vegetable oil
1 teaspoon vanilla
1 cup packed brown sugar
⅓ cup Kahlúa (coffee liquor)
1¼ cups chopped pecans

GLAZE

3 tablespoons margarine
1 cup powdered sugar

2 tablespoons Kahlúa
½ cup chopped pecans

Place cake mix in a medium mixing bowl. Add eggs, one at a time, beating well after each addition. Add sour cream and next 3 ingredients. Blend well. In a separate bowl, combine sugar, Kahlúa, and pecans. Add half of cake batter to Kahlúa mixture and blend well. Layer mixtures, alternately, in a Bundt pan, ending with Kahlúa mixture. Swirl with a knife to marbleize. Bake at 350° for 60 minutes. Remove immediately from pan. Cool completely before glazing. To make glaze, cream margarine and sugar. Add Kahlúa. Mixture should be watery. If too stiff, add a small amount of milk. Drizzle over cake and sprinkle with pecans.

Yield: 10 servings

Crystal M. Garcia

GRANDMOTHER RANKIN'S POUND CAKE

2 sticks margarine or butter
1¾ cups sugar
5 eggs

2 cups all-purpose flour
2 teaspoons lemon extract

Cream margarine and sugar. Add eggs alternately with flour, starting and ending with an egg. Add lemon extract. Pour into a greased Bundt pan. Place in a cold oven and heat to 300°. Bake 1 hour, 15 minutes.

Susan Rankin

LEMON POUND CAKE WITH FRUIT SAUCE

Cake can be eaten without fruit sauce - delicious!

CAKE

2 sticks unsalted butter, softened
2 ⅔ cups sugar
6 eggs, room temperature
3 cups sifted unbleached all-
  purpose flour
½ teaspoon salt

¼ teaspoon baking soda
1 cup sour cream or crème
  fraîche
1 teaspoon vanilla
zest of 2 lemons

SAUCE

7 tablespoons kirsch, divided
½ cup cold water, divided
1½ cups mixed fresh or frozen
  berries
3 tablespoons honey
1 tablespoon freshly squeezed
  lemon juice
½ teaspoon vanilla

12 fresh figs, halved
2 ripe peaches, peeled and sliced
2 nectarines, peeled and sliced
1½ cups strawberries, hulled
1½ cups raspberries
6 tablespoons sugar
juice and zest of 4 lemons
whipped cream for garnish

Line the bottom of a 9-inch tube pan with parchment paper. Grease and flour paper and sides of pan. In a mixing bowl, cream butter and sugar, scraping sides occasionally, until light and fluffy. Add eggs, one at a time, and continue to beat until smooth and silky. Sift together flour, salt, and baking soda. Add dry ingredients and sour cream, alternately, to butter mixture. Beat until smooth. Add vanilla and zest. Pour into prepared pan. Bake at 350° for 60 minutes or until a toothpick inserted in the center comes out clean. Let stand 5 minutes, then turn out of pan onto a rack to cool.

To make sauce, combine 1 tablespoon kirsch, 2 tablespoons water, and next 4 ingredients in a food processor or blender. Puree and strain juice, discarding pulp. Combine figs and next 4 ingredients in a bowl. Pour juice over fruit. In a small saucepan, combine remaining 6 tablespoons kirsch, remaining 6 tablespoons water, sugar, juice, and zest. Bring to a boil. Reduce heat and simmer 3 minutes. Cool and add to fruit mixture. To serve, place a slice of cake on each plate. Top with cream and spoon sauce around cake.

Yield: 10 to 12 servings

Note: Cake and sauce can be prepared up to 2 days in advance. Keep the cake tightly covered and store the sauce in the refrigerator. Heat sauce slightly before serving.

Substitute fruit of choice for the fruit to be pureed or the sliced fruit.

Colleen Curran Hook

ANDREA'S FUDGE CAKE AND GLAZE

Wonderful recipe for chocolate lovers.

CAKE

12 ounces semi-sweet chocolate
⅓ cup prepared espresso or
  strong coffee
2 sticks unsalted butter

2 cups sugar
6 egg yolks
1 cup all-purpose flour
6 egg whites

GLAZE

4 ounces semi-sweet chocolate
2 tablespoons unsalted butter,
  melted

powdered sugar (optional)

Heat chocolate and espresso in the top of a double boiler until chocolate melts. Cool. Cream butter and sugar in a bowl. Mix in egg yolks, one at a time. Stir in flour. In a separate bowl, beat egg whites until stiff. Fold chocolate mixture into egg white. Fold into butter mixture. Pour into a greased and floured 9-inch springform or removable-bottom pan. Bake at 350° for 60 to 70 minutes or until top is crusty and cracked and middle is moist. Cool and transfer to a serving plate. To make glaze, melt chocolate in the top of a double boiler over hot, but not boiling, water. Whisk in butter. Pour over cake and smooth as needed. Place a doily on top and sift with sugar. Remove doily.

Yield: 10 to 12 servings

Loreita McCormick

CINNAMON CHOCOLATE CAKE

CAKE

¼ cup cocoa powder
½ cup vegetable shortening
1 stick butter or margarine
1 cup water
2 cups all-purpose flour
2 cups sugar

1 teaspoon baking soda
2 teaspoons cinnamon
2 eggs
½ cup buttermilk
dash of salt
1 tablespoon vanilla

ICING

1 stick butter or margarine
¼ cup cocoa powder
6 tablespoons milk
dash of salt

1 teaspoon vanilla
1 (16-ounce) package powdered
  sugar
1 cup chopped nuts (optional)

Combine cocoa and next 3 ingredients in a saucepan. Bring to a boil, stirring constantly. Remove from heat. Sift together flour and next 3 ingredients. Add cocoa mixture to dry ingredients. Beat well with an electric mixer. Add eggs and next 3 ingredients. Mix thoroughly. Pour into a greased and floured 9X13 inch pan. Bake at 350° for 30 minutes or until the top springs back when touched. To make icing, combine butter and next 3 ingredients in a saucepan. Bring to a boil. Remove from heat and stir in vanilla, sugar, and nuts. Mix well. Spread over warm cake.

Yield: 12 to 15 servings

Note: This cake does not freeze well.

Madelaine McLelland

EL CHAPOTE CHOCOLATE CAKE

For my family, holidays and other occasions have often been enjoyed outdoors. Growing up in South Texas, we always anticipated going to our family picnic grounds at El Chapote (a piece of ranch land named for its wild persimmon trees) for a holiday feast. The cake recipe that follows is a hearty, moist cake that can withstand the ruggedness of the outdoors in South Texas. It is a fitting dessert or snack for those who have worked up an appetite after a round of volleyball, a brisk walk, or several swings at a piñata.

CAKE

1½ cups sugar
2 cups all-purpose flour
1 teaspoon baking soda
¼ cup cocoa powder

1 cup mayonnaise
1 cup cold water
1 teaspoon vanilla

FROSTING

2 cups sifted powdered sugar
3 tablespoons cocoa powder
3 tablespoons butter or
   margarine, softened

¼ cup hot coffee
1 cup chopped pecans, lightly
   toasted

Combine sugar and next 3 ingredients in a mixing bowl. Add mayonnaise. Combine water and vanilla and stir into batter. Pour into a greased and floured 9X13 inch glass dish. Bake at 325° for 25 minutes. Cool. To prepare frosting, combine sugar and next 3 ingredients. Mix with an electric mixer. Stir in nuts. Spread over cooled cake.

Yield: 30 servings

Carla Conley Haynes

RED VELVET CAKE

A Texas original developed by the famous Nieman Marcus store in Dallas.

CAKE

2½ cups cake flour
1 teaspoon baking soda
1½ cups sugar
2 eggs
1½ cups vegetable oil

1 teaspoon vinegar
1 teaspoon vanilla
4 teaspoons red food coloring
1 cup buttermilk

ICING

3-3½ cups powdered sugar
1 (8-ounce) package cream
cheese

1 stick margarine, melted
1 cup chopped nuts (optional)

Sift together flour and baking soda in a large bowl. In a separate bowl, beat sugar and next 3 ingredients. Add sugar mixture to dry ingredients. Stir in vanilla and food coloring. Slowly mix in buttermilk. Pour into 2 greased and floured 8-inch round pans. Bake at 350° for 25 to 30 minutes. Cool completely before frosting. To make icing, blend sugar and cream cheese. Mix in margarine. Stir in nuts. Spread between layers and on top of cake. Let icing dribble down sides.

Ellen Sigrist

CHEESECAKE WITH
WARM APPLE-MACADAMIA SAUCE

CRUST

2 cups all-purpose flour
1 stick butter, softened
½ cup sugar
1 egg

1 teaspoon baking powder
1 envelope vanilla sugar, or 1
   teaspoon vanilla extract

FILLING

6 eggs, separated
1 cup sugar
3 (8-ounce) packages cream
   cheese

1 (3-ounce) package cook and
   serve vanilla pudding (not
   instant)
1 cup sour cream
1 teaspoon vanilla

APPLE-MACADAMIA SAUCE

6-8 Granny Smith apples, peeled
   and sliced
lemon juice
4-6 tablespoons butter

⅔-1 cup packed brown sugar
3-4 tablespoons macadamia nut
   liqueur, or other nut-flavored
   liqueur

Combine all crust ingredients and mix to form a firm pastry dough. Pat into a greased 9-inch springform pan, making dough ½-inch thick on bottom and halfway up the sides of pan. Set aside. To make filling, combine egg yolks and next 5 ingredients in a mixer until creamy and smooth. Beat egg whites until stiff and fold into yolk mixture. Pour over crust. Bake at 325° for 1 hour, 15 minutes to 1 hour, 30 minutes or until cake has risen substantially and the center is firm when shaken. Cool slightly in pan, then loosen cake from edge of pan with a knife. Invert pan, with cake still in it, onto a rack. Loosen pan and lift off bottom of pan. Retighten sides of pan and let cool on rack. Flip cake onto a serving plate and carefully remove sides of pan, using a knife to loosen cake as needed. To make sauce, sprinkle apple slices with lemon juice to prevent browning. Sauté apple slices in butter. Stir in brown sugar and let dissolve. Add liquor and let bubble until alcohol smell is gone. Serve sauce warm over cooled cheesecake.

Yield: 12 to 16 servings

Note: Substitute apple juice for the liquor, if desired.

Melissa McAllen Guerra
Santillana Ranch
Linn, Texas

PUMPKIN CHEESECAKE

Great for the Holidays!

CRUST

1½ cups crushed vanilla wafers
¼ cup sugar

4 tablespoons butter, melted

FILLING

3 (8-ounce) packages cream
  cheese, softened
¾ cup granulated sugar
¼ cup packed brown sugar
¼ cup whipping cream
5 eggs

1 teaspoon cinnamon
½ teaspoon nutmeg
¼ teaspoon ground cloves
¼ teaspoon ground ginger
1 (16-ounce) can pumpkin

TOPPING

6 tablespoons butter
1 cup packed brown sugar

1 cup coarsely chopped walnuts

Combine crust ingredients. Press firmly on the bottom and sides of a 9-inch springform pan. To prepare filling, beat cream cheese until light and fluffy. Mix in sugars and cream. Add in eggs, one at a time. Mix in cinnamon and next 4 ingredients. Pour into springform pan. Bake at 350° for 60 minutes. Add topping. To make topping, cream butter and sugar. Stir in walnuts. Gently spoon over cheesecake. Bake 15 minutes longer. Chill overnight.

Yield: 12 to 16 servings

Mary Vance Jones

CHEESECAKE FLAN

Sinfully delicious! This dessert combines Mexican and American classics: flan and cheesecake. It's topped off with a sweet caramelized glaze and fresh fruit.

1 cup sugar
2 (8-ounce) packages cream
  cheese, softened
5 egg yolks
1 teaspoon vanilla
1 (14-ounce) can sweetened
  condensed milk

1 cup milk
½ teaspoon salt
2 small oranges, peeled and
  thinly sliced
½ cup strawberries, sliced
  (optional)
12 pecan halves (optional)

Heat sugar in a 1-quart saucepan over medium heat, stirring constantly, until melted and light caramel colored. Immediately pour into a greased 9-inch round pan and coat bottom. In a large bowl, beat cream cheese and egg yolks until smooth. Gradually beat in vanilla and next 3 ingredients until blended. Pour into pan. Place in a 10X14 inch baking pan. Fill pan halfway with hot water. Bake at 350° for 50 minutes or until set. Remove from hot water and cover. Refrigerate 3 hours or until chilled. Loosen flan from sides of pan. Invert onto a dessert platter, allowing caramel topping to drip from pan onto flan. Garnish with orange, strawberries, and pecan halves.

Yield: 12 servings

Carlota M. Gutierrez

Rio Grande Valley Pink Grapefruit Pie

Makes a wonderful, light, festive ending to a hearty meal.

4 medium to large pink or red
  grapefruit
1 cup sugar
1¾ cup water or strained
  grapefruit juice
2 tablespoons cornstarch

⅛ teaspoon salt
1 (3-ounce) package strawberry
  gelatin
1 (8- or 9-inch) pie crust, baked
1 cup whipping cream, whipped

Peel grapefruit, separate sections, and remove membranes. Place sections in a strainer over a bowl overnight. Cook sugar and next 3 ingredients until thick and clear. Add gelatin and stir until dissolved. Brush gelatin mixture over pie crust. Chill gelatin mixture and crust. When gelatin starts to thicken, add grapefruit sections. Pour into pie crust and chill until set. Top with cream.

Yield: 8 servings

Note: Pie can be made with navel orange sections and orange gelatin.

Coylie Koelle and Vi Norton

Lemon Chess Pie

This is so easy because it can all be done by hand in one bowl! And men love it!

2 cups sugar
¼ teaspoon salt
1 tablespoon all-purpose flour
1 tablespoon cornmeal
4 eggs

4 tablespoons butter, melted
¼ cup lemon juice
¼ cup milk
zest of 1 lemon
1 pie crust, unbaked

Combine sugar and next 3 ingredients in a bowl. Add eggs and next 4 ingredients. Mix well using a wire whisk. Pour into pie crust. Bake at 350° for 40 minutes.

Yield: 8 servings

Carol Lynn Looney

LEMON PECAN PIE

A "lemon twist" to an old favorite.

3 eggs, lightly beaten
5 tablespoons butter or
  margarine, melted
1 cup chopped pecans

1½ cups sugar
6 tablespoons fresh lemon juice
1 pie crust, unbaked

Combine egg and next 4 ingredients. Pour into pie crust. Bake at 350° for 45 to 55 minutes or until set.

Yield: 8 servings

Mary Kittleman

MANGO LIME PIE

pastry for (9-inch) 2-crust pie
5-8 ripe mangos, peeled
2 tablespoons fresh lime juice
¾ cup sugar, plus extra for
  topping

⅓ cup all-purpose flour
¼ teaspoon cinnamon, plus
  extra for topping
2 tablespoons butter

Divide pastry in half. Roll each half into a circle. Line a 9-inch pie pan with 1 circle. To prepare mangos for pie, remove skin with a vegetable peeler. Slice pulp of the fruit away from the flat seed in the center, along the same plane as the basic contour of the fruit. Slice mangos, as uniformly as possible, to equal 5 cups. Combine mango and lime juice in a large bowl. Add sugar, flour, and cinnamon and toss. Turn into pie pan. Dot with butter. Cover with second crust. Seal and flute edges. Cut slits in top crust for steam to escape. Combine a small amount of cinnamon and sugar. Sprinkle over crust. Bake at 425° for 40 to 45 minutes or until crust is browned and juice begins to bubble through slits. If crust is getting too brown, loosely cover with foil during last 15 minutes of baking.

Yield: 8 servings

Note: Ripe mangos give slightly when squeezed, no matter what color the outside is.

Monica Burdette
The Inn at El Canelo
Raymondville, Texas

STRAWBERRY-KIWI TART

CRUST

1 stick butter
⅓ cup sugar

½ teaspoon vanilla
1 cup all-purpose flour

FILLING

1½ cups whipping cream
½ cup sugar
3 egg yolks

1 teaspoon vanilla or 3
  tablespoons Cointreau

TOPPING

1½-2 cups fresh whole
  strawberries
2 kiwi fruit, peeled and sliced

apricot jam
lemon juice

Combine all crust ingredients in a food processor. Pat into a greased 9-inch flan pan. Bake at 350° for 20 minutes or until brown. Cool. Combine all filling ingredients and pour into cooled crust. Bake at 325° for 35 minutes. Cool. Arrange strawberries and kiwi slices in circles on cooled tart. Place 1 strawberry in the center. Heat jam and a small amount of lemon juice. Brush jam mixture over fruit.

Yield: 8 servings

Mary F. Lary

SPICED WATERMELON PIE

watermelon rind	1 cup chopped pecans
1 cup sugar	⅛ teaspoon salt
1 teaspoon cinnamon	2 teaspoons all-purpose flour
¼ teaspoon allspice	¼ cup cider or white vinegar
¼ teaspoon nutmeg	2 pie crusts, unbaked

Cut away outer green part and any red pulp on rind. Cut rind into ¼-inch cubes to measure 2 cups. Place in a saucepan. Add water to cover and bring to a boil. Reduce heat and simmer until tender and transparent. Drain. Add sugar and next 7 ingredients to rind. Stir well. Line a pie pan with 1 pie crust. Pour rind mixture into pan. Cover with second crust and seal. Cut slits in top crust for steam to escape. Bake at 450° for 10 minutes or until browned. Reduce heat to 350° and bake 40 to 45 minutes or until filling sets.

Yield: 8 servings

Christina M. Garcia

BUTTERMILK PIE

This recipe has been used in my family for many years! My mother learned to cook from her mother-in-law, and this was one of my grandmother's recipes.

3 eggs	1½ teaspoons vanilla
2 cups sugar	½ teaspoon salt
1 stick butter, melted	1 cup buttermilk
¼ cup all-purpose flour	1 (9-inch) pie crust, unbaked

Mix eggs and sugar together. Add butter and next 4 ingredients. Pour into pie crust. Bake at 350° for 45 minutes or until center is set.

Yield: 8 servings

Kathryn Kaplan

OLD ORIGINAL BOOKBINDER'S APPLE WALNUT PIE

A tasty, rich apple pie from the famous Bookbinder's restaurant in Philadelphia.

CRUST

1¾ cups all-purpose flour
¼ cup sugar
1 teaspoon cinnamon

1 stick unsalted butter, cold and cut into pieces
5-6 tablespoons ice water

FILLING

1 cup granulated sugar
½ cup all-purpose flour
pinch of salt
1 (16-ounce) container sour cream

2 eggs, lightly beaten
2 teaspoons vanilla
8 cups peeled and sliced baking apple

STREUSEL TOPPING

½ cup packed brown sugar
½ cup granulated sugar
½ cup all-purpose flour
1 teaspoon cinnamon

pinch of salt
1 stick unsalted butter, softened
1 cup chopped walnuts

Combine flour, sugar, and cinnamon in a bowl and blend. Cut in butter with a pastry blender or 2 knives until mixture resembles coarse crumbs. Gradually add ice water, tossing mixture with a fork, until moistened. Gather dough into a ball and flatten. Wrap in plastic and refrigerate 60 minutes. Roll out dough on a well-floured surface into a circle large enough to line a 10-inch pie pan. Place crust in pan. Trim and flute edge high, as filling is generous.

To make filling, combine sugar, flour, and salt in a large bowl. Mix well. Add sour cream, eggs, and vanilla. Stir until blended. Place apple in a large bowl. Pour sour cream mixture over apple and gently mix until evenly coated. Pour into pie pan. Place on a baking pan. Bake at 450° for 10 minutes. Reduce heat to 350° and bake 30 minutes longer.

Meanwhile, prepare topping by combining brown sugar and next 4 ingredients in a medium bowl. Mix well. Cut in butter with a pastry blender or 2 knives until blended. Mix in walnuts. Crumble topping evenly over hot pie. Bake at 350° for 20 to 25 minutes longer or until topping is lightly browned and center is set. Cool on a rack.

Yield: 8 servings

Note: Cover and refrigerate leftovers.

Patricia G. Chapa

FUDGE-MALLOW PIE

3 (1-ounce) squares semi-sweet
  chocolate
1½ sticks butter
1¼ cups sugar
¾ cup sifted all-purpose flour
3 eggs

1½ cups colored miniature
  marshmallows
½ cup milk chocolate chips
1 (9-inch) pie crust, unbaked
1 cup chopped pecans

Melt semi-sweet chocolate and butter over low heat. Add sugar, flour, and eggs. Stir until well blended, about 50 strokes. Add marshmallows and milk chocolate chips. Pour into pie crust. Sprinkle pecans over top. Bake at 350° for 25 minutes. Remove from oven and cool 60 minutes. Chill several hours before serving. Filling will be fudge-like when chilled.

Yield: 8 servings

Hilda Lewin

RUM CHIFFON PIE

6 egg yolks
1 scant cup sugar
1 (¼-ounce) package unflavored
  gelatin
½ cup cold water

1 cup whipping cream, whipped
¼ cup rum
1 graham cracker pie crust
chocolate shavings (optional)

Beat egg yolks until light. Mix in sugar. Soak gelatin in water in a saucepan until dissolved. Bring to a boil over low heat. Pour over egg mixture and stir briskly. Fold in cream and rum. Pour into pie crust. Refrigerate. Sprinkle with chocolate shavings before serving.

Yield: 8 servings

Anne Armstrong
Former U.S. Ambassador to the Court of St. James
Armstrong Ranch

TEXAS CHOCOLATE CHIP COOKIES

They say everything is BIG in Texas! Our idea of a chocolate chip is a Hershey's Kiss!

1 stick butter, softened
½ cup packed dark brown sugar
¼ cup granulated sugar
2 tablespoons wheat germ
¼ teaspoon salt
1 teaspoon vanilla
1 egg

½ teaspoon baking soda
1 cup plus 1 teaspoon all-purpose flour
1 cup pecan halves or chunks
2 cups Hershey's Kisses, with or without almonds

Combine butter and next 4 ingredients in a bowl. Mix with a wooden spoon until creamy. Add vanilla, egg, and baking soda and blend until smooth. Mix in flour until smooth. Add pecans and Kisses. Cover and chill several hours. Use 2 heaping tablespoons of dough to make 1 cookie. Drop dough onto foil-lined baking sheets, 4 to 6 cookies per sheet. Bake at 350° for 10 to 12 minutes. Cool slightly on pan. Transfer cookies to paper towels to finish cooling.

Yield: 12 to 15 cookies

Note: Doubling this recipe is not recommended.

Mariella Gorena

NORWEGIAN BUTTER COOKIES

A true butter cookie.

6 sticks unsalted butter, softened
1½ cups sifted powdered sugar
1½ teaspoons salt

5 cups sifted cake flour
1 cup sliced almonds
½ teaspoon almond extract

Cream butter with an electric mixer until very light and fluffy. Add sugar, salt, and flour. Mix well. Stir in almonds and extract. Drop by teaspoonfuls onto an ungreased baking sheet. Bake at 350° for 10 to 12 minutes or until just starting to brown around the edges.

Yield: 110 cookies

Note: Like most butter cookies, the flavor of these improves when stored for several weeks before serving.

Marilyn Putz

Shortbread Sugar Cookies

COOKIES

2 sticks butter, softened
2 cups sugar
2 eggs
1 teaspoon vanilla

½ teaspoon salt
2 teaspoons baking powder
4 cups all-purpose flour

POWDERED SUGAR ICING

2 cups sifted powdered sugar
½ teaspoon almond extract

⅓ cup milk
food coloring

Cream butter and sugar in a large bowl. Add eggs and vanilla and mix well. In a separate bowl, sift salt, baking powder, and flour. Gradually add dry ingredients to butter mixture by hand. Divide dough into 4 sections and place in an airtight container. Chill at least 3 hours or overnight. Roll each section to ⅛-inch thickness on a floured surface. Cut into shapes with cookie cutters. Place on a lightly greased baking sheet. Bake at 400° for 5 to 7 minutes. Cool on a wire rack. To make icing, combine sugar, almond extract, and milk. Icing should be the consistency of thin glue. Pour icing into bowls large enough for dipping cookies and add food coloring. To decorate, dip top of cookies into icing. Remove quickly and let icing drip. Place on wax paper.

Kathryn Kaplan

NUN'S COOKIES

In 1989, a family friend gave us this recipe, calling it "The World's Best Cookies". A girl that worked for us had grown up in Tampico and said the Nuns there made and sold cookies that tasted like these - from then on we called them the "Nun's Cookies".

2 sticks butter	1 cup crushed corn flakes
1 cup granulated sugar	½ cup grated coconut
1 cup packed brown sugar	½ cup chopped nuts
1 egg	3½ cups sifted flour
1 teaspoon vanilla	1 teaspoon salt
1 cup vegetable oil	1 teaspoon baking soda
1 cup rolled oats	

Cream butter and sugars until light. Add egg and vanilla and mix well. Mix in oil. Stir in oats and next 3 ingredients. Add flour, salt, and baking soda and mix well. Form into walnut-size balls and flatten on an ungreased baking sheet. Bake at 325° for 12 minutes. Cool on baking sheet.

Yield: 3 to 4 dozen

Jennifer Wiltsie and Toni Leadbetter
Nuevo Restaurant

LACE COOKIES

2 cups rolled oats	2 eggs, beaten
2 cups sugar	1 teaspoon vanilla
½ teaspoon salt	1 cup chopped pecans, walnuts,
1 tablespoon all-purpose flour	or roasted peanuts
2 sticks butter, melted	

Combine oats and next 3 ingredients. Pour butter over mixture and stir until sugar dissolves. Add egg and vanilla. Mix well. Stir in nuts. Drop by ½-teaspoonfuls, 1 inch apart, onto a foil-lined baking sheet. Bake at 325° for 10 to 12 minutes or until lightly browned. Cool on foil and peel off.

Ray Schaleben

CHOCOLATE CHIP BARS

1 cup all-purpose flour
1 cup rolled oats
¾ cup packed brown sugar
1 stick margarine
1 (14-ounce) can sweetened
  condensed milk

1 cup chopped pecans or
  walnuts
1 (6-ounce) package chocolate
  chips

Blend flour and next 3 ingredients in a food processor. Press three-fourths of mixture into a greased 9X13 inch pan. Bake at 350° for 10 minutes. Remove from oven and spread milk over crust. Sprinkle with nuts and then chocolate chips. Sprinkle remaining crust mixture over top. Bake at 350° for 25 to 30 minutes. Cool and cut into bars.

Yield: 24 bars

Madelaine McLelland

TURTLE BROWNIES

40-50 caramels
⅔ cup evaporated milk, divided
1 (18-ounce) package German
  chocolate cake mix

2 sticks butter, softened
1½ cups chopped nuts
1½ cups milk chocolate chips

Melt caramels and ⅓ cup milk in the top of a double boiler. Combine remaining ⅓ cup milk, cake mix, butter, and nuts. Mix well. Pour half of cake mixture into a greased 9X13-inch pan. Bake at 350° for 10 minutes. Sprinkle chocolate chips over top. Drizzle with caramel mixture. Drop and pat remaining half of cake mixture over top. Bake 25 minutes longer. Cool. Refrigerate 30 minutes before cutting.

Yield: 36 to 40 bars

Mary R. Ashley

BEST FUDGE

2 cups milk
2 cups sugar
¼ cup cocoa powder
pinch of salt

¼ teaspoon vanilla
1 stick butter
3 tablespoons peanut butter
(optional)

Combine milk and next 3 ingredients in a saucepan. Bring to a boil over medium heat, stirring constantly. Boil until mixture reaches soft-ball stage (234°-240°). Remove from heat and add vanilla and butter. Beat until mixture loses its gloss. Stir in peanut butter. Pour into a 9X9 inch baking pan that has been sprayed with nonstick cooking spray. Cut into 1-inch squares. Store in an airtight container at room temperature.

Yield: 81 (1-inch) squares

John Cozad

BUTTERSCOTCH CASHEW CHEWS

1 stick plus 1 tablespoon butter,
  divided
¾ cup sugar
½ teaspoon salt
1½ cups all-purpose flour

1 (6-ounce) package
  butterscotch chips
½ cup light corn syrup
1 teaspoon water
1 (10- to 12-ounce) can whole
  cashews

Cream 1 stick butter and sugar. Mix in salt and flour. Press into the bottom of a greased 9X13 inch pan. Bake at 350° for 15 to 20 minutes. While baking, melt butterscotch chips with corn syrup, water, and remaining 1 tablespoon butter. Pour over baked crust. Sprinkle cashews over top and press lightly into mixture. Bake 10 minutes longer. Cool before cutting into squares.

Robb Peterson

LOU TOWER'S BUTTERMILK PRALINES

U.S. Senator John Tower was first nominated as the Republican Party's candidate at a 1960 state convention held at the Fairway Hotel in McAllen, Texas. The Republican Party was so small at the time that it was not even required to hold county primaries. It is ironic that the convention in McAllen was the beginning of the Party's return to power in Texas, because the Rio Grande Valley was, and still continues to be, the Democratic stronghold of the state.This recipe was used during Tower's 1966 campaign. His wife, Lou, and volunteers all over the state, walked door to door during the campaign and left door hangers that had the wonderful recipe on them. Maybe one reason Senator Tower continued to win elections was because Lou's praline recipe was so good!

2 cups sugar	**2 tablespoons butter**
1 cup buttermilk	**2½ cups pecans**
1 teaspoon baking soda	**1 teaspoon vanilla**
½ teaspoon salt	

Combine sugar and next 3 ingredients in a large saucepan. Quickly bring to a boil, stirring constantly until mixture takes on a creamy tinge (210°). Add butter and pecans. Cook over medium heat, stirring frequently, to soft-ball stage (234°-240°). Remove from heat and add vanilla. Beat until mixture loses its gloss. Working very quickly, drop mounds onto foil. Pralines harden fast and are very dark in color.

Yield: 2 dozen pralines

Use a candy thermometer to be sure to reach required temperatures.

Doris Bentley
The Grill Room
South Padre Island, Texas
Shan Rankin and Marion Conlin

APPLE-BERRY CRISP

Best made the same day.

4 cups peeled and sliced apple
1½ teaspoons cinnamon
1 teaspoon salt
¼ cup cold water

½ cup fresh cranberries or
   blueberries
¾ cup sifted flour
1 cup sugar
5 tablespoons butter

Place apple in a greased 6X10X2 inch baking dish or a deep dish pie pan. Sprinkle with cinnamon and salt. Pour water over apple and top with berries. Blend flour, sugar, and butter using a pastry blender. Distribute mixture over berries. Bake at 350° for 40 to 45 minutes. If desired, serve with whipped cream or ice cream.

Yield: 6 to 8 servings

Kathryn Kaplan

BLUEBERRY CRUNCH

2 cups all-purpose flour
2 sticks margarine, softened
1 cup pecan pieces
1 (16-ounce) package powdered
   sugar

1 (8-ounce) package cream
   cheese, softened
1 (12-ounce) container frozen
   whipped topping, thawed
1 (20- to 24-ounce) can
   blueberry pie filling

Combine flour, margarine, and pecan pieces. Press into a 9X13 inch pan. Bake at 350° for 30 minutes or until golden brown. Mix sugar, cream cheese, and topping together. Spread over crust. Top with pie filling. Chill 1 to 2 hours.

Yield: 8 servings

Cathy Conley Swofford

EASY FRESH FRUIT COBBLER

Especially good with fresh peaches!

1 stick margarine or butter
1¾ cups sugar, divided
¾ cup all-purpose flour
1½ teaspoons baking powder
¼ teaspoon salt

½ cup milk
3 cups fresh fruit of choice
cinnamon or nutmeg to taste
   (optional)

Melt margarine in an 8X12 inch glass dish. Sift together ¾ cup sugar and next 3 ingredients. Add milk and mix well. Pour over melted butter; do not stir. Add fruit. Sprinkle remaining 1 cup sugar over fruit. Dust with cinnamon or nutmeg. Bake at 350° for 45 to 60 minutes or until top browns. Serve with vanilla ice cream.

Yield: 8 servings

Variation: Canned fruit may be used, but decrease sugar sprinkled over fruit to ¾ cup.

Billie Brown

MANGO MOLD

3 (3-ounce) packages orange
   gelatin
1 cup water, boiling

1 (8-ounce) package cream
   cheese
1 (30-ounce) can mangoes

Place gelatin in a bowl. Add water and stir until dissolved. Add cream cheese. Blend mangoes in a blender. Add to gelatin mixture. Stir 1 minute to blend. Pour into a mold and chill 3 hours or until set. Unmold and cut into wedges or slices.

Nancy Boultinghouse

TEXAS MELONS IN RUM-LIME SAUCE

1 medium cantaloupe, balled	1 teaspoon lime zest
1 small honeydew melon, balled	6 tablespoons lime juice
1 cup blueberries	½ cup light rum (optional)
⅔ cup sugar	mint sprigs for garnish
⅓ cup water	

Place melon balls and blueberries in a serving bowl and chill. In a small saucepan, combine sugar and water. Bring to a boil and simmer 5 minutes. Add zest and cool to room temperature. Stir in juice and rum. Pour over fruit and cover. Chill several hours. Garnish with mint sprigs before serving.

Yield: 4 servings

Paula Fouchek
Texas Fresh Promotional Board

EASY STRAWBERRIES ROMANOFF

A spiced up version of a culinary classic.

1 (16-ounce) container sour cream	⅓ cup raisins (optional)
	⅛ teaspoon nutmeg
⅓ cup packed brown sugar	⅛ teaspoon cinnamon
2 teaspoons brandy extract	2 quarts strawberries, hulled

Combine sour cream and next 5 ingredients and refrigerate up to 2 weeks. When ready to serve, place strawberries in dessert dishes and top with a generous helping of cream sauce.

Yield: 6 servings

Phyllis Hutchins

Strawberry Mold

1 (10-ounce) package frozen
sliced strawberries, thawed
few drops of lemon juice
1 (3-ounce) package strawberry
gelatin

1½ cups hot water
1 (3-ounce) package cream
cheese
milk
⅓ cup chopped pecans

Sprinkle strawberries with lemon juice. Combine gelatin and water. Allow to cool, but not set. Beat cream cheese with enough milk to reach the consistency of heavy cream. Combine strawberries, gelatin mixture, cream cheese mixture, and pecans. Pour into a mold. Chill until set.

Nancy Boultinghouse

Wild Mustang Grape Jelly

Mustang grape vines grow in many parts of South Texas. Even though the ripe grapes are sour and not very good to eat, they can be used to make a very delicious jelly that has a beautiful deep red color.

Mustang Grape Juice

3 pounds very ripe mustang
grapes, stemmed

½ cup water

Combine grapes and water in a saucepan. Bring to a boil. Reduce heat and simmer, covered, for about 10 minutes. Strain juice by pouring mixture into a jelly bag or through several layers of dampened cheesecloth over a colander. Twist bag at the top to squeeze out juice.

Jelly

4 cups mustang grape juice
7 cups sugar (3 pounds)

1 (3-ounce) package liquid fruit
pectin

Combine juice and sugar in a large saucepan or a Dutch oven. Bring to a boil, stirring constantly. Stir in pectin. Bring to a rolling boil and cook 1 minute, stirring constantly. Remove from heat, skim foam, and pour quickly into hot jars. Seal with lids or paraffin.

Margaret H. McAllen
McAllen Ranch

CANDIED GRAPEFRUIT PEEL

Mr. and Mrs. T. M. Melden moved to Mission, Texas, in 1912. Mrs. Melden, my mother-in-law, was an exceptionally good cook and she worked out many of her own recipes. She devised a Candied Grapefruit Peel that was a favorite of all her family, especially when she made it at Christmas time.

2 firm grapefruit, zest removed
3 cups sugar, plus extra for
coating

3 tablespoons light corn syrup
1 cup water

Peel zested grapefruit. Place peel in a large saucepan with cold water to cover. Bring to a boil and cook 5 minutes. Drain and repeat 4 times. Peel should now be tender and have lost some of its bitterness. If not, boil 5 minutes longer and drain. Transfer to paper towels to dry slightly. Slice peel into thin strips. Combine sugar, syrup, and water in a saucepan. Bring to a boil and cook 5 minutes. Add peel and cook gently until peel is transparent. Remove peel from saucepan a few pieces at a time and toss in sugar to coat well. Add more sugar to peel as placing it in a single layer on wax paper to crystallize. Store in an airtight container. Peel will keep a very long time.

Mary Lil Melden

GRAPEFRUIT JELLY

6 cups fresh grapefruit juice
13 cups sugar
1 (3-ounce) package liquid fruit
pectin, or one (1¾-ounce) box
powdered pectin

4-5 drops red food coloring, or
as desired

Combine grapefruit juice and sugar in a saucepan. Bring to a boil and cook 12 to 15 minutes. Add pectin and boil 1 minute longer. Stir in food coloring. Pour into sterilized jelly jars. Seal with paraffin.

Shirley Bair

 SOUR ORANGE JELLY

2½ cups fresh sour orange juice, strained
zest of 1 orange

4½ cups sugar
½ (3-ounce) package liquid fruit pectin

Combine juice and zest. Let stand 5 to 10 minutes. Strain juice through a cheesecloth into a saucepan. Add sugar and bring to a boil. Add pectin and bring to a rolling boil. Cook 1½ minutes. Remove from heat and skim foam. Pour into jelly jars. Seal with paraffin.

Yield: 5 large, or 10 to 12 small jars

Margaret Looney

 PAPAYA MARMALADE

A tropical treat. Papaya is an excellent source of Vitamins A, C, and B complex. Delicious served in slices with a bit of lime juice. Also very good in fruit salads. Tough cuts of beef can be wrapped in papaya leaves to cook and will be very tender.

5 pounds papaya, peeled, seeded, and chopped
juice of 3 oranges

juice of 1 lemon
5 pounds sugar

Combine all ingredients in a saucepan. Bring to a boil and cook until papaya is transparent. Pour into hot, sterilized jars and seal.

Fedora Guerra

POTS DE CRÈME

1 (6-ounce) package chocolate chips
2 tablespoons sugar
dash of salt
1 egg

¾ cup milk, heated, but not boiling
½ cup whipping cream, sweetened and whipped

Combine chocolate chips and next 4 ingredients in a blender. Blend 1 minute. Pour into demitasse cups. Chill 2 hours or until set. Top with cream.

Yield: 6 servings

Lois Keefe

MIMMIE'S CRÈME BRÛLÉE

1 quart whipping cream	⅛ teaspoon salt
2 teaspoons vanilla	1 cup plus 3 tablespoons packed
9 egg yolks	light brown sugar
1 cup plus 2½ tablespoons	
granulated sugar	

Heat cream over medium heat in a saucepan until hot, but not scalded. Add vanilla. In a large bowl, beat egg yolks and granulated sugar with an electric mixer until thick and pale. Beat in cream mixture and salt until combined. Pour into an 8-cup, 2-inch deep ovenproof dish. Place dish in a pan and add hot water to pan half way up sides of dish. Bake at 325° for 30 minutes or until a knife inserted in the center comes out clean. Cool on a wire rack. Sprinkle brown sugar over the top by forcing sugar through a sieve over the custard. Broil about 6 inches from the heat source until sugar melts. Chill at least 60 minutes.

Yield: 10 servings

Note: This custard is delicious served with fresh blackberries or raspberries. Variation: For individual servings, divide among ¾-cup ramekins and bake the same as above.

Mary F. Lary

JOE'S FLOWERPOT DESSERT

1 (20-ounce) package chocolate	3½ cups cold milk
sandwich cookies	1 (12-ounce) container frozen
1 (8-ounce) package cream	whipped topping, thawed
cheese, softened	1 (8X10 inch) new flower pot
2 tablespoons butter or	and new garden shovel
margarine, softened	1 silk flower spray
1 cup powdered sugar	speckled jelly beans (optional)
3 (4-ounce) packages instant	
vanilla pudding	

Process cookies in a food processor or blender until fine. In a mixing bowl, beat cream cheese, butter, and sugar until smooth. In a separate bowl, mix pudding and milk until well blended. Fold in whipped topping and add to cream cheese mixture. Line flower pot with foil. Alternate layers of cookie crumbs and pudding mixture in flower pot, ending with crumbs. Chill several hours or overnight. Decorate with silk flower spray and a few jelly beans to look like small stones. Use garden shovel to serve.

Yield: 12 servings

Jose Luis Garcia

Salsas, sauces, salads & soups

The Early Days

Was Phillips in the wagon with a cap on and little Bill Hull beside him. Marion Gladys Hall & Mr Hall

McChesney's Store at McAllen & grocery wagon

Above: *Gathering in front of McChesney's Store in McAllen circa 1910.*

Cover page: *McAllen really began to take off during the 1920s.*

Below: *The original moving vans—ox carts were common along the border up until the 1920s.*

The Early Days

Ιn the sweltering May heat of 1846, cannons roared and sabers clashed in the Rio Grande Valley, as American and Mexican armies collided on the prairies of Palo Alto and in the thickets of Resaca de la Palma in what was the single most defining event in the area's history—the Mexican War. The fierce struggle culminated in the

establishment of the Rio Grande River as the new border between Texas and Mexico.

When the Mexican War ended in 1848, Laredo was the only town that existed on the northern banks of the Rio Grande. Until then, ranching had been the only way of life in the region. For the conveniences of town life, ranch owners maintained second homes in Mexican towns south of the river like Reynosa, Camargo, and Mier.

Things began to change when county authorities established a ferry connection between Reynosa and what would later become the town of Hidalgo on the U.S. side of the river. John Young, a businessman from Scotland, and John McAllen, a businessman from Ireland, received the concession to operate the ferry. It proved a lucrative business, and people began to make frequent trips back and forth. By the 1850s, the river became a busy

Top: Forts established after the Mexican War, like Ft. Ringgold at Davis Landing (now Rio Grande City), brought in soldiers and an Anglo influence to the Valley.
Bottom: Enticed by the adventure and opportunity of living on one of the last "frontiers," many of these WWI soldiers decided to stick around, bringing their wives from home, or marrying local girls and building their lives in the emerging towns along the border.

thoroughfare, as steamboats carrying freight and passengers made their way through its muddy waters.

At the same time, towns began sprouting up around newly established U.S. military forts near the river. These included Brownsville and Davis Landing (now Rio Grande City). Laredo, once a Mexican town, now thrived under U.S. governance, and those who chose not to become U.S. citizens moved across the river to found Nuevo Laredo.

In the 1860s, during the Civil War, the Valley's commercial significance grew as it became a "back door" for the Confederacy's cotton trade. Steamboats continued to crowd the river, and commerce

Above: Probably in Matamoros, this early Mexican street shows the elegant brick building style with French-influenced iron grill work popular from the mid-1800s until the turn of the century.
Right: First National Bank and Cage's Newsitorium occupied this quaint structure at the corner of Cage and Business 83 in Pharr. Photo taken April 6, 1918. A modified version of this building still stands.
Below: Early Edinburg, with the Old Hidalgo County Jail in the background. The jail is now the home of Hidalgo County Historical Museum.

thrived. The era of the steamboat soon gave way to the age of the railroad in the early 1900s, and urban life began to develop very quickly. Most of the Valley towns that exist today were organized along those newly laid railroad tracks. The towns were named after the railroad executives, bankers, and land developers—those responsible for the economic

Main St. McAllen Tex.

This page: Three views of Main Street McAllen. Above, looking south, around 1919. Above right, looking south from Business 83, c.1935. Below, looking north c. 1935.

prosperity that was taking the region by storm.

Early town life experienced a period of frenzied organization during those years, as people began to flood the region via rail. They came from all over the world. There were communities of Poles, Swedes, Scots, Irish, Italians, Asians and others. Slowly the Valley became a veritable melting pot of cultures which, when blended with the strong Spanish and Mexican influence of the region, resulted in the unique social tapestry that still exists today.

The largest influx of people in the U.S. came from the midwest. They came to develop Valley farmland now connected to northern markets, via rail, and towns were developed to serve those farms.

By 1920, agriculture had become the main economic force in these borderlands, and the newly established towns soon developed into full-fledged farming communities. Although agriculture remains the largest economic base in the region, many of the towns, now small- and medium-sized cities, have

Above: An early shot of Point Isabel (most likely taken from the lighthouse) shows a newly constructed dock. c. 1912 (?)
Below: The domes of San Benito Bank and Trust Co. c.1910.
Inset: New small towns, like Donna, arranged themselves like a string of pearls along the railroad track all up and down the Valley.

diversified their economies, capitalizing on the latest opportunities so accessible to them on the Mexican border. Today's explosion of industry and population in these cities is a testament to the age-old perseverance and spirit of entrepreneurship that was born during those early town days in Mesquite Country.

Above Left: *This ingenious palapa made from live palms served as the Missouri Pacific train stop at Llano Grande (between Mercedes and Weslaco, on Business 83) around 1911.*
Left: *Some towns were born at auction. Elsa, advertised in 1927 as "The Planned Valley Town," was started at this gathering where speculative investors rubbed elbows with "just plain folk" to buy a piece of the future from land developers.*
Below: *Busy downtown Harlingen pictured around 1910.*

PICO DE GALLO

Traditional "salsa" served on many kinds of tacos - or serve with corn tortilla chips as an appetizer.

4 large, red tomatoes, coarsely or finely chopped
1 medium onion, finely chopped
1 large, fresh jalapeño pepper, seeded and finely minced
½ cup finely chopped fresh cilantro
juice of 10 to 12 small Mexican limes, or 6 to 8 regular limes
salt and pepper to taste

Combine all ingredients in a mixing bowl.

Variation: For variety, add 2 or 3 chopped ripe avocados.

Monica Burdette
The Inn at El Canelo
Raymondville, Texas

FRESH TOMATO PICANTE SAUCE

1 fresh tomato
25 chili piquins, or to taste
2 cloves garlic
½ teaspoon salt
½ teaspoon black pepper
1 tablespoon olive oil

Mash tomato in a *molcajete* leaving a few chunks. Transfer to a bowl. Add chili piquins and garlic to *molcajete* and mash. Add to tomato. Stir in salt, black pepper, and oil. Chill before serving.

Gillespie Baker

SALSA PICANTE

3 fresh jalapeño peppers, or to taste
1 medium onion, quartered
1 (8-ounce) can tomato sauce
1 (8-ounce) can tomato juice

Combine all ingredients in a blender or food processor. Process until ground, but do not liquefy. If too thick, add more juice. If too thin, add extra onion.

Allen Dreyer
Big-R Bar-B-Que Restaurant

GRAPEFRUIT *PICO DE GALLO*

3 large Texas Rio Red grapefruit,
peeled and sectioned
1 small red bell pepper, diced
2 tablespoons minced fresh
cilantro

¼ cup diced green onion, or
other onion
¼ teaspoon crushed red pepper
flakes
pinch of salt

Cut grapefruit sections into ½-inch pieces. Place in a 2-quart glass or pottery bowl. Add bell pepper and remaining 4 ingredients. Stir gently to mix. Chill at least 60 minutes before serving.

Yield: 6 servings

Note: Goes good with breakfast tacos, brunch, or BBQ.

Barbara Steidinger
Texas Agri-Women, Inc.

PAPAYA-MANGO SALSA

If fresh mangoes and papaya are not available, look in the produce section of the store for jarred fruit, or for canned fruit in the grocery section.

1 cup peeled, seeded, and
chopped papaya
1 cup peeled, seeded, and
chopped mango
½ cup chopped jícama
½ cup chopped red onion
¼ - ½ cup chopped fresh
cilantro

1 fresh jalapeño pepper, seeded
and chopped
1 tablespoon lime juice
1 clove garlic, crushed
¼ cup finely chopped peanuts
⅛ teaspoon salt
dash of black pepper

Combine all ingredients in a medium bowl.

Yield: 3 cups

Note: Excellent with grilled meats such as pork or chicken.

Gilda dela Garza

Mango Relish

Fabulous fresh, zippy taste!

3 large mangoes, peeled and finely diced
1 red onion, finely diced
4 green onions, thinly sliced
¼ cup fresh lime juice
1 tablespoon grated fresh ginger
2 cloves garlic, minced
2 fresh Chile de Ristra or Anaheim peppers, finely chopped

Combine all ingredients and mix well. Serve with fish or shrimp.
Yield: 6 servings

Barbara Steidinger
Texas Agri-Women, Inc.

Pear and Chili Chutney

Great served along-side meats - especially pork.

2½ pounds firm pears, peeled and chopped
1 cup chopped white onion
3 tablespoons seeded and minced jalapeño pepper
2 Anaheim peppers, roasted, skinned, seeded, and coarsely chopped
2 red bell peppers, roasted, skinned, seeded, and coarsely chopped
1½ cups apple cider vinegar
¾ cup packed light brown sugar
¾ cup packed dark brown sugar
2 teaspoons turmeric
1½ teaspoons minced fresh ginger
1 tablespoon honey
1 tablespoon soy sauce
½ teaspoon salt
1½ teaspoons dry mustard
2 teaspoons cornstarch
2 teaspoons water

Combine pear and next 13 ingredients in a nonreactive saucepan over medium-high heat. Dissolve cornstarch in water and stir into mixture. Bring to a boil. Reduce heat and simmer 15 minutes or until pear begins to break apart. Cool. Transfer to jars and cover. Store in refrigerator up to 2 weeks.

Madelaine McLelland

Ninfa's Green Sauce

3 medium-size green tomatoes,
  coarsely chopped
4 tomatillos, chopped
1-2 jalapeño peppers, stemmed
  and coarsely chopped
3 small cloves garlic

3 medium-size ripe avocados,
  peeled and sliced
4 sprigs cilantro
1 teaspoon salt
1 cup sour cream

Combine tomato and next 3 ingredients in a saucepan. Bring to a boil. Reduce heat and simmer 10 to 15 minutes or until tomatoes are soft. Cool slightly. In batches, combine tomato mixture, avocado, cilantro, and salt in a food processor and puree. Transfer to a bowl. Stir in sour cream. Cover with plastic and chill. Serve with warm tortillas.

Yield: 4 to 5 cups

Julie Flores

Chimichurri Sauce

This version of a South American classic uses the Rio Grande Valley's specialty - Texas Rio Red grapefruit - but any fresh grapefruit can be substituted.

2 sprigs cilantro
1 sprig parsley
½ cup balsamic vinegar
¾ cup fresh Texas Rio Red
  grapefruit juice
1 cup virgin olive oil
¼ cup chopped fresh garlic
2 tablespoons Worcestershire
  sauce

1 tablespoon Tabasco sauce
1½ tablespoons ground cumin
1½ tablespoons chili powder
1 tablespoon black pepper
1½ teaspoons salt
¼ cup chopped red onion
juice of 2 lemons

Combine all ingredients in a food processor. Blend until well mixed. Use as a marinade for meat and seafood, or serve on the side.

Barbara Steidinger
Texas Agri-Women, Inc.

COOKED PICANTE SAUCE

Best with fresh picked chiles. At our house, we have to fight the mocking-birds for the chiles.

½ cup chopped onion
3 cloves garlic, pressed
1 tablespoon olive oil
24 green chile piquins

1 (14½-ounce) can diced
   tomatoes, undrained
1½ tablespoons vinegar
1 teaspoon salt

Sauté onion and garlic in oil. Place chile piquins and a small amount of water in a *molcajete* and grind. Add to sautéed mixture. Add tomatoes, vinegar, and salt to mixture. Simmer about 45 minutes. Serve hot or cold. Store in refrigerator.

Yield: 2 cups

Note: Delicious with tortilla chips, on eggs, rice, tamales - all types of Mexican dishes.

Marcia Ross

RIO GRANDE VALLEY CITRUS SAUCE

This zingy sauce is excellent served on chicken, pork, shrimp, or fish.

1 stick butter
1 cup cider vinegar
1 cup tomato puree
3 tablespoons prepared
   horseradish
juice of 3 limes
juice of 1 medium orange

3 tablespoons packed brown
   sugar
1 tablespoon Worcestershire
   sauce
1 teaspoon salt
1 orange, peeled, sectioned, and
   chopped

Combine butter and next 8 ingredients in a saucepan. Bring to a boil. Reduce heat and simmer, stirring frequently, for 40 minutes or until mixture thickens. When ready to serve, add orange. Serve warm or cold.

Yield: 2 cups

The Honorable Kika de la Garza
89th Member of Congress
15th Congressional District
Served 1965-1996

MUSTARD SAUCE

For a spicier taste, substitute ½ cup horseradish mustard for half of the prepared mustard.

1 cup prepared mustard	⅔ cup sugar
2 tablespoons coarse mustard	2 eggs, beaten
1 cup vinegar	1 teaspoon white pepper

Combine prepared mustard and next 3 ingredients in the top of a double boiler. Let stand several hours without cooking. Add eggs to mixture and stir well. Add pepper. Cook until thick. Store in refrigerator up to 5 days.

Yield: about 2 cups

Note: Great served as an accompaniment to venison or other meat.

Kathryn Kaplan

MUSHROOM STEAK SAUCE

Great on steak, but can also be used on roasted chicken.

6 tablespoons margarine	1 (7-ounce) can sliced
6-8 shallots, chopped	mushrooms, undrained
2½ tablespoons all-purpose flour	pinch of black pepper

Melt margarine in a saucepan. Add shallot and sauté until transparent. Stir in flour. Cook and stir 5 minutes. Add mushrooms and pepper and cook until thickened.

Yield: 4 servings

Nancy Boultinghouse

AVOCADO AND MUSHROOM PIQUANT

Tastes great with grilled meats.

2 avocados, peeled and sliced
8 ounces mushrooms, stemmed
½ cup oil
3 tablespoons tarragon vinegar
2 tablespoons lemon juice
2 tablespoons water

1 tablespoon chopped fresh
  parsley
1-2 cloves garlic, minced
¾ teaspoon salt
freshly ground black pepper
Bibb lettuce

Combine avocado and mushrooms in a bowl. Place oil and next 7 ingredients in a blender. Puree and pour over vegetables. Chill several hours, spooning oil mixture over vegetables several times. Serve on lettuce.

Mary Vance Jones

BROCCOLI SALAD

1 large head broccoli, cut into
  florets
1 onion, sliced into thin rings
½ cup golden raisins
1 (8-ounce) can sliced water
  chestnuts
1 cup sliced celery

½ cup sliced carrot
½ cup cashews
½ cup mayonnaise
2 tablespoons vinegar
1 tablespoon sugar
10 slices bacon, crisply cooked
  and crumbled

Combine broccoli and next 6 ingredients in a bowl. Blend mayonnaise, vinegar, and sugar and pour over broccoli mixture. Toss and chill. Sprinkle with bacon before serving.

Sue Wilson

CABBAGE SLAW

¾ cup sugar
1 teaspoon prepared mustard
1 teaspoon celery seed
1½ teaspoons salt

1 cup vinegar
1 cup corn oil
1 head cabbage, diced
1 large onion, sliced into rings

Combine sugar and next 4 ingredients in a saucepan. Bring to a boil and remove from heat. Stir to dissolve. Add oil. Place cabbage and onion in a bowl. Pour sugar mixture over top. Refrigerate 24 hours.

Kenneth Schauer

JÍCAMA AND ORANGE SALAD

SALAD
½ cup pecans
1 head Boston or Bibb lettuce
2 oranges, peeled and sliced

1 red onion, very thinly sliced
1 cup julienned jícama

DRESSING
¾ cup vegetable oil
¼ cup vinegar

½ teaspoon salt
½ teaspoon ground cumin

Toast pecans in an oven at 350° for 5-10 minutes or until fragrant. Line a serving platter or individual salad plates with lettuce. Top with orange slices, onion, jícama, and pecans. To make dressing, whisk together all ingredients. Drizzle over salad.

Yield: 6 to 8 servings

Colleen Curran Hook

SWEET RELISH POTATO SALAD

5 pounds potatoes, peeled and
cubed
5 carrots, peeled
salt and pepper to taste
2 cups mayonnaise

1 teaspoon prepared mustard
⅓ cup sweet pickle relish
10 hard-cooked eggs, chopped
paprika

Cook potato and carrots in boiling water for 15 minutes. Drain and cool. Finely chop carrots. Combine potato, carrot, salt, pepper, and next 3 ingredients. Add eggs. Chill and sprinkle with paprika to garnish.

Yield: 20 servings

Karen Valdez

SENSATION SALAD I

½ cup canola oil
½ cup olive oil
2½ tablespoons lemon juice
1½ tablespoons vinegar
2 cloves garlic, pressed
¾ teaspoon salt

2 large or 3 small heads lettuce, torn into bite-size pieces
1 bunch parsley, chopped
1 cup grated Romano cheese
¼ cup crumbled blue cheese
freshly ground black pepper to taste

Combine canola oil and next 5 ingredients to make a dressing. Combine lettuce and parsley in a bowl. Pour dressing over top and toss until well coated. Sprinkle with cheeses and toss. Season with black pepper.

Yield: 1¼ cups dressing

Barbara Steidinger
Texas Agri-Women, Inc.

SENSATION SALAD II

This is my dinner party salad, introduced to me by friends from Alexandria, Louisiana. It is simple and good to serve at large dinner parties. Just prepare the lettuce and parsley early in the day. Pour the dressing on before serving.

8 ounces Romano cheese, freshly grated
2 cups canola oil
juice of 2 lemons
juice of 3 cloves of garlic

lettuce, torn into bite-size pieces
fresh parsley, chopped
freshly ground black pepper to taste
salt to taste

Combine cheese and next 3 ingredients in a 1-quart jar. Shake to mix. Store indefinitely in refrigerator. Combine lettuce and parsley in a bowl. Pour dressing over top and toss until well coated. Season with pepper and salt.

Yield: 6 servings per head of lettuce

Note: Use a salad spinner to dry lettuce and parsley after rinsing. The drier the better. Chop parsley quickly and efficiently in a food processor.

Barbara Steidinger
Texas Agri-Women, Inc.

Spinach Salad

Super easy - super good!

1 (10-ounce) bag fresh spinach, rinsed and torn into bite-size pieces
1 red onion, thinly sliced
2-3 red or green pears, unpeeled and thinly sliced
1 (8-ounce) package crumbled blue cheese
1 (8-ounce) bottle poppy seed salad dressing
pine nuts (optional)
bacon bits (optional)

Toss spinach and next 4 ingredients together in a bowl. Sprinkle with pine nuts and bacon bits.

Yield: 6 to 8 servings

Becky Gerling

Another Spinach Salad and Dressing

This salad is so good that it was submitted separately by 2 people.

Salad

1 (10-ounce) bag or 3 bunches fresh spinach, rinsed and dried
2 cups fresh bean sprouts
1 (8-ounce) can water chestnuts, drained
4 hard-cooked eggs, sliced
4 ounces bacon, cooked and crumbled (optional)

Dressing

1 cup vegetable oil
¾ cup sugar
2 teaspoons Worcestershire sauce
2 teaspoons onion salt
¼ cup vinegar
⅓ cup ketchup

Combine all salad ingredients and toss. Combine all dressing ingredients in a blender and mix. Pour over salad just before serving.

Yield: 4 to 6 servings

Julie Flores and Mariella Gorena

FRESH FRUIT AND SPINACH SALAD WITH RASPBERRY VINAIGRETTE

RASPBERRY VINAIGRETTE DRESSING

1 cup raspberry wine vinegar
½ cup sugar
2 tablespoons sesame seed
2 tablespoons poppy seed

1 tablespoon Worcestershire
sauce
1 tablespoon paprika
2½ cups vegetable oil

SALAD

2 avocados, peeled and sliced
2 cups raspberry vinaigrette
dressing
1 (10-ounce) bag fresh spinach,
rinsed and stemmed

2 heads Boston lettuce, rinsed
and torn into bite-size pieces
3 kiwi, peeled and sliced
1 pint strawberries, sliced
2 tablespoons sliced almonds,
toasted

Mix together vinegar and next 5 ingredients. Slowly mix in oil until thick. To prepare salad, marinate avocado in dressing. Combine spinach and remaining 4 ingredients in a bowl. Remove avocado from dressing, reserving dressing, and add to bowl. Toss. When ready to serve, pour reserved dressing over salad.

Note: To toast almonds, place on baking sheet in 350° oven for 5 - 10 minutes or until fragrant.

Sergio Rodriguez
Executive Chef
Catering by Don Strange
San Antonio, Texas

BLACK-EYED PEA SALAD

This tasty dish is sure to become a tradition on New Year's Day at your house!

4 (14-ounce) cans black-eyed
  peas, drained
1 bell pepper, chopped
1 bunch green onion, chopped
¼ cup pimiento-stuffed green
  olives
¼ cup olive oil

¼ cup cider vinegar
2 tablespoons red wine vinegar
½ teaspoon garlic salt
½ teaspoon dried basil
1 teaspoon black pepper
dash of hot pepper sauce

Place peas and next 3 ingredients in a mixing bowl. Combine oil and remaining 6 ingredients in a glass jar. Cover tightly and shake vigorously. Pour over pea mixture. Toss gently to coat. Cover and chill 2 to 3 hours, or preferably overnight. Store up to several days in the refrigerator.

Kathryn Kaplan

WHITE BEAN SALAD

1 cup dried white beans, cooked,
  or two (16-ounce) cans great
  Northern beans
1 large red onion, very thinly
  sliced
salt to taste

½ cup virgin olive oil
¼ cup red wine vinegar, or to
  taste
½ cup chopped fresh parsley
kalamata olives for garnish
  (optional)

Drain beans, rinse well, and drain again. Place beans and onion in a bowl. Add salt, oil, and vinegar. Stir in parsley and let stand at least 60 minutes at room temperature. Stir well and adjust seasonings as needed. Garnish with olives before serving. Serve cold or at room temperature.

Yield: 4 to 6 servings

Laura Martinez Ilgun

BLACK BEAN AND AVOCADO SALAD

1 cup dried black beans
3 cups water
1 tablespoon chili powder, or to taste
4 cloves garlic, mashed

1 tablespoon tamari sauce
sea salt or regular salt to taste
1 ripe avocado
1 ear corn, kernels removed
¼ cup chopped fresh cilantro

Soak beans in 3 cups water overnight. Discard water and rinse beans. Remove any stones. Place beans in a saucepan. Add enough water to cover. Add chili powder and garlic. Bring to a boil. Reduce heat and simmer 35 to 50 minutes or until tender. Add water as needed to keep beans covered. As beans start to soften, let water cook off so all water has evaporated when beans are done. Season beans with tamari sauce and salt. Cool in refrigerator. Scoop out avocado in chunks with a spoon. Add avocado, corn kernels, and cilantro to beans. Mix well.

Yield: 4 servings

Zoila Martinez

LETTUCE AND FRITO SALAD WITH AVOCADO DRESSING

AVOCADO DRESSING

½ cup mashed avocado
1 tablespoon lemon juice
½ cup sour cream
⅓ cup vegetable oil

1 clove garlic, crushed
½ teaspoon salt
½ teaspoon chili powder
¼ teaspoon hot pepper sauce

SALAD

½ cup chopped or thinly sliced black olives
¼ cup chopped onion
5 chicken thighs, boiled and cubed

½ medium head lettuce, torn into bite-size pieces
1 tomato, cubed
1 cup small corn chips

Mix together all dressing ingredients. To make salad, combine olives, onion, and chicken meat. When ready to serve, add lettuce, tomato, and chips. Pour dressing over salad and toss to mix.

Gilda de la Garza

FLAVORFUL BEEF AND BLACK BEAN SALAD

½ cup fresh lime juice, divided
2 tablespoons olive oil, divided
2 tablespoons fresh orange juice
1 tablespoon packed brown
   sugar
1 tablespoon packed chopped
   fresh thyme
1 clove garlic, crushed
¼ teaspoon crushed red pepper
   pods

1 (1-pound, 1-inch thick)
   boneless top sirloin beef steak
1 large orange, peeled and cut
   into ½-inch slices
1 (16-ounce) can black beans,
   drained and rinsed
2 green onions, thinly sliced
4 cups sliced romaine lettuce,
   sliced ¼-inch thick
prepared salsa, chilled

Combine 6 tablespoons lime juice, 1 tablespoon oil, and next 5 ingredients
for a marinade. Place steak in a plastic bag. Add marinade, seal bag, and turn
to coat. Refrigerate 30 minutes. Separate each orange slice into sections.
Combine orange, beans, green onions, remaining 2 tablespoons lime juice,
and remaining 1 tablespoon oil. Remove steak from marinade, discarding
marinade. Broil steak 3 to 4 inches from the heat source. Cook 16 to 20
minutes for rare to medium, turning once. Trim excess fat from steak and
carve into ⅛-inch thick slices. Arrange lettuce on a 12-inch platter. Spoon
bean mixture onto lettuce around the edge. Place beef in center. Serve with
salsa.

Yield: 4 servings

National Cattlemen's Beef Association
Chicago, Illinois

TACO SALAD

1 pound ground beef
1 (15-ounce) can Ranch-style
   beans, drained
¼ teaspoon salt
1 medium onion, chopped
4 tomatoes, chopped

1 medium head lettuce, chopped
6 ounces cheddar cheese, grated
1 (10-ounce) bag corn chips
1 avocado, cut into bite-size
   pieces

Brown beef. Add beans and salt. Simmer 10 minutes. Place beef mixture in a
bowl. Add onion, tomato, and lettuce. Mix in cheese, chips, and avocado
and serve.

Yield: 4 servings

Note: Serve plain or in a pita shell with hot sauce or salad dressing.

Dora Brown

SHRIMP PARADISE SALAD

SALAD

1 quart water
2 tablespoons salt
½ pound large shrimp, peeled
and deveined
1 large pineapple, halved
lengthwise

1 avocado, peeled and sliced
1 tablespoon lemon juice
2 large oranges, peeled and
sectioned

SHRIMP PARADISE DRESSING

2 tablespoons lemon juice
2 tablespoons dry white wine
1 teaspoon honey

½ teaspoon salt
½ teaspoon paprika
½ cup olive or vegetable oil

Combine water and salt in a saucepan and bring to a boil. Add shrimp and cook 2 minutes. Pour shrimp into a colander to drain and cool. Transfer to refrigerator to chill. Remove core and pulp from pineapple, reserving shells for serving. Sprinkle avocado with lemon juice to prevent discoloration. Fill pineapple shells with pineapple pulp, avocado, and orange. Arrange shrimp on top. Serve with Shrimp Paradise Dressing. To make dressing, combine all dressing ingredients in a jar, shake well, and chill.

Yield: 6 servings

Nancy Boultinghouse

DORA'S SHRIMP SALAD

1 cup mayonnaise
1½ tablespoons wine vinegar
salt and pepper to taste
1 pound peeled and cooked
shrimp

1 small head lettuce, cut into
bite-size pieces
3 hard-cooked eggs, chopped
1 small onion, finely chopped
½ cup celery, finely chopped

Combine mayonnaise and vinegar in a large bowl. Add salt, pepper, and remaining 5 ingredients. Chill.

Yield: 4 servings

Dora Brown

TORTELLINI SALAD

SALAD

2 (8-ounce) packages cheese
tortellini
1 red onion, chopped
1 cup feta or Havarti cheese

1 (2¼-ounce) can chopped black
olives
1 cup chopped red bell pepper

MUSTARD VINAIGRETTE

2 cloves garlic, crushed
2 tablespoons Dijon mustard
½ cup red wine vinegar
1 teaspoon black pepper

1 cup olive oil
½ cup slivered fresh basil
½ cup chopped fresh parsley

Cook tortellini according to package directions. Drain. Combine tortellini, onion, and next 3 ingredients. To make vinaigrette, place garlic and next 3 ingredients in a small bowl. Mix well. Slowly whisk in oil in a steady stream. Add basil and parsley. When ready to serve, combine salad and vinaigrette and toss.

Lynn Wright Parker

CRAB AND PASTA SALAD

½ cup chopped celery
¼ cup chopped green onions
4 ounces crabmeat, or to taste
1 (10-ounce) package pasta
shells, cooked al dente and
chilled

1 tablespoon seasoned salt
1 tablespoon black pepper
½ - ¾ cup Miracle Whip

Combine celery and next 3 ingredients in a bowl and mix. Season with seasoned salt and pepper. Mix well. Stir in salad dressing until pasta is coated. Refrigerate overnight to allow flavors to blend.

Julie Flores

COLD PASTA AND CHICKEN SALAD

1 (8-ounce) package vermicelli
1 cup garlic vinaigrette salad
dressing, divided (La
Martinique Famous French
dressing is recommended)
10 fresh mushrooms, sliced

1 cup broccoli florets, blanched
10 cherry tomatoes (optional)
2 cups cubed cooked chicken
⅓ cup chopped fresh basil, or
1½ teaspoons dried
⅓ cup pine nuts, toasted

Cook pasta and drain. While still hot, combine pasta and ⅓ cup dressing in a mixing bowl. Chill at least 3 hours. Place remaining ⅔ cup dressing in a separate bowl. Stir in mushrooms, broccoli, and tomatoes. Chill. When ready to serve, add chicken to pasta mixture and toss. Add vegetable mixture, basil, and pine nuts and toss.

Yield: 4 to 6 servings

Linda Y. Thompson

CONFETTI CHICKEN SALAD

Very colorful and fresh tasting salad.

2 cups cubed, cooked chicken
1 cup cooked rice, cooled
1 cup frozen green peas, thawed
½ cup diced water chestnuts
¼ cup diced celery
¼ cup chopped bell pepper
¼ cup chopped onion

¼ cup chopped fresh cilantro
(optional)
1 cup canned corn
¼ cup chopped pimiento
½ cup bottled green goddess
dressing
¼ cup sour cream

Combine all ingredients. Cover and chill.

Yield: 6 to 8 servings

Lucille dela Garza

CHICKEN ROTELLE SALAD
WITH CILANTRO VINAIGRETTE

CILANTRO VINAIGRETTE

¼ cup red wine vinegar
¾ teaspoon salt
¼ teaspoon coarsely ground
  black pepper
½ - ¾ cup extra virgin olive oil

2 teaspoons sesame oil
2 cloves garlic, slightly crushed
1 large bunch cilantro, leaves
  only

CHICKEN AND PASTA

2 pounds boneless, skinless
  chicken thighs or breasts
Bolner's Fiesta Fajita Seasoning
½ cup bell pepper, cut into
  strips
½ cup red bell pepper, cut into
  strips

½ cup yellow bell pepper, cut
  into strips
1 bunch green onions, sliced
1 (12-ounce) package rotelle
  (spiral) pasta, cooked al dente
1-2 teaspoons crushed red
  pepper flakes, or to taste

Combine vinegar, salt, and pepper in a food processor. Blend 45 to 60 seconds or until foamy. Add oils. Process 60 seconds or until very creamy. Add garlic and cilantro and process 30 to 45 seconds or until cilantro is finely minced. To prepare salad, place chicken on a baking sheet. Sprinkle both sides with fajita seasoning. Bake at 350° for about 15 minutes. Turn and bake another 10 minutes or until thoroughly cooked. Cool and cut into strips or chunks. Place peppers and onions in a glass baking dish. Microwave 5 minutes and cool. Combine chicken, vegetable mixture, and pasta in a large salad bowl. Pour vinaigrette over top and toss. Add pepper flakes and toss.

Yield: 6 to 8 servings

Note: Look for Bolner's Fiesta Fajita Seasoning in the spice section of the grocery store. If not available, substitute salt, pepper, and garlic powder.

Serve with Parmesan Herb Bread (page 72).

Monica Burdette
The Inn at El Canelo
Raymondville, Texas

CRUNCHY CHICKEN SALAD

1 cup chopped pecans, toasted
5½ cups chopped cooked
 chicken
3 hard-cooked eggs, chopped
1 cup chopped celery
1 cup cubed sweet pickles
1 cup seedless green grapes,
 halved
1 cup mayonnaise

1 (8-ounce) can water chestnuts,
 drained and chopped
1 (8-ounce) can pineapple
 tidbits, drained and chopped
½ cup pimiento-stuffed green
 olives, chopped
1 small onion, chopped
1 (2-ounce) jar diced pimiento,
 drained
1 tablespoon lemon juice

Bake pecans at 350° for 5 to 10 minutes or until fragrant. Combine pecans
and remaining 12 ingredients. Mix well and chill. Serve in lettuce cups or use
for sandwiches.
Yield: 12 servings

Nancy Boultinghouse

SPANISH SALAD

3 cups shredded cooked chicken
½ cup cubed salami
3 medium boiled potatoes,
 peeled and diced
1 bell pepper, seeded and
 coarsely chopped
½ cup chopped pimiento
1 cup cooked green peas
2 radishes, thinly sliced
2 tablespoons capers, drained

½ cup quartered pimiento-
 stuffed green olives
3 tablespoons dry sherry
½ cup extra virgin olive oil
¼ cup white wine vinegar
¼ teaspoon white pepper
1 large head Boston lettuce
2 hard-cooked eggs, chopped
6-8 spears asparagus, cooked
8 sprigs parsley
1 medium onion, sliced into
 rings

Combine chicken and next 8 ingredients in a large bowl. Toss once. Combine sherry and next 3 ingredients in a jar. Close tightly and shake until well
mixed. Pour over chicken mixture and toss. Cover and chill 4 hours. Line a
serving platter with Boston lettuce. Add egg to salad and toss lightly. Drain
excess dressing from bowl. Transfer salad to serving plate. Garnish with
asparagus, parsley, and onion.
Yield: 6 to 8 servings

Kathy Escamilla

Jennifer's Turkey Salad

6 cups chopped cooked turkey
1 cup chopped celery
1 cup seedless red grapes,
  halved
¼ cup chopped fresh parsley
¼ cup chopped green onions

1 cup mayonnaise
1 tablespoon fresh dill
salt and pepper to taste
½ cup sliced almonds, toasted
  (optional)

Combine turkey and next 6 ingredients and mix well. Season with salt and pepper. Garnish with almonds.

Variation: Top salad with breadcrumbs and cheddar cheese and serve warm.

Jennifer Wright

Chilled Quail Salad

¼ cup finely chopped celery
¼ cup finely chopped onion
⅛ cup chopped pimiento
⅛ cup chopped bell pepper
¼ cup chopped black olives

1½-2 cups shredded, boiled quail
  meat
1 tablespoon Accent flavor
  enhancer
½ cup mayonnaise
salt and pepper to taste

Combine all ingredients. Chill overnight.

Sandra Catlett

Poppy Seed Dressing

1½ cups sugar
2 teaspoons dry mustard
2 teaspoons salt
⅔ cup vinegar

3 tablespoons onion juice
2 cups vegetable oil
3 tablespoons poppy seed

Combine sugar and next 3 ingredients. Add onion juice and stir thoroughly. Slowly beat in oil with an electric mixer until thick. Add poppy seed and beat a few minutes longer. Store in refrigerator.

Yield: 3½ cups

Note: Dressing can be prepared in a blender.

Linda Browder

RASPBERRY VINAIGRETTE

1 cup raspberry vinegar
1 tablespoon finely minced
  shallot
2 tablespoons sugar

1 tablespoon dried tarragon
2 tablespoons fresh or frozen
  strained raspberry puree
3 cups vegetable oil

Combine vinegar and next 4 ingredients. Mix in oil.

Yield: about 1 quart

Note: Pour dressing over a lettuce salad and garnish with fresh whole raspberries.

Lisa Harms
Santa Fe Steakhouse
McAllen, Texas

HONEY MUSTARD DRESSING

Make 24 hours ahead. Goes on any salad or as a dipping sauce.

3 cups mayonnaise
⅓ cup vegetable oil
⅓ cup prepared mustard
⅓ cup honey

2 tablespoons apple cider
  vinegar
½ teaspoon onion salt
cayenne pepper to taste

Combine all ingredients. Mix thoroughly and chill.

Yield: 1 quart

Ron Speier
Yacht Club
Port Isabel, Texas

CHEESE SOUP

¼ cup chopped onion
pinch of celery flakes
1 stick margarine
1 cup all-purpose flour
1 quart milk
1 quart chicken broth

⅓ cup chopped cooked carrot
1 tablespoon dry mustard
¼ teaspoon cayenne pepper
1½ pounds processed cheese
    loaf, grated
salt and pepper to taste

Sauté onion and celery flakes in margarine in a large saucepan. Blend in flour. In a separate saucepan, slowly bring milk and broth to a boil, but do not scald. Gradually whisk hot liquid into flour mixture. Stir in carrot and next 3 ingredients. Season with salt and pepper. Slowly bring to a boil, stirring constantly.

Yield: 6-8 servings

Variation: For variety, add a 10-ounce package frozen chopped broccoli with the carrot.

Julie Flores

MUSHROOM SOUP

4 tablespoons unsalted butter
1 medium onion, finely chopped
1 pound mushrooms, chopped
3 tablespoons all-purpose flour

1 quart beef broth
pinch of white pepper
pinch of nutmeg
1½ cups whipping cream

Melt butter in a large saucepan. Add onion and sauté until transparent. Add mushrooms and cook until tender. Blend in flour. Stirring constantly, add broth and bring to a boil. Add pepper and nutmeg. Remove from heat and stir in cream. Serve immediately.

Yield: 4 to 6 servings

Shan Rankin

TEXAS GAZPACHO

This recipe comes from Rio Ranch Restaurant in Houston. This was part of a menu planned for a special media luncheon for the Texas Fresh Promotional Board in May of 1993.

3 Texas 1015 onions, or other
  sweet onions
½ bunch celery
3 carrots
3 bell peppers
4 red bell peppers
4 zucchini

2 serrano chili peppers
8 ounces Roma tomatoes
⅓ cup red wine vinegar
2 (32-ounce) cans V-8 juice
1½ teaspoons salt
1½ teaspoons white pepper
¼ teaspoon sugar

Chop onions and next 7 ingredients into 1-inch pieces. Place vegetables in a food processor and chop into small pieces. In a large bowl, combine vinegar and V-8 juice. Add chopped vegetables, salt, white pepper, and sugar. Cover and chill several hours. Serve cold.

Yield: 10 to 12 servings

Paula Fouchek
Texas Fresh Promotional Board

MEXICALI BEAN SOUP

½ cup chopped onion
1 clove garlic, minced
2 tablespoons vegetable oil
2 (16-ounce) cans red kidney
  beans, drained
1 (14½-ounce) can tomatoes,
  chopped
1 (16-ounce) can cream-style
  corn

1 (4-ounce) can green chilies,
  rinsed, seeded, and chopped
1 tablespoon instant chicken
  bouillon
1 teaspoon ground cumin
6 cups water
2 teaspoons salt
¼ teaspoon black pepper
grated cheddar cheese

Sauté onion and garlic in oil in a 5-quart Dutch oven until softened. Stir in beans and next 8 ingredients. Cover and simmer 25 minutes. Top individual serving with cheese and serve immediately.

Yield: 4 servings

Dora Brown

MINESTRONE

6 tablespoons margarine
3 large carrots, sliced
2 medium stalks celery, sliced
2 medium onions, diced
1 small clove garlic, minced
1 medium head cabbage, sliced
1 (14½-ounce) can tomatoes, undrained
2 quarts water
⅓ cup dry rice
1 teaspoon salt
2 teaspoons Worcestershire sauce
¼ teaspoon dried oregano
¼ teaspoon freshly ground black pepper
3-4 potatoes, peeled and cut into bite-size pieces
4 instant beef bouillon cubes
2 large zucchini, cut into bite-size pieces
2 (15-ounce) cans kidney beans, drained
1 (10-ounce) package frozen chopped spinach
½ cup Parmesan or Romano cheese (optional)

Melt margarine in a large pot. Add carrot and next 4 ingredients. Cook and stir until lightly browned. Add tomatoes and next 9 ingredients. Bring to a boil. Reduce heat and cover. Simmer about 30 minutes. Add beans and spinach. Cook until heated through. Sprinkle cheese over individual servings.

Yield: 8 to 10 servings

Marilyn Moffitt

ACCIDENTAL PINTO BEAN SOUP

"This was developed after being too generous with the water used for cooking beans. They were seasoned so well I didn't want to discard so much good broth, so I froze the broth and developed this recipe. It has become one of our favorite cold weather soups, and now I always cook beans with the soup broth in mind."

BEANS AND BEAN BROTH
dry pinto beans

SOUP
½ onion, chopped
2 cloves garlic, chopped, or to taste
3-4 small hot green chili peppers, or to taste

1 tablespoon vegetable oil or bacon fat
2 quarts bean broth
1 cup mashed beans
2 dry corn tortillas, cut into small pieces

Place beans in a saucepan. Add enough water to allow for 2 quarts of broth when beans are cooked. Season as desired. Cook beans until tender. Drain beans, reserving broth. Mash beans to equal 1 cup. To make soup, sauté onion, garlic, and peppers in oil until softened. Add broth and beans. Simmer 30 minutes or until flavors blend. Add tortillas and continue cooking, stirring occasionally, until tortillas softened.

Yield: 4 servings

Note: The beans and tortillas thicken the soup, the broth will thin it. Adjust amounts of these ingredients to reach desired consistency.

Josephine Stone

BLACK BEAN SOUP

1 cup dried black or turtle
  beans, rinsed
8 cups chicken broth, divided,
  preferably homemade
1 large bay leaf
1 large onion, coarsely chopped
1 tablespoon olive oil
1 garlic clove, minced
1 cup canned tomatoes, drained
  and chopped

3 tablespoons dry red wine
1 teaspoon sugar
¼ teaspoon freshly ground black
  pepper
1½ cups dry elbow macaroni
2 very large red bell peppers,
  roasted, peeled, and diced
minced parsley for garnish
minced green onion for garnish

Soak beans overnight. Drain beans and place in a large pot. Cover with 3 cups broth and bring to a boil. Reduce heat and add bay leaf. Simmer 2 hours or until beans are almost tender. In a medium saucepan over medium heat, sauté onion in olive oil for 5 minutes or until softened. Add garlic and cook 1 minute. Add onion mixture and tomatoes to beans. Cook about 60 minutes or until beans are tender, adding broth as needed. Stir in wine, sugar, black pepper, and remaining broth. Cook macaroni in lightly salted boiling water for 6 minutes. Drain. When almost ready to serve, add macaroni and bell pepper to soup. Simmer over medium-low heat until macaroni is cooked al dente. Remove bay leaf and adjust seasonings as desired. Garnish with minced parsley and green onions.

Yield: 6 servings

Victoria Shawn Stephen

BLACK BEAN AND SHRIMP SOUP

The recipe for this deliciously different soup originated at "La Floridita Restaurant" in Havana, Cuba.

1 pound dried black beans
5 tablespoons butter
1 large onion, finely chopped
10 cups chicken broth
⅓ cup frozen orange juice
  concentrate, thawed

1 clove garlic, crushed
1½ teaspoons salt
2 pounds shrimp, peeled and
  deveined
2 green onions, sliced

Soak beans overnight. Melt butter in a saucepan. Add onion and sauté. Drain beans. Add beans, chicken broth and next 3 ingredients. Simmer 2 hours. Sauté shrimp and green onions in a skillet. Spoon soup into individual serving bowls. Top with shrimp mixture.

Yield: 6 servings

Hilda Lewin

TORTILLA SOUP

1 yellow onion, finely chopped
4 tablespoons butter
salt and pepper to taste
3 tablespoons chopped fresh
  cilantro
4 cups corn
2½ quarts chicken broth

1 (8-ounce) can tomato sauce
2 teaspoons ground cumin
1 teaspoon garlic powder
cayenne pepper to taste
tortilla chips
grated Monterey Jack cheese
sliced avocado (optional)

Sauté onion in butter until tender. Add salt, pepper, and next 7 ingredients. Cook until heated. When ready to serve, crumble tortilla chips into individual serving bowls. Add cheese and avocado. Pour soup over top.

Yield: 8 to 10 servings

Variation: To serve as a main course, add 4 or 5 cooked and shredded chicken breasts.

Julie Flores

CALDO MAYA
CHICKEN TORTILLA SOUP

MEAT AND BROTH

1 whole chicken, or 6 chicken
  breasts
salt and pepper to taste
1 medium onion, coarsely
  chopped
2 stalks celery, coarsely chopped

1 tomato, coarsely chopped
  (optional)
¼ cup chopped fresh cilantro
½ teaspoon ground cumin
cayenne pepper to taste

SOUP

1 medium onion, chopped
2 stalks celery, chopped
3 carrots, chopped
1 poblano chili pepper
sliced avocado for garnish

chopped fresh cilantro for
  garnish
sliced green onion tops for
  garnish
6 corn tortillas, cut into strips
  and fried crisp

Combine chicken, salt, pepper, and next 6 ingredients in a large pot. Add water to cover and bring to a boil over medium-high heat. Reduce heat and cover. Simmer 60 minutes or until chicken is tender. Remove chicken, skin and debone, and chop meat. Strain, reserving broth and discarding vegetables. To make soup, return reserved broth and meat to pot. Add onion, celery, and carrot. Simmer 60 minutes to 1 hour and 30 minutes or until vegetables are crisp-tender. Meanwhile, roast poblano pepper over a burner until dark and blistered. Soak in ice water or place on a cold, wet towel to remove skin; chop. Add pepper to soup when ready to serve. Garnish individual servings with avocado and remaining 3 ingredients.

Yield: 10 to 12 servings

Mike Fain
State Game Warden
Kenedy County

EL MIRADOR'S MEXICAN SOUP

BROTH

2½ quarts water
5 cloves garlic
3 sprigs oregano
2 whole cloves
1 tablespoon ground cumin
1 teaspoon black pepper

3 bay leaves, broken
1-2 sprigs basil (omit if fresh
   basil not available)
5 instant chicken bouillon cubes
1 (3-pound) frying chicken, cut
   up

SOUP

juice of 2 limes
1 medium zucchini, chopped
1 yellow onion, sliced
2 stalks celery, chopped
1 carrot, chopped
1 bell pepper, chopped

1 (17-ounce) can garbanzo
   beans, drained
Mexican rice (optional)
2 avocados, sliced, for garnish
salsa for garnish

Bring water to a boil in a large pot. Add garlic and next 8 ingredients. Simmer 60 minutes to 1 hour and 30 minutes, skimming foam from top occasionally. Remove chicken, skin, and debone. When cool, shred meat and set aside. Strain broth and chill. Remove hardened fat from top of broth. Prepare broth the day before serving. Heat the defatted broth in a pot. Add lime juice and next 5 ingredients. Cook 20 minutes or until just crisp-tender. Add shredded chicken and garbanzo beans. To serve soup, spoon rice into individual serving bowls, if using. Add soup to bowls. Garnish with avocado and salsa.

Yield: 8 servings

Note: Broth can be prepared 1 to 2 days in advance.

Colleen Curran Hook

GAME CALDO
GAME SOUP

This recipe was multiplied by 5 and tested by 87 people at a church function. Must have been good - there was nothing left! Good way to use game cuts that are tough or too small to make into steaks.

1 large onion, diced	4-6 carrots, thickly sliced
2-3 cloves garlic, minced	3-4 stalks celery, thickly sliced
olive oil for sautéing	2-3 ears corn, thickly sliced
2 quarts water	2-4 potatoes, cut into large cubes
2 pounds game stew meat, cubed	1 small cabbage, quartered and
1 tablespoon ground cumin	then halved
salt and pepper to taste	1 (14½-ounce) stewed tomatoes
3-4 large zucchini, thickly sliced	½ cup chopped fresh cilantro

Sauté onion and garlic in oil. Add water and bring to a boil. Add meat, cumin, salt, and pepper. Cook 60 minutes. Stir in zucchini and next 6 ingredients. Cook 45 minutes. Add cilantro and cook 15 to 20 minutes longer. Add extra water as needed during cooking to maintain desired consistency.

Yield: 15 to 18 servings

Note: Use meat such as venison, nilgai, or elk. Add any other vegetables of choice to soup.

Variation: For a thicker version of this soup, omit the cabbage. Add 1 cup dry barley and cook 45 minutes before adding vegetables.

Mike Fain
State Game Warden
Kenedy County

PORTUGUESE SOUP

2 cups chopped red onion
6 cloves garlic, chopped
6 tablespoons vegetable oil
1 pound link sausage, sliced
2½ quarts beef broth
1 (16-ounce) can kidney beans,
  undrained

1 head cabbage, chopped
12 small new potatoes,
  quartered
¼ - ½ cup vinegar
2 cups ketchup
salt and pepper to taste
cayenne pepper to taste

Sauté onion and garlic in oil until transparent. Add sausage and brown. Drain off fat. Add broth and next 5 ingredients. Bring to a boil, stirring occasionally. Reduce heat and simmer 45 minutes. Season with salt, pepper, and cayenne pepper.

Yield: 1 gallon

Mike Fain
State Game Warden
Kenedy County

COWBOY STEW

Very hearty, "stick-to-your-ribs" stew. Sure to become a favorite with the "menfolk".

6 slices bacon
1 cup chopped onion
½ cup chopped bell pepper
2 cloves garlic, minced
1½ pounds ground beef or
  venison
12 tomatoes, peeled and diced,
  with juice

2½ cups water
1 teaspoon salt
black pepper to taste
2 tablespoons chili powder
1 cup cooked corn
1 cup cooked pinto beans
1 cup peeled and cubed potatoes
1 cup dry Texas-shaped pasta

Fry bacon until crisp in a large pan or Dutch oven. Transfer bacon to paper towels to drain. Add onion, bell pepper, and garlic to bacon drippings and sauté over medium heat. Add beef and cook until browned. Reduce heat and add tomato and next 4 ingredients. Cover and cook slowly for 30 minutes. Add corn and remaining 3 ingredients. Cook 20 minutes or until potatoes and pasta are tender. When ready to serve, crumble bacon and sprinkle over top.

Yield: 8 to 10 servings

Carol Campbell Steer

JOHN TOWER CHILI

This recipe was used by Senator John Tower of Texas at an April 4, 1974 chili cook-off in Washington D.C.

3 pounds chili meat
1 (15-ounce) can tomato sauce
1 cup water
1 teaspoon hot pepper sauce
3 heaping tablespoons chili powder or ground chili peppers
1 heaping tablespoon dried oregano
1 heaping teaspoon ground cumin

2 onions, chopped
minced garlic to taste
1 teaspoon salt
1 teaspoon cayenne pepper
1 teaspoon paprika
12 red bell peppers, chopped
4-5 chili pods, crushed
2 heaping tablespoons all-purpose flour

Sear meat in a large pot until juice accumulates. Add tomato sauce and water. Stir in hot pepper sauce and next 10 ingredients. Simmer 1 hour, 15 minutes. Mix flour with enough cold water to form a thin paste. Stir into chili. Simmer 30 minutes longer.

Shan Rankin

CHUNKY BEEF AND CORN CHILI

SPICY SEASONING MIX

3 tablespoons chili powder
2 teaspoons ground coriander
2 teaspoons ground cumin
1½ teaspoons garlic powder

¾ teaspoon dried oregano,
  crushed
½ teaspoon cayenne pepper

CHILI

2 teaspoons vegetable oil
1 pound lean beef cube steaks,
  cut into 1-inch cubes
4½ teaspoons spicy seasoning
  mix, divided

1 medium onion, chopped
salt (optional)
1 (28-ounce) can peeled plum
  tomatoes, undrained
2 cups frozen corn

Combine all seasoning mix ingredients in an airtight container. Shake well to blend. To make chili, heat oil in a Dutch oven over medium heat for 5 minutes. Sprinkle beef with 2 teaspoons seasoning mix. Add beef and onion to oil and sauté 2 to 3 minutes. Season with salt, if desired. Add tomatoes and break them apart with a spoon. Stir in corn and remaining 2½ teaspoons seasoning mix. Bring to a boil. Reduce heat to medium-low. Simmer, uncovered, for 18 to 20 minutes.

Yield: about ⅓ cup seasoning mix, 4 servings chili

Variation: Substitute one (15-ounce) can kidney, pinto, or black beans, drained and rinsed, or 2 cups cooked cubed potatoes for the corn.

National Cattlemen's Beef Association
Chicago, Illinois

HOWLIN' CHILI BLANCO

1 pound white beans (2 cups)
2½ quarts chicken or veal broth
2 cloves garlic, minced
2 medium onions, chopped, divided
1 tablespoon vegetable oil
2 (4-ounce) cans chopped green chiles
1 (28-ounce) can whole tomatoes, quartered
2 teaspoons dried oregano
¼ teaspoon ground cloves
¼ teaspoon cayenne pepper
4-8 pounds veal stew meat, coarsely chopped
salt and pepper to taste
8 ounces Monterey Jack cheese, grated
1 bunch green onions, chopped

Soak beans overnight in enough water to cover. Drain beans and place in a large pot. Add broth, garlic, and half the onion. Bring to a boil. Reduce heat and simmer 2 hours or until beans are very tender. Add extra broth as needed. Heat oil in a skillet. Add remaining onion, chiles, and next 5 ingredients and sauté. Stir into bean mixture. Season with salt and pepper. Serve topped with cheese and green onions.

Yield: 12 to 16 servings

Sergio Rodriguez
Executive Chef
Catering by Don Strange
San Antonio, Texas

Coquina Soup

Coquinas are also called "Periwinkles". They are a finger-tip size mollusk in delicate pastel colors. They roll in with the surf and immediately burrow into the wet sand. The eye must be quick and the hand must be quick, also, to scoop them up from shallow pools or dig into the sand for them. Collecting them can be fun if you make it a game for your children!

6 quarts coquinas, still in shells   chopped fresh parsley
black pepper to taste   toasted croutons (optional)
butter

Place *coquinas* in a colander or sieve and dip into the surf to remove sand. Wash in fresh water and place in a large kettle. Add hot water to cover. Bring to a boil and simmer a few minutes. Season with pepper, butter, and parsley. Ladle broth into individual bowls. Sprinkle croutons on top. Serve hot or cold.

Yield: 1 quart broth

Note: After they are boiled, coquina shells will settle to the bottom of the kettle.

Entrees

EDINBURG COURT HOUSE HIDALGO CO TEX

Bricks and Mortar:
Yesterday's Buildings

Bricks and Mortar

Architecture in the Rio Grande Valley is as diverse as the culture. Each structure tells its own story, but all bear the undeniable mark of the river and the resourcefulness of the people who settled here. One of the oldest structures still standing is the Treviño Fort, located in San Ygnacio. This 1830's structure is listed in the National Register of Historic Places and has high walls which once protected its inhabitants from Indian raids. It is built of sandstone and is simple and unrefined, with massive hand-hewn mesquite wood doors.

Structures dating back to the 1700s can be found in the ghost town of Guerrero Viejo. This abandoned town is the area's very own Atlantis, having been inundated by the rising waters of nearby Falcon Dam. During dry spells, the architecture of

Above: The Treviño Fort at San Ygnacio in nearby Zapata County—one of the area's oldest standing structures.
Cover page: Razed in 1954 after the existing courthouse was finished, the old Hidalgo County Courthouse in Edinburg epitomized the popular Texas Mission Revival style.
At left: Don Chencho Rosales, who lived to be 115, pictured in front of the Point Isabel Lighthouse which he helped construct as a boy.
At right: The abandoned church at Guerrero Viejo rises out of Falcon Lake during dry spells.
Below: Mexican troops of 1874 assemble in front of Mier's main catholic church, still standing.

DID YOU KNOW?

AT ITS ZENITH, THE CITY OF GUERRERO, TAMAULIPAS, MEXICO BOASTED A POPULATION OF 16,000. A CENTER FOR CULTURE AND TRADE ON THE RIVER BETWEEN LAREDO AND MATAMOROS, GUERRERO'S STONE BUILDINGS AND BUSTLING STREETS WERE TYPICAL OF PROSPEROUS MEXICAN CITIES OF THE DAY. ALL BUT FORGOTTEN WHEN IT WAS FLOODED IN THE 1950S TO CREATE FALCON LAKE, GUERRERO NOW SHOWS HER WEATHERED SPOILS OF PAST GLORY ONLY WHEN LAKE LEVELS DROP. WHEN DRY, THE ABANDONED CITY IS OVERRUN BY HISTORY BUFFS AND CURIOUS SIGHTSEERS WANTING A CHANCE TO LOOK AT THE WATER-LOGGED RUINS BEFORE THE LAKE RECLAIMS IT.

this once beautiful town is eerily revealed. Its centerpiece is an imposing stone church known as the Templo de Nuestra Señora del Refugio, which bears the unmistakable beauty and detail of Spanish architecture.

In the 1850s, the boom of the river trade made the Rio Grande a thriving international boundary. Its waters, frequented by enterprising boatmen of all flags and languages, brought new needs and tastes to the region. Out of this era came the rich, heady architecture of the Mexican border city of Matamoros. The distinctly French influence evident in the ornate iron balconies and detailed brick façades of downtown Matamoros make it unlike any other commercial center on the border, and rather reminiscent of New Orleans. Its U.S. sister city of Brownsville boasts late 19th century architectural wonders like La Madrileña and La Nueva Libertad, the city's oldest bank building. The Public Market and Town Hall of Brownsville, constructed in 1850, is Texas' oldest municipal building in continuous use.

In the city of Roma, the town square remains perhaps the most alluring plaza on the north side of the river. Around this National Historic

DID YOU KNOW?

IN 1883, DR. WILLIAM CRAWFORD GORGAS WAS ASSIGNED AS THE NEW ASSISTANT POST SURGEON AT THE FORT BROWN ARMY HOSPITAL LOCATED IN WHAT IS NOW BROWNSVILLE, TEXAS. THE AREA WAS SUFFERING FROM AN EPIDEMIC OF YELLOW FEVER IN THOSE DAYS, AND GORGAS WAS DETERMINED TO FIND THE CAUSE. AFTER CONDUCTING UNAUTHORIZED AUTOPSIES OF YELLOW FEVER VICTIMS AT THE HOSPITAL, HE WAS ABLE TO DETERMINE THAT THE DEADLY DISEASE WAS MOSQUITO BORNE, NOT PASSED ON BY HUMAN CONTACT, AS WAS PREVIOUSLY BELIEVED. THIS DISCOVERY LATER FACILITATED THE COMPLETION OF THE PANAMA CANAL BY PREVENTING THE WIDESPREAD YELLOW FEVER DEATHS OF CONSTRUCTION WORKERS. CONSTRUCTION ON THE CANAL HAD PREVIOUSLY BEEN DELAYED AND NEARLY ABANDONED BECAUSE OF THE TRAGIC TOLL THE EPIDEMIC HAD TAKEN ON CREWS. THE ORIGINAL FORT BROWN HOSPITAL BUILDING, WHERE GORGAS HAD MADE THE MOMENTOUS DISCOVERY, LATER BECAME PART OF TEXAS SOUTHMOST COLLEGE AND THE UNIVERSITY OF TEXAS AT BROWNSVILLE. IT WAS APTLY NAMED GORGAS HALL AND NOW HOUSES ADMINISTRATIVE OFFICES.

Above: The graceful colonnades of Ft. Brown buildings echo Spanish influence in Valley architecture.
Left: La Borde House in Rio Grande City still functions as a bed and breakfast, looking much the same as it did in this c. 1917 photo.

Landmark, commercial, religious, and public buildings 120 years or older repose gracefully. Many bear the mark of the talented regional architect Heinrich Portscheller—originally from Germany—evidenced by the ornately detailed façades of molded brick. Fort Ringgold, in nearby Rio Grande City, includes many distinctive 19th century structures. Among these is an 1850s frame home in which Robert E. Lee reputedly stayed prior to the Civil War.

The prosperity of late steam-era agricultural development and railroad commerce fueled another phase of construction. Indeed, some of the era's most significant and lasting structures are the pump houses and train depots of the region. These include the Hidalgo pump house (1912), which once watered over 40,000 acres (soon to be restored for use as a visitor center); Edinburg's Southern Pacific station, built in the Spanish

Above: Roma, as seen from across the river in Mexico in this late 1800s illustration.
Below: "General Lee Slept Here," so the story goes about this simple frame home located in Ft. Ringgold, Rio Grande City.
Below right: Visitors by rail were greeted by the sight of these stately Spanish-style depots. Brownsville (shown here), McAllen and Edinburg all have beautifully restored depot buildings serving various uses today.

> ## "MAKE BUILDINGS, NOT WAR"
>
> THE FAMED ARCHITECT OF ROMA AND RIO GRANDE CITY, HEINRICH PORTSCHELLER, WAS ORIGINALLY FROM GERMANY. IN 1865, WHILE IN HIS EARLY TWENTIES, PORTSCHELLER LEFT GERMANY FOR MEXICO TO AVOID COMPULSORY MILITARY SERVICE. IRONICALLY, UPON HIS ARRIVAL IN MEXICO, HE WAS IMMEDIATELY DRAFTED INTO MAXIMILIAN'S ARMY! HE LATER DESERTED.

Colonial Revival style, now the Chamber of Commerce; the Brownsville depot, now housing the Historic Brownsville Museum; and the McAllen depot, now a law office.

The Valley is, indeed, blessed with a rich architectural heritage—one designed by the collective hands of the many who came here seeking a better life. Unfortunately, many of the area's architectural treasures were, until recently, allowed to fall into ruin. But the call for preservation is growing louder each day, and the future of one of this area's most significant legacies is looking brighter in today's Mesquite Country.

Above: Stately hotels, like the Casa de Palmas in McAllen, helped early towns lure potential investors to an area. c. 1918

Above inset: *William Jennings Bryan, famous speaker, celebrity and failed presidential candidate owned a country home in Mission around 1909 (shown here in the 60s or 70s).*

Below: *Though mislabeled as a monastery in this old photo, the picturesque St. Peter's Novitiate actually served as a seminary for the Oblate Fathers, builders of nearby La Lomita mission for which the town of Mission is named.*

DID YOU KNOW?

FAMOUS GANGSTER AL CAPONE BUILT HIS MOTHER A HOME IN MERCEDES. RUMOR HAS IT THE ARCHITECT DESIGNED THE HOME SO THAT NONE OF THE DOORS, WINDOWS OR HALLWAYS WERE ALIGNED, DENYING AN INTRUDER A "STRAIGHT SHOT" THROUGH THE HOUSE.

MILANO'S FETTUCCINE ALFREDO

Here is one of Mrs. Milano's personal favorites of the specialties at Milano's - a Valley-famous restaurant.

16 ounces fresh fettuccine
8 tablespoons butter
2 pints whipping cream

¼ cup Parmesan cheese, plus
  extra for topping
¼ cup grated Romano cheese
black pepper to taste

Bring water to a boil in a saucepan. Add fettuccine and boil 3 minutes. Drain well. Combine butter and remaining 4 ingredients in a separate saucepan. Bring to a boil and cook until mixture thickens. Add fettuccine and heat thoroughly. Top with Parmesan cheese and serve immediately.
Yield: 4 servings

Giovanna Milano
Milano's Restaurant
Weslaco, Texas

CRUSTLESS QUICHE FLORENTINE

Good, basic, quick.

1 (10-ounce) package frozen
  chopped spinach, thawed and
  squeezed dry
4 tablespoons butter or
  margarine, melted (optional)
3 eggs, beaten

3 tablespoons all-purpose flour
1 (16-ounce) container small
  curd cottage cheese, drained
10 ounces cheddar cheese,
  grated

Combine all ingredients and pour into a greased 9- or 10-inch quiche pan. Bake at 325° for 1 hour, 15 minutes.
Yield: 8 servings

Ruth Penn

MARTHA'S SPINACH CRÊPES

Serve with crusty French bread and a crisp salad for an elegant ladies' luncheon.

CRÊPE BATTER

1 cup all-purpose flour
2 eggs
½ cup milk
½ cup water

¼ teaspoon salt
2 tablespoons butter or
    margarine, melted

CRÊPES

crêpe batter
1 (10-ounce) package frozen
    chopped spinach
4 tablespoons butter or
    margarine
3 tablespoons all-purpose flour
1 cup milk
½ teaspoon salt

⅛ teaspoon nutmeg
⅛ teaspoon black pepper
4-5 ounces Swiss cheese, diced
    or grated
1 teaspoon grated onion
melted butter or margarine for
    topping
Parmesan cheese for garnish

Combine all batter ingredients in a blender in order listed. Blend 30 seconds. Scrape down sides and blend 30 to 60 seconds or until smooth. Refrigerate 2 hours. To make crêpes, use an electric crêpe maker or a nonstick skillet. Pour batter onto heated cooking surface, using only enough to make a large thin circle. Cook on one side only. As crêpes finish cooking, place between layers of wax paper to prevent sticking. Cook and drain spinach. Melt butter in a saucepan. Blend in flour. Slowly stir in milk and cook until thickened. Add spinach, salt and next 4 ingredients. Mix well. Spoon spinach mixture into crêpes. Roll up crêpes and place in a greased pan. Brush each crêpe with melted butter and sprinkle with Parmesan cheese. Bake at 375° for 15 to 20 minutes.

Yield: 4 to 6 servings

Note: Cooked crêpes can be frozen.

Martha Kirkendall

AJI DE GALLINA

CHICKEN AND BROTH

1 (4½-pound) chicken or hen	1 onion
1 quart water	1 carrot
1 leek	salt to taste

ENTREE

¾ cup vegetable oil, divided	3 tablespoons pureed hot chili
1 onion, finely chopped	pepper
1 clove garlic, crushed	1 cup grated cheese
½ teaspoon cumin seed	½ cup chopped nuts
2 cups soft breadcrumbs	2 pounds peeled and boiled
1 cup evaporated milk	white potatoes

Combine chicken and next 5 ingredients in a saucepan. Bring to a boil and cook until chicken is tender. Remove chicken, skin and debone, and shred meat. Strain broth and reserve. To prepare entree, heat ½ cup oil in a skillet. Add onion, garlic, and cumin seed and sauté until browned. Soak breadcrumbs in milk. Add to onion mixture and simmer 15 minutes. Place in a blender and blend until creamy. Return to skillet. Fry chili pepper in remaining ¼ cup oil in a separate skillet. Add chili pepper, shredded chicken, cheese, and nuts to onion mixture. Simmer 10 minutes, thinning with reserved broth and adding salt as needed. The sauce should be thick. Garnish with potatoes and serve with rice.

Yield: 6 servings

Rosanna Robalino

CHICKEN RANCHERO

1 large onion, diced	1 (12-ounce) can evaporated
4 tablespoons butter or	milk
margarine	10 corn tortillas
¼-½ (7-ounce) can jalapeño	chicken broth or melted butter
peppers, finely diced	2 cups cubed cooked chicken
1 (10¾-ounce) condensed cream	8 ounces cheddar cheese, grated
of chicken soup	

Sauté onion in butter briefly. Add pepper and cook until onion is transparent. Add soup and milk and heat slowly. Dip tortillas in broth or melted butter. Use some of tortillas to line the bottom of a casserole dish. Pour some of soup mixture over tortillas. Add a layer of chicken. Repeat layers 3 times. Top with cheese. Bake at 350° for 20 to 25 minutes or until browned and bubbly.

Yield: 8 servings

Note: Serve with a green salad with avocado and hot garlic bread.

Sandra Perez-Spencer

CILANTRO CHICKEN

2 large onions, chopped	2 bunches cilantro, stemmed
4 tablespoons butter	and chopped
8 chicken breasts, cubed	salt and pepper to taste
1 (10-ounce) bottle white wine	
Worcestershire sauce, divided	

Brown onion in butter in a skillet over medium heat. Before onion is completely cooked, add chicken and cook until done. Add half the bottle of Worcestershire sauce. Stir in cilantro. Add remaining Worcestershire sauce to taste. Season with salt and pepper. Serve immediately.

Yield: 8 servings

Note: Serve with corn tortillas, white rice, chopped avocado, tomato, and onion, grated cheese, and other taco condiments.

Mark Dizdar

CHICKEN MONTEREY

These wonderful caterers from Edinburg (home of the Hidalgo County Historical Museum), not only serve lunch at the monthly HCHM Board of Trustee meetings, they also prepare fabulous goodies for elegant and casual HCHM functions.

MONTEREY JACK CHEESE SAUCE

2 tablespoons margarine
¼ cup all-purpose flour
dash of salt
⅛ teaspoon white pepper
2 cups hot milk

8 ounces Monterey Jack cheese, grated
½ teaspoon paprika
½ teaspoon dry mustard
½ teaspoon Worcestershire sauce

ENTREE

4 chicken breasts, boned and skinned
2 cups canned or homemade refried beans, divided

2 fresh jalapeño peppers, seeded, deveined, and halved
sprigs cilantro for garnish

Melt margarine in a saucepan. Blend in flour, salt, and pepper. Cook and stir 5 to 10 minutes over low heat. Slowly stir in milk until smooth. Bring to a boil, stirring constantly. Strain if sauce is lumpy. Stir in cheese until melted. Add paprika, mustard, and Worcestershire sauce. Beat with a whisk until smooth. To prepare entree, flatten chicken by pounding and place in a baking pan. Bake at 350° to 375° for 15 minutes or until done. Spread ½ cup beans over chicken. Pour cheese sauce over top. Garnish with pepper halves. Bake 5 minutes longer to reheat. Garnish with cilantro. Serve immediately.

Yield: 4 servings

Note: Serve with rice or potatoes and grilled vegetables or a salad. Tastes great with "Marqués de Riscal Rioja" 1988 wine.

Gloria Gonzalez
Professional Food Service Management
at The University of Texas at Pan American
Edinburg, Texas

CHICKEN IN ENCHILADA SAUCE

Not to be confused with Chicken Enchiladas!

ENCHILADA SAUCE

2 tablespoons vegetable oil
½ cup chopped onion
2 cloves garlic, minced
1 (14½-ounce) can peeled
  tomatoes

1 (8-ounce) can tomato sauce
1 (4-ounce) can green chiles
1 teaspoon ground cumin
½ teaspoon salt
1 tablespoon chili powder

CHICKEN

¼ cup masa harina
¼ teaspoon garlic powder
¼ teaspoon black pepper
salt to taste

2 tablespoons vegetable oil
6 chicken breasts
4 ounces colby cheese, grated
10 round tortilla chips, crushed

Heat oil in a saucepan. Add onion and sauté 2 minutes. Add garlic and sauté 1 minute. Blend tomatoes, tomato sauce, and chiles in a food processor or blender until smooth. Add to saucepan. Stir in cumin, salt, and chili powder. Bring to a boil. Reduce heat and simmer 15 minutes. To prepare chicken, combine masa harina and next 3 ingredients in a pie pan. Heat oil in a skillet over medium-high heat. Dredge chicken in masa harina mixture. Sauté in skillet for 4 to 5 minutes on each side or until golden. Chicken does not need to be cooked through. Transfer to a baking dish. Pour sauce over chicken. Bake, uncovered, at 375° for about 25 minutes. Sprinkle with cheese and chips. Bake 10 minutes longer or until cheese melts.

Yield: 6 servings

Note: Masa harina, the mix used to make corn tortillas, is available at grocery stores.

**Monica Burdette
The Inn at El Canelo
Raymondville, Texas**

PHYLLO-WRAPPED CHICKEN BREASTS

We served this at a ladies' luncheon at church; it was a big hit.

1½ cups mayonnaise	salt and pepper
1 cup chopped green onions	36 sheets phyllo dough
⅓ cup lemon juice	4 tablespoons butter, melted
2 cloves garlic, minced	⅓ cup freshly grated Parmesan
2 teaspoons dried tarragon	cheese
12 chicken breasts, boned and	chopped fresh parsley for
skinned	garnish

Combine mayonnaise and next 4 ingredients. Pound chicken to flatten to ¼- to ½-inch thickness. Sprinkle lightly with salt and pepper. Place a sheet of phyllo dough on a flat surface. Brush with butter. Place a second sheet on top of first and brush with butter. Repeat with a third sheet. Spread 1 to 2 tablespoons mayonnaise mixture on both sides of a chicken breast. Place chicken in corner of phyllo dough and roll up to form a package. Place on an ungreased baking dish. Repeat with remaining chicken breasts. Brush rolls with butter and sprinkle with cheese. Bake at 375° for 20 to 25 minutes or until golden. Serve hot. Baste with butter from bottom of pan. Garnish with parsley.

Yield: 12 servings

Bonnie Brown

MILANO'S CHICKEN MARSALA

Milano's Restaurant in Weslaco has been a Valley institution for several decades. This is one of Mrs. Milano's favorites.

2 chicken breasts, cut into strips	2 teaspoons chopped fresh
all-purpose flour for dredging	parsley
2 tablespoons olive oil	4 fresh basil leaves, chopped
salt and pepper to taste	1 tablespoon capers
	½ cup Marsala wine

Dredge chicken in flour. Heat oil in a skillet. Add chicken, salt, pepper, and next 3 ingredients. When chicken is almost done, add wine. Simmer 5 to 10 minutes or until chicken is thoroughly cooked. Serve with hot pasta.

Yield: 2 servings

Giovanna Milano
Milano's Restaurant
Weslaco, Texas

DIJON CHICKEN IN PHYLLO

6 chicken breasts, cut into strips
salt and pepper to taste
2½ sticks butter, melted, divided
½ cup Dijon mustard
1 pint whipping cream

10-12 sheets phyllo dough
½ cup breadcrumbs, toasted
1 egg
1 teaspoon water

Season chicken with salt and pepper. Sauté chicken in 1 stick butter in a skillet for 7 minutes. Transfer to a plate. Add mustard to skillet and stir to deglaze. Whisk cream into mustard. Cook over low heat until reduced by a fourth. Stir in any chicken juices that have collected on the plate. Place chicken in a bowl. Pour cream sauce over top and toss to coat. Lay a sheet of phyllo dough on a dish towel. Working rapidly, brush some of remaining 1½ sticks melted butter over dough. Sprinkle with 1 tablespoon breadcrumbs. Continue layering sheets of dough on top of each other, buttering and adding crumbs to each sheet. Do not add crumbs to top layer. Arrange chicken on the bottom ⅓ of the long side of dough layers, leaving a 2-inch border around edges. Turn in bottom and sides of dough and then roll, using dish towel to help, in jelly roll fashion. Place on an ungreased jelly-roll pan. Beat egg and water together and brush over top. Bake at 450° for 12 to 15 minutes. Slice and serve.

Mary Vance Jones

CHICKEN ANGELO

8 chicken breasts, boned and
   skinned
3 eggs, beaten
1 cup seasoned breadcrumbs
1 stick margarine or butter

12 ounces fresh mushrooms,
   sliced, divided
1 pound Muenster cheese, sliced
1 (10½-ounce) can condensed
   chicken broth
hot cooked rice

Soak chicken in egg for 2 hours in refrigerator. Remove chicken and dredge in breadcrumbs. Heat margarine in a skillet. Add chicken and brown. Place in a 9X13 inch baking pan. Sprinkle with half the mushrooms and cover with cheese. Sprinkle remaining mushrooms over the top and pour broth over all. Cover with foil. Bake at 350° for 30 minutes, basting occasionally. Remove foil and bake 15 minutes. Serve over hot rice.

Yield: 8 servings

Note: Cut calories by skipping the breadcrumbs and margarine. Poach or brown chicken with nonstick cooking spray.

Helene Bleibdry

BAKED CHICKEN CHABLIS

This recipe was selected for inclusion in "The Entertainment Guide and Cookbook" for the American Women's Club of the Philippines. Dianne was a missionary there.

CHICKEN

8 chicken breasts, boned and skinned
seasoned flour
1 stick butter
1 cup sliced green onions

1 cup mushroom buttons, stems, and pieces
2 cups marinated artichoke hearts

SAUCE

3 tablespoons butter
2 tablespoons seasoned flour

2 cups chicken broth
1 cup rosé or white wine

Dust chicken in flour. Melt butter in a shallow baking pan. Place chicken in pan. Bake, uncovered, at 350° for 45 minutes. Meanwhile, make sauce by melting butter in a saucepan. Blend in flour. Add broth and wine. Cook and stir until thickened and smooth. When chicken is done, sprinkle with onions, mushrooms, and artichoke hearts. Pour sauce over top. Bake 20 minutes longer.

Yield: 4 servings

Dianne McVeigh

CHICKEN ROLL-UPS

1½ sticks butter or margarine,
  melted
2 cloves garlic, minced
1 cup fine dry breadcrumbs
1 tablespoon finely chopped
  fresh or dried parsley
⅔ cup Parmesan cheese
½ teaspoon salt
¼ teaspoon black pepper
8 chicken breasts, boned and
  skinned
juice of 2 lemons
paprika

Stir together butter and garlic. Combine breadcrumbs and next 4 ingredients. Mix well. Dip chicken in butter mixture and then dredge in breadcrumb mixture. Fold together long sides of chicken. Tuck short ends under and secure with a toothpick. Place chicken rolls, seam-side down, in a greased 9X13 inch pan. Sprinkle with lemon juice and paprika. Bake at 350° for 60 minutes or until done.

Yield: 8 servings

Anne Addington

ROAST CHICKEN WITH MUSHROOMS AND CREAM

1 (5-pound) roasting chicken
salt and freshly ground pepper
  to taste
crushed garlic to taste
1 orange, unpeeled and
  quartered
1 cup whipping cream, divided
8 ounces mushrooms

Rub chicken inside and out with salt, pepper, and garlic. Put orange in chicken cavity. Place chicken, breast-side up, in a greased casserole dish. Bake at 425° for 20 minutes. Reduce heat to 350°. Pour ½ cup cream over chicken. Bake 20 minutes. Pour remaining ½ cup cream over chicken and roast 60 minutes longer. Place mushrooms around chicken in dish and bake 15 minutes.

Mary Vance Jones

PERUVIAN CHICKEN STEW

The mixture of Indian and Spanish cookery in Peru has evolved over the centuries into a cuisine with a tremendous variety of dishes and a delicious blend of flavors.

1 medium chicken, cut into 6
  pieces
2 tablespoons vegetable oil
1½ cups chopped onion
1 clove garlic, crushed
1 (8-ounce) can tomato sauce
¾ cup Sauterne wine

¼ cup raisins
½ cup peas
½ cup diced carrot
salt and pepper to taste
6 white potatoes, boiled and
  peeled

Brown chicken in oil in a medium saucepan. Remove chicken. Add onion and garlic and sauté. Add tomato sauce and next 4 ingredients. Mix well and season with salt and pepper. Place chicken on top and cover. Simmer 15 minutes or until meat is done. Add potatoes. Serve with rice.

Yield: 6 servings

Rosanna Robalino

SWEET 'N SOUR BAKED CHICKEN

4 tablespoons butter or
  margarine
½ cup chopped onion
½ cup coarsely chopped bell
  pepper
½ cup coarsely chopped carrot
½ cup chopped celery
¾ cup ketchup
1 cup pineapple juice
2 tablespoons vinegar

¼ cup packed brown sugar
2 teaspoons soy sauce
½ teaspoon garlic salt
½ teaspoon salt
¼ teaspoon black pepper
1 cup pineapple chunks, drained
1 (3-pound) broiling chicken,
  cut up, or boneless chicken
  breasts

Melt butter in a medium skillet. Add onion and next 3 ingredients. Sauté 5 minutes. Stir in ketchup and next 7 ingredients. Bring to a boil, stirring constantly. Add pineapple chunks. Arrange chicken, skin-side up in a 9X13 inch baking pan. Pour sauce over chicken and cover. Bake at 400° for 45 minutes. Uncover and bake 30 minutes or until chicken is done.

Yield: 4 to 6 servings

Nancy Boultinghouse

CHICKEN SPAGHETTI

CHICKEN AND BROTH

1 frying chicken
1 onion, quartered

2-3 cloves garlic
2 bay leaves

ENTREE

1 stick butter
1 stalk celery, diced
2-3 onions, diced
2-3 bell peppers, diced
1 (28-ounce) can tomatoes, undrained
1 (8-ounce) can tomato sauce

1 cup water
1 (16-ounce) package spaghetti
1-2 (7-ounce) cans sliced mushrooms, drained
grated cheddar or Parmesan cheese

Combine chicken and next 3 ingredients in a large saucepan. Add water to cover and bring to a boil. Cook until meat falls from the bone. Remove chicken, skin, debone, and chop meat. Strain broth and reserve. To prepare entree, melt butter in a skillet. Add celery, onion, and pepper and sauté. Stir in tomatoes, tomato sauce, and water. Simmer 3 to 4 hours or until liquid reduces. Cook spaghetti in reserved broth. Drain. Add spaghetti, chicken, and mushrooms to tomato sauce. Top with cheese.

Yield: 6 to 8 servings

Margaret Looney

BBQ SMOKED STUFFED HENS

2 medium onions, chopped
1 cup chopped fresh parsley
1 pound chorizo
4 cups cooked rice

4 Cornish game hens
salt and pepper to taste
4 slices bacon

Sauté onion and parsley for 5 minutes or until softened. Crumble in chorizo and brown. Remove from heat and drain excess liquid. Add rice and mix thoroughly. Stuff mixture into hen cavities. Season hens with salt and pepper. Wrap with bacon and secure with a toothpick. Cook in a BBQ pit for 30 to 60 minutes or until golden brown.

Yield: 4 servings

Note: Any type of sausage can be used for the stuffing, or try it with shrimp or crawfish tails. Serve with Crunchy Romaine Tossed Salad.

Doug Dillard

DEEP-FRIED TURKEY

Have you ever tried frying an entire turkey!?! You won't believe how juicy and tasty it turns out! The secret to this recipe's great flavor is using a cattle syringe to inject the seasonings throughout the bird. This is the key to a bird with a kick. Doug also says to buy "Tex-Joy" seasoning if you can find it.

2 sticks butter
2 tablespoons hot pepper sauce, or to taste
3 tablespoons Worcestershire sauce

2 tablespoons Tex-Joy steak seasoning, or seasoned salt
2 tablespoons garlic powder
1 tablespoon celery salt
1 (8 to 10-pound) turkey
3-4 gallons peanut oil

Melt butter in a saucepan. Add hot pepper sauce and next 4 ingredients. Using a large syringe, inject butter mixture throughout turkey. Place oil in a pot large enough to immerse turkey. Heat oil to 300° to 325°. Immerse turkey in oil and cook 3 to 4 minutes per pound. Do not exceed 4 minutes per pound. Oil should maintain a constant temperature while cooking. Remove turkey from oil and cool slightly.

Note: A propane "Fish Fryer", available at large sporting goods stores works well for frying the turkey.

Doug Dillard

CANELO FAJITAS

6 pounds lean beef skirt steak   ⅓ cup lemon juice
⅓ cup sherry   ½ teaspoon sesame oil
⅓ cup soy sauce   Bolner's Fiesta Fajita Seasoning

Cut all connective tissue and gristle from meat. Cut away as much fat as possible. Combine sherry and next 3 ingredients. Pour into an empty soy sauce bottle, replacing plastic stopper. Sprinkle a little of sherry mixture into a zip-top plastic bag. Place a single layer of beef in the bag. Sprinkle generously with sherry mixture, then season with fajita seasoning. Continue beef and seasoning layers to about 3 layers. Use another bag if needed. Close bag and turn several times to coat all surfaces. Refrigerate several hours or overnight, turning occasionally. Sear beef over a very hot grill. Transfer to a roasting pan and cover tightly. Cool at room temperature and then refrigerate several hours, if desired. Warm in a 250° oven for 1 to 2 hours before serving. Slice beef against the grain into about ½-inch strips. Return to roasting pan and keep warm until ready to serve. Serve in fresh flour tortillas folded in half, topped with Pico de Gallo (page 112) and Guacamole (page 228). Serve with Arroz a la Mexicana (page 264) and Frijoles a la Charra (page 265).

Yield: 10 servings

Note: Look for Bolner's Fiesta Fajita Seasoning in the spice section of the grocery store. If not available, substitute salt, pepper, and garlic powder. It is not necessary to use all the sherry mixture. Store extra in the refrigerator indefinitely.

**Monica Burdette
The Inn at El Canelo
Raymondville, Texas**

PEPPERED BEEF TENDERLOIN WITH MUSTARD AND HORSERADISH SAUCE

SAUCE

1 cup sour cream
3 tablespoons Dijon mustard

2 tablespoons prepared horseradish

BEEF

2 teaspoons whole black peppercorns
2 teaspoons whole white peppercorns
2 teaspoons whole green peppercorns
2 teaspoons coarse salt

3 tablespoons Dijon mustard
2 tablespoons butter, softened
1 cup loosely packed chopped fresh Italian parsley
1 (2-pound) beef tenderloin, trimmed
fresh parsley sprigs for garnish

Whisk together all sauce ingredients in a small bowl. Cover and refrigerate up to 2 days until ready to use. To prepare beef, coarsely grind peppercorns in a spice grinder or pepper mill. Transfer peppercorns to a bowl. Mix in salt. In a medium bowl, whisk together mustard, butter, and parsley. Rub over entire tenderloin. Roll tenderloin in peppercorn mixture, coating completely. If desired, cover and refrigerate up to 24 hours. Place on a rack in a shallow baking pan. Roast at 450° for 35 minutes or until a thermometer inserted in the center registers 130° for rare. Let stand 10 minutes before slicing. Arrange on a platter and garnish with parsley sprigs. Serve with sauce.

Yield: 6 servings

Variation: For a uniquely Texas flavor, substitute cilantro for parsley.

Jennifer Wright

BEEF TENDERLOIN

1 beef tenderloin, well
trimmed, ½ pound per person
1 tablespoon ground thyme
1 teaspoon white pepper
1 tablespoon seasoned salt

1 teaspoon garlic salt
½ teaspoon dried oregano
salt to taste
¼ cup Worcestershire sauce
1 cup water

Place beef on a large sheet of foil. Rub in thyme. Combine pepper and next 3 ingredients and sprinkle over beef. Roll beef through spices on the foil. Wrap and refrigerate 12 hours. Remove from refrigerator and unwrap 2 hours before cooking. Place in a foil-lined pan. Sprinkle with salt and Worcestershire sauce. Add water to pan. Bake at 400° for 40 minutes or until beef reaches desired degree of doneness.

Katherine Zeigler

PEPPERED RIB-EYE STEAKS

4 (1½-inch thick) beef rib-eye
steaks
1 tablespoon olive oil
1 clove garlic, crushed
1 tablespoon paprika
2 teaspoons ground thyme

2 teaspoons ground oregano
1½ teaspoons black pepper
1 teaspoon salt
1 teaspoon lemon pepper
1 teaspoon cayenne pepper

Brush steaks with oil. In a small bowl, combine garlic and remaining 7 ingredients. Sprinkle seasoning mixture over steaks and press into both sides. Cover and chill 60 minutes. Grill steaks, turning once, over medium hot coals. Cook 14 to 18 minutes for rare, 18 to 22 minutes for medium, 24 to 28 minutes for well done.

Yield: 4 servings

Mary Cozad-Schach

GARLIC PEPPER ROUND ROAST

1 beef eye of round roast, fat trimmed	chopped garlic black pepper

Cover roast with garlic and pepper. Place on a broiler pan. Bake at 275° to 300° until roast reaches medium rare.

Note: If cooked on too high a heat, meat will be tough. This method can also be used with pork roast, except add rosemary and cook until well done.

Shan Rankin

SOUTHWESTERN-STYLE BEEF POT ROAST

2 large cloves garlic, crushed	1 (14½-ounce) can peeled whole tomatoes, cut up
1 tablespoon chili powder	
1 teaspoon ground cumin	2 pounds medium-size red potatoes, peeled and quartered
1 teaspoon salt	
½ teaspoon cracked black pepper	1 tablespoon cornstarch
	2 tablespoons water
1 (3 to 3½-pound) boneless beef shoulder pot roast	1 (4-ounce) can chopped green chilies, undrained
1 tablespoon vegetable oil	2 tablespoons chopped fresh parsley
1 large onion, chopped	

Combine garlic and next 4 ingredients to form a paste. Rub evenly over roast. Brown roast in oil in a Dutch oven over medium-high heat. Pour off drippings. Add onion and tomato. Reduce heat to low and cover tightly. Simmer 1 hour, 30 minutes to 2 hours or until meat is almost tender. Add potatoes and cover. Cook 35 minutes or until meat and potatoes are tender. Transfer roast and potatoes to a warm platter. Skim off fat from cooking liquid. Dissolve cornstarch in water and stir into liquid. Add chilies and bring to a boil. Boil 1 minute, stirring constantly. Stir in parsley. Trim excess fat from roast before carving. Serve roast and potatoes with sauce.

Yield: 9 or 10 servings

Note: A boneless beef shoulder pot roast will yield three (3-ounce) cooked and trimmed servings per pound.

National Cattlemen's Beef Association
Chicago, Illinois

DWAYNE'S FAVORITE RUMP ROAST

1 boneless rump roast; beef,
venison, nilgai, or elk
1 (10¾-ounce) can condensed
cream of mushroom soup

1 (1½-ounce) package dry onion
soup mix
water or white wine (optional)

Place roast in a roasting pan. Spoon soup over roast and sprinkle with soup mix. Cover and bake at 325° for about 3 hours, depending on the size of the roast. Use pan juices for gravy. Add water to gravy to thin to desired consistency.

Yield: 6 to 8 servings

Variation: Add peeled and chopped carrot and potato to pan 30 minutes before end of cooking time.

Shirley Bair

OVEN-BARBECUE BRISKET

This is an easy version of barbecue brisket done entirely in the kitchen - no grill required. A great dish for an outdoor buffet.

2 cups water, divided
1 (6 to 8-pound) boneless beef
brisket, fat trimmed
salt and pepper
Worcestershire sauce

garlic powder
liquid smoke (optional)
2 tablespoons all-purpose flour
1-2 cups bottled barbecue sauce

Pour ½ cup water into a roasting pan sprayed with nonstick cooking spray. Place roast in pan. Sprinkle liberally with salt, pepper, and next 3 ingredients. Bake, uncovered, at 425° for 15 to 20 minutes. Reduce temperature to 275° and add 1 cup water to pan. Cover and bake 5 hours. Remove from pan and trim any excess fat. Combine flour and remaining ½ cup (cold) water and stir into pan drippings. Brown brisket, if desired, by broiling to desired color. Pour barbecue sauce over meat. Cool. Slice meat into ½-inch or thinner slices. Arrange slices, overlapping, in a glass baking dish. Pour pan drippings mixture over top. Reheat at 350° for 30 minutes. Serve in baking dish.

Note: Brisket can be baked the day before and sliced and reheated when ready to serve. Increase reheating time to 45 minutes or until heated through.

Cecilia Gutierrez

TEXAS BARBECUE BEEF BRISKET

2 teaspoons paprika
1 teaspoon freshly ground black
  pepper, divided
1 (6 to 8-pound) boneless beef
  brisket, fat trimmed
1 cup water
1 tablespoon butter or
  margarine

1 medium onion, grated
1½ cups ketchup
1 tablespoon fresh lemon juice
1 tablespoon Worcestershire
  sauce
1 teaspoon hot pepper sauce

Soak oak, pecan, mesquite, or hickory wood chips in water for 30 minutes. Prepare briquettes and add wood chips. Combine paprika and ½ teaspoon pepper. Rub evenly over beef. Place beef, fat-side down, in a 9X11½ inch disposable aluminum pan. Add water to pan and cover tightly with foil. Place on center grill of cooker over very low coals. Cover and cook 5 hours, turning brisket every 1 hour, 30 minutes. Remove excess fat from pan as it accumulates. Add extra water as needed. Periodically add just enough briquettes to keep coals at an even temperature. Remove brisket from pan, reserving pan drippings. Place directly on grill, fat-side down, over coals. Cover and cook 30 minutes. Meanwhile, skim fat from drippings, reserving 1 cup drippings. Melt butter in a saucepan over medium heat. Add onion and sauté until crisp-tender. Add reserved pan drippings, remaining ½ teaspoon pepper, ketchup, and remaining 3 ingredients. Simmer about 15 minutes, stirring occasionally. Trim excess fat from brisket and carve across the grain into thin slices. Serve brisket with sauce.

Yield: 18 to 24 servings

Note: Coals should be in a single layer with space between each briquette. To check temperature, cautiously hold hand about 4 inches above coals. Very low coals will force removal of hand in 6 to 7 seconds.

Variation: Water Smoker Method: Prepare smoker according to manufacturer's directions. Place beef brisket, fat-side up, in center of cooking rack. Cover smoker and smoke-cook at a low to moderate temperature for 4 hours, 30 minutes to 5 hours or until tender.

National Cattlemen's Beef Association
Chicago, Illinois

SWISS STEAK PIPERADE

1 (1¾-pound,¾-inch thick) full-
cut beef round steak or
boneless shoulder steak
1 tablespoon vegetable oil
¾ teaspoon salt
½ teaspoon dried thyme
¼ teaspoon black pepper
1 large onion, chopped
1-2 medium jalapeño peppers,
cut into ⅛-inch slices

¼ cup water
4 medium tomatoes, chopped
½ bell pepper, cut into 1-inch
pieces
½ yellow bell pepper, cut into 1-
inch pieces
3 cups cooked farfalle (bow tie
pasta)
1 tablespoon chopped fresh
parsley

Brown beef in oil in a large, ovenproof frying pan or Dutch oven. Pour off any pan drippings. Season steak with salt, thyme, and black pepper. Top with onion and jalapeño pepper. Add water and cover tightly. Bake at 325° for 45 minutes. Add tomato and bell peppers. Cover and cook 30 minutes or until beef and vegetables are tender. Remove beef to a warm platter. Reduce pan liquid, stirring frequently, on stove over high heat for 8 to 10 minutes or until slightly thickened. Carve beef and add to sauce. Serve over farfalle. Garnish with parsley.

Yield: 6 servings

Variation: For a milder version, discard seeds and ribs of jalapeño pepper and finely chop.

**National Cattlemen's Beef Association
Chicago, Illinois**

MEXICAN BEEF TIPS

2 pounds beef rib-eye roast, cut
into thin strips
6 cloves garlic, chopped, divided
½ teaspoon black pepper
½ teaspoon ground cumin
2 teaspoons salt
2 tablespoons olive oil
1 cup chopped onion
2½ pounds Roma tomatoes,
chopped
6 serrano chili peppers, seeded
and chopped

Combine beef, 4 cloves garlic, and next 3 ingredients in a storage container. Cover and refrigerate overnight. Heat oil in a Dutch oven. Add onion, remaining 2 cloves garlic, and beef and sauté 10 minutes or until browned. Add tomato and chili pepper and cook, uncovered, for 45 to 60 minutes or until sauce is thickened and meat is tender.

Yield: 6 to 8 servings

Note: Serve with Spanish rice and tortillas.

Kathryn Kaplan

ROAST BEEF QUESADILLAS

1 small onion, thinly sliced
¼ cup chopped bell pepper
½ cup medium salsa, divided
¾ cup grated Colby-Jack cheese
4 (7-inch) flour tortillas
6 ounces deli roast beef, thinly
sliced

Place onion and bell pepper in a small microwave-safe bowl. Cover and microwave on high power for 3 to 4 minutes, stirring halfway through cooking time. Stir in 3 tablespoons salsa. Divide cheese among tortillas. Arrange beef over cheese. Top each with equal amounts of vegetable mixture. Fold tortillas over to close. Heat a 10-inch nonstick skillet over medium heat for 5 minutes. Cook 2 quesadillas at a time in skillet for 2 to 2½ minutes, turning once. Serve with remaining salsa.

Yield: 4 quesadillas

Note: A mixture of grated Monterey Jack and colby or cheddar cheese can be substituted for the Colby-Jack.

Variation: Microwave Method: Place 2 quesadillas at a time on a 12-inch microwave-safe plate. Cover with moistened paper towels. Microwave on high power for 1 to 1½ minutes or until hot.

National Cattlemen's Beef Association
Chicago, Illinois

HOT 'N SPICY BEEF BACK RIBS

7 pounds beef back ribs
¾ cup water, divided
1 cup ketchup
2 tablespoons fresh lemon juice

1 teaspoon cinnamon
1 teaspoon hot pepper sauce
½-1 teaspoon crushed red
  pepper flakes

Place each rib rack, meat-side down, in center of a double-thick rectangle of heavy-duty foil. Foil should be twice the length of the rack plus 8 inches. Use ¼ cup water to sprinkle over rib racks. Bring opposite sides of foil together over top of ribs. Fold edges over 3 to 4 times, pressing crease in tightly each time, and allowing some air space. Flatten foil at both ends and crease to form triangles. Fold over toward packet several times, pressing tightly to seal. Place packets on a grill over low to medium hot coals. Place cover on cooker and grill 1 hour, 30 minutes, turning packets every 30 minutes. Meanwhile, combine remaining ½ cup water, ketchup, and remaining 4 ingredients in a small saucepan. Bring to a boil and reduce heat. Cook slowly, stirring occasionally, for 10 to 12 minutes. Remove ribs from foil and place directly on grill over medium hot coals. Cook 30 to 40 minutes, turning and brushing with sauce occasionally. Serve ribs with remaining sauce.

Yield: 8 to 10 servings

Note: To check temperature, cautiously hold hand about 4 inches above coals. Low to medium coals will force removal of hand in 4 to 5 seconds.

Beef back ribs will yield one to one and a quarter (3-ounce) cooked, trimmed servings per pound.

Variation: Open Cooker Method: Prepare ribs in foil packets and place on grill over medium coals. Increase cooking time to 2 hours, turning packets every 30 minutes. Continue with remaining procedure as above.

National Cattlemen's Beef Association
Chicago, Illinois

ALCACHOFAS RELLENAS
STUFFED ARTICHOKES

MEAT STUFFING

1 tablespoon vegetable oil
½ cup finely chopped onion
2 cloves garlic, minced
½ cup finely chopped bell
pepper
2 tomatillos, finely chopped
(optional)

1 pound lean ground meat
salt and pepper to taste
cayenne pepper to taste
2 tablespoons raisins
2 tablespoons chopped pecans
or walnuts

STUFFED ARTICHOKES

4 artichokes

Meat Stuffing

Heat oil in a skillet. Add onion and next 3 ingredients. Cook, stirring often, for about 5 minutes. Add meat and cook until most of liquid evaporates. Add salt, pepper, and remaining 3 ingredients. Cook until flavors blend. To prepare stuffed artichokes, place artichokes upright on a rack in a large pot or Dutch oven. Fill with water halfway up sides of artichokes. Add a little vinegar or lemon juice to the water. Bring to a boil. Reduce heat and cover. Steam until an outer leaf easily pulls off. When cool enough to handle, remove small center leaves and dig out the inedible prickly part of artichokes. Do not detach the heart from the center. Leave most of the leaves intact. Cool completely and fill with stuffing. Microwave briefly to reheat.

Yield: 4 servings

Variation: For a cold entree, fill cooled artichokes with cold chicken, shrimp, tuna, or egg salad. For the egg salad, mix 2 boiled, chopped eggs per artichoke with chopped onion, sliced green olives, mayonnaise, Dijon mustard, garlic pepper, and cayenne pepper.

**Helen Groves
King Ranch**

MEXICAN LASAGNA

2 pounds lean ground beef
1 small onion, chopped
1 clove garlic, minced
1½ cups picante sauce
1 (10-ounce) package frozen
  spinach, thawed and squeezed
  dry
1 (8-ounce) can tomato sauce
2 medium tomatoes, seeded and
  chopped

1 large red bell pepper, diced
1 tablespoon lime juice
1½ teaspoons salt
12 corn tortillas
1 cup sour cream
¾ cup grated Monterey Jack
  cheese
¾ cup grated cheddar cheese
½ cup sliced black olives

Brown beef with onion and garlic. Drain. Add picante sauce and next 6 ingredients. Simmer, uncovered and stirring occasionally, for 15 minutes. Arrange 6 tortillas, overlapping as necessary, on the bottom and sides of a lightly greased 9X13 inch baking dish. Top with half the beef mixture. Cover with remaining tortillas. Spread sour cream evenly over tortillas. Add remaining beef mixture. Bake at 350° for 30 minutes or until hot and bubbly. Sprinkle with cheeses. Let stand 10 minutes. Cut into squares and garnish with olives.

Yield: 8 servings

Betty Aguirre

VEAL PICCATA

1½ pounds veal round
salt and pepper to taste
all-purpose flour for dredging
4 tablespoons butter
1½ tablespoons olive oil
2 cloves garlic, minced
8 ounces fresh mushrooms,
  sliced

2 tablespoons fresh lemon juice
½ cup dry white wine
2 teaspoons capers
3 tablespoons minced fresh
  parsley
½ lemon, thinly sliced for
  garnish

Sprinkle veal with salt and pepper on both sides. Dredge in flour. Heat butter and oil in a large skillet. Add veal and brown on both sides. Remove veal and add garlic and mushrooms to skillet. Sauté 1 minute. Return veal to skillet. Add lemon juice and wine. Cover and simmer 20 minutes. Stir in capers and transfer to a serving platter. Sprinkle with parsley and garnish with lemon slices.

Yield: 4 servings

Variation: Chicken can be substituted for veal for another tasty dish.

Mary Vance Jones

GRILLED SALMON SOUTHWEST WITH FRESH CORN RELISH AND BLACK BEANS

FRESH CORN RELISH

3 ears corn, kernels removed
1 red bell pepper, diced
½ red onion, diced
1-2 fresh jalapeño peppers, seeded and diced

½ bunch cilantro, chopped
1 lime, halved
olive oil
salt and pepper to taste

BLACK BEANS

1 (16-ounce) bag black beans
3 tomatoes, blanched, peeled, seeded, and diced

1 clove garlic
sour cream

SALMON

2 pounds salmon fillets
olive oil

sea salt and pepper

Combine corn kernels and next 4 ingredients in a bowl. Squeeze lime juice over vegetables. Slowly add enough oil to bind vegetables. Season with salt and pepper. To prepare beans, simmer beans in water until tender. Drain. Combine beans, tomato, and garlic in a bowl. When ready to serve, top with sour cream. Prepare salmon by rinsing fillets with cool water. Pat dry. Rub fillets with oil, salt, and pepper. Grill 10 minutes for a 1-inch thick fillet. Serve salmon topped with corn relish and with beans on the side.

Yield: 4 to 5 servings

Colleen Curran Hook

POACHED SALMON WITH CUCUMBER TARRAGON SAUCE

SALMON

1 onion, sliced
3 carrots, chopped
¼ stalk celery, chopped
2 bay leaves
2 lemons, halved
2 quarts water

1 whole salmon, washed, butterflied, and backbone removed
thinly sliced lemon, limes, and cucumbers for garnish

CUCUMBER TARRAGON SAUCE

2 cucumbers, seeded and finely chopped
1 cup mayonnaise
1 cup sour cream
2 tablespoons fresh chopped parsley

2 tablespoons fresh chopped tarragon
pinch of salt
pinch of white pepper
1 tablespoon lemon juice

Combine onion and next 5 ingredients in a large poaching pan. Bring to a boil. Place salmon on top and reduce heat. Simmer, adding water as needed, 30 minutes or until fish flakes easily with a fork. Drain liquid and refrigerate salmon until chilled. Transfer salmon from pan to a lettuce-lined serving tray. Remove skin from salmon. Spread sauce over top and garnish. To make sauce, combine all ingredients.

Sergio Rodriguez
Executive Chef
Catering by Don Strange
San Antonio, Texas

SOUTH PADRE FISH KABOBS

3 bell peppers
3 medium onions
1 pound small mushrooms
5 strips bacon, cut into 1-inch
 squares

1 link spicy polish sausage, cut
 into ¾-inch slices
3 pounds kingfish fillets, as
 thick as possible, cut into 1-
 inch cubes
blackened redfish seasoning

Cut bell peppers and onions in half, and then cut halves into quarters. Arrange bell pepper, onion, mushrooms, and next 3 ingredients on skewers, placing a piece of bacon on both sides of fish. Sprinkle kabobs with seasoning. Roast or grill until fish is cooked.

Yield: 6 or 7 servings

Ruby dela Garza Krautkremer

MESQUITE GRILLED REDFISH

½ cup olive oil
juice of 4 limes
4 cloves garlic, crushed
dash of cayenne pepper

black pepper to taste
seasoned salt to taste
4-6 redfish fillets

Combine oil and next 4 ingredients. Sprinkle seasoned salt over fillets. Dip or marinate fillets in oil mixture. Grill over mesquite coals, or cook on a gas grill or under a broiler.

Yield: 4 to 6 servings

Note: Other fish can be used, but redfish holds together best when cooking.

Mike Fain
State Game Warden
Kenedy County

BAKED ORANGE ROUGHY

We are so lucky to get the recipe for this house specialty at Santa Fe Steakhouse!

4 orange roughy fillets
½ cup pesto sauce with garlic
sun-dried tomatoes, packed in
    oil
1 (6-ounce) jar artichoke hearts
pine nuts

1 zucchini, cut into long strips
1 red onion, sliced
1 lemon
Cajun seasoning to taste
4 teaspoons butter

Place each fillet on a sheet of parchment paper or foil. Spread pesto sauce evenly over fillets. Sprinkle with tomatoes, artichoke hearts, and pine nuts. Lay a slice of zucchini on either side of each fillet. Top with an onion slice. Squeeze lemon over fillets and season with Cajun seasoning. Place 1 teaspoon butter on top of each. Fold paper or foil over the top and seal edges. Place on a baking sheet. Bake at 400° for 25 minutes.

Yield: 4 servings

Lisa Harms
Santa Fe Steakhouse
McAllen, Texas

STUFFED FLOUNDER

1 whole flounder, scaled
1 medium onion, chopped
1 stalk celery, diced
4 tablespoons butter or
    margarine, plus extra for
    topping

1 (6-ounce) can crabmeat
1 cup cooked small shrimp
cracker crumbs
1 egg, beaten
lemon slices for garnish
paprika for garnish

To prepare fish, use a sharp knife to make a cut, 6 to 8 inches long, along the backbone. Cut into meat on both sides of backbone to form a pocket. Sauté onion and celery in butter. Remove from heat and mix in crabmeat and shrimp. Add enough cracker crumbs to fill pockets. Stir in egg to bind ingredients together. Stuff mixture into fish pockets. Place several pats of butter on top of dressing. Place fish on a foil-lined baking sheet. Garnish with lemon slices and paprika. Bake at 350° to 375° for 35 to 40 minutes. Serve with extra melted butter and lemon slices.

Nancy Boultinghouse

COSTA RICA DELIGHT

2 tablespoons vegetable oil
1 cup diced onion
1 cup diced celery
⅛ teaspoon filé powder
dash of salt
½ teaspoon cayenne pepper, or
    1 teaspoon sage
8 ounces fresh or canned
    mushrooms, chopped

3 pounds fish fillets, thinly
    sliced
2 cups dry breadcrumbs
2 eggs
1 lemon, halved
4 tablespoons butter, melted,
    divided
paprika
dried tarragon

Heat oil in a skillet. Add onion and celery and sauté until softened. Stir in filé powder and salt. Add cayenne pepper if you like it hot, otherwise use sage. Add mushrooms and cover. Steam 5 minutes. Place a single layer of fillets in a greased casserole or baking dish. Place breadcrumbs in a mixing bowl. Mix in onion mixture and eggs. Spoon a ½-inch layer of breadcrumb mixture over fillets. Add a second layer of fillets. Cover with remaining breadcrumb mixture. Top with a final layer of fillets. Squeeze lemon over fish. Baste with 2 tablespoons melted butter. Sprinkle with paprika and tarragon. Cover and bake at 375° for 30 minutes. Baste with remaining 2 tablespoons butter. Broil until top of fish is crisp. Serve hot.

Yield: 4 to 6 servings

Nancy Boultinghouse

SHRIMP PAESANO

SHRIMP

1 pound jumbo shrimp, peeled
    and deveined
half-and-half

all-purpose flour for dredging
dry breadcrumbs for dredging
olive oil

SAUCE

1 egg yolk
juice of ½ lemon
1 stick butter, divided

2 cloves garlic, minced
chopped fresh parsley
chopped fresh chives

Soak shrimp in half-and-half for 10 minutes. Remove and drain shrimp, re-serving half-and-half. Dredge shrimp in flour. Dip in reserved half-and-half, and then dredge in breadcrumbs. Sauté in oil over medium heat for 5 minutes. Transfer to broiler and broil until golden. Drain and serve topped with sauce. To prepare sauce, combine egg yolk and lemon juice in a heavy saucepan. Add 4 tablespoons butter and stir over low heat until melted. Add garlic and remaining 4 tablespoons butter. Stir briskly until butter melts and sauce thickens. Add parsley and chives.

Yield: 2 or 3 servings

Mary Vance Jones

SHRIMP VERMOUTH

1 tablespoon butter
½ pound large shrimp, peeled
    and deveined
½ teaspoon minced shallot
¼ cup dry vermouth
black pepper to taste

pinch of saffron
½ cup cream, or regular or
    canned milk
½ cup fish or chicken broth
1 teaspoon hollandaise sauce
    (optional)

Melt butter in a skillet. Add shrimp and shallot and sauté 3 minutes. Remove shrimp and cover loosely with foil. Add vermouth and pepper to skillet. Cook about 8 minutes. Add saffron and simmer until slightly reduced. Add cream and simmer until thickened. Strain cream sauce into another pan. Add enough broth to reach desired consistency. Bring to a boil. Add hollandaise sauce if cream sauce is too thin. Place shrimp in the center of a rice ring. Pour sauce over top.

Yield: 2 servings

Kathryn S. Cain

GULF COAST SHRIMP BAKE

1½ sticks butter
1 large bell pepper, chopped
1 medium onion, chopped
2 large tomatoes, chopped
juice of 1 lemon
2 tablespoons seasoning blend
¼ teaspoon garlic powder
½ teaspoon Italian seasoning
3 bay leaves
½ cup picante sauce
2 stalks celery, chopped

¼ teaspoon ground cumin
⅔ cup BBQ sauce
½ cup steak sauce
1 tablespoon fresh chopped
  cilantro
½ cup ketchup
1 cup water
⅔ cup dry white wine
3 pounds large shrimp, peeled
  and deveined

Place butter in a baking pan and melt in a 375° oven. Add bell pepper, onion, and tomato and bake until softened. Add lemon juice and next 13 ingredients. Mix well. Add shrimp. Bake 30 minutes or until shrimp are pink. Baste with pan juices about every 10 minutes. Do not overcook. Serve hot on a large platter with warm French bread.

Yield: 4 servings

Sandra Medina

SHRIMP AND CRAB CREOLE

1 stick butter or margarine
3 tablespoons bacon fat
1 large onion, chopped
1 bunch green onions, chopped
1 cup chopped celery
1 small bell pepper, chopped
3-4 (14½-ounce) cans stewed
   tomatoes

3-4 bay leaves
salt and pepper to taste
garlic powder to taste
1 pound shrimp, peeled and
   deveined
1 pound crabmeat
1 tablespoon filé powder
dash of hot pepper sauce

Heat butter and bacon fat in a skillet. Add onion and next 3 ingredients and sauté until softened. Add tomatoes and bay leaves. Simmer 1 hour, 30 minutes to 2 hours. Add salt, pepper, and garlic powder. Add shrimp and remaining 3 ingredients. Simmer 30 minutes. Remove bay leaves and serve over rice.

Yield: 6 to 8 servings

Variation: Fish can be used instead of crab, but add fish during final 20 minutes of cooking and do not stir.

Bonnie Brown

CRAB AU GRATIN

1 stalk celery, finely chopped
1 onion, finely chopped
4 tablespoons butter
½ cup all-purpose flour
1 (12-ounce) can evaporated
   milk

2 egg yolks
salt and pepper to taste
1 pound crabmeat
½ cup grated cheddar cheese

Sauté celery and onion in butter until tender. Blend in flour. Slowly stir in milk. Cook until thickened. Add egg yolks, salt, and pepper. Cook 5 minutes. Stir in crabmeat. Pour into a casserole dish. Top with cheese. Bake at 350° for 10 to 15 minutes or until cheese melts.

Yield: 8 to 10 servings

Mike Fain
State Game Warden
Kenedy County

CHUCKWAGON PORK ROAST WITH TANGY SAUCE

PORK ROAST

½ teaspoon salt
½ teaspoon garlic salt

½ teaspoon chili powder
1 (4-pound) pork loin

TANGY SAUCE

1 cup apple jelly
1 cup ketchup

2 teaspoons vinegar
2 teaspoons chili powder

Combine salt, garlic salt, and chili powder and rub into pork. Roast at 325° for 2 hours or until a meat thermometer inserted in the center registers 160°. To make sauce, combine all ingredients in a saucepan. Bring to a boil and simmer 2 minutes. About 15 minutes before pork is done, brush with sauce. Add ½ cup of pan drippings to remaining sauce and serve with pork.

Yield: 12 servings

Variation: Substitute other pork cuts, if desired. Pork tenderloin should roast 30 minutes, and baby back ribs need to cook 20 minutes.

Sergio Rodriguez
Executive Chef
Catering by Don Strange
San Antonio, Texas

LOMO DE PUERCO
PORK LOIN

1 pork loin
1 cup chopped ham
1 cup chopped bacon
1 (12-ounce) can crushed
  pineapple, juice reserved

1 cup chopped prunes
salt and pepper to taste
garlic powder to taste
1 cup cooking sherry

Cut slits, about 1 to 1½ inches apart, in the top of the pork loin. Stuff each opening with ham and next 3 ingredients. Pinch each opening closed as much as possible. Season pork with salt, pepper, and garlic powder. Place in a baking dish and pour sherry and reserved pineapple juice over the top. Cover and bake at 350° for about 2 hours.

Tracey L. Garrido

SWEET 'N SOUR PORK

1½ pounds lean pork shoulder
  or chops, cut into strips
vegetable oil
¼ cup water
¼ cup packed brown sugar
2 tablespoons cornstarch

1 (20-ounce) can sweetened
  pineapple chunks, juice
  reserved
¼ cup vinegar
1 tablespoon soy sauce
½ teaspoon salt
¾ cup bell pepper strips
¼ cup thinly sliced onion

Brown pork in oil. Add water and cover. Simmer 60 minutes or until tender. Combine brown sugar and cornstarch in a saucepan. Stir in reserved pineapple juice, vinegar, soy sauce, and salt. Cook and stir over low heat until thickened. Pour over hot pork. Let stand 10 minutes. Add pineapple, bell pepper, and onion. Cook 2 to 3 minutes. Serve over chow mein noodles or hot rice.

Nancy Boultinghouse

BAKED STUFFED PORK CHOPS

SAVORY STUFFING

2 tablespoons butter or
  margarine
⅓ cup finely chopped onion
½ cup chopped celery
1½ cups soft bread cubes
¼ cup raisins

2 tablespoons chopped fresh
  parsley
1 teaspoon salt
½ teaspoon dried marjoram
⅛ teaspoon black pepper
3 tablespoons apple juice

PORK CHOPS

4 (1 to 2-inch thick) rib pork
  chops

Savory Stuffing
1 teaspoon seasoned salt

Melt butter in a skillet. Add onion and celery and cook 8 minutes or until tender. Add bread cubes and sauté until lightly browned. Remove from heat. Stir in raisins and next 5 ingredients. Toss mixture lightly. To prepare pork, cut into side of chop opposite the bone to form a pocket. Pat chops dry with paper towels. Fill pockets with stuffing. Stand chops on rib bones on a rack in a shallow roasting pan. Sprinkle with seasoned salt. Pour water into pan to a ½-inch depth. Water should not touch pork. Cover with foil. Bake at 350° for 45 minutes. Remove foil and bake 45 to 55 minutes or until pork is tender and browned.

Yield: 4 servings

Nancy Boultinghouse

BBQ PORK RIBS WITH BROTH BASTING SAUCE

1 teaspoon salt
1 teaspoon dry mustard
2 bay leaves, finely crumbled
1 teaspoon chili powder
½ teaspoon paprika
1 teaspoon hot pepper sauce
½ cup Worcestershire sauce

½ cup cider vinegar
3 cups beef broth
⅓ cup vegetable oil
1 tablespoon soy sauce
1 clove garlic, chopped
3-4 pounds pork ribs

Blend salt and next 4 ingredients in a large saucepan. Slowly stir in hot pepper and Worcestershire sauces until mustard dissolves. Stir in vinegar and next 4 ingredients. Bring to a boil and cook a few minutes. Pour into a container and cover. Refrigerate overnight. When ready to cook, place ribs on a grill over hot coals and brush with basting sauce. Baste ribs frequently while cooking.

Jay Ellison

TERIYAKI PORK RIBS BOTANA

¼ cup olive oil
¼ cup soy sauce
2 tablespoons ketchup
1 tablespoon vinegar

¼ teaspoon freshly ground black
pepper
2 cloves garlic, crushed
pork rib racks, cut lengthwise in
half or thirds

Whisk together oil and next 5 ingredients in a bowl to make a sauce. Place ribs in a freezer zip-top plastic bag(s). Pour sauce into bag(s). Flatten to remove excess air and zip closed. Place flat on a baking sheet and refrigerate several hours or overnight, turning every few hours. Open corner of bag and pour sauce into a bowl. Grill ribs over hot coals to sear. Move to cooler part of grill and brush with sauce. Cover grill and cook 30 minutes, basting every 10 minutes. Transfer to a deep baking dish. Pour remaining sauce over ribs and cover tightly with foil. Bake at 275° to 300° for 2 hours. Remove from oven. Loosen foil and let ribs stand 20 minutes before slicing between ribs. Cut carefully to prevent tender ribs from falling from the bone.

Note: Have the butcher cut the raw ribs in lengthwise strips.

**Monica Burdette
The Inn at El Canelo
Raymondville, Texas**

LONE STAR LAMB TACOS

PAPAYA CORIANDER RELISH

1 teaspoon honey
1 papaya, peeled, seeded, and
    finely chopped
1 bell pepper, finely chopped

1 bunch cilantro, finely chopped
dash of salt
juice of 1 lemon

TACOS

1 leg of lamb or boneless leg
    roast of lamb
1 teaspoon salt
1 teaspoon garlic powder

1 teaspoon paprika
¼ teaspoon cinnamon
¼ teaspoon ground cloves
60-75 small flour tortillas

Combine all relish ingredients and refrigerate 2 hours. To prepare tacos, rub lamb with salt and next 4 ingredients. Roast at 350° for 2 to 2½ hours or until tender. Slice meat into small strips. Serve in warm flour tortillas with Papaya Coriander Relish.

Yield: 20 to 25 servings

Sergio Rodriguez
Executive Chef
Catering by Don Strange
San Antonio, Texas

VENISON MOO SHEE CRÊPES

3 tablespoons rice wine
⅓ cup soy sauce
2 tablespoons sugar
1 tablespoon baking soda
1 teaspoon sesame oil
¼ cup cornstarch, plus extra to thicken sauce
1½ pounds venison, julienned
1½ pounds pork, julienned, bone and trimmed fat reserved

salt and pepper
2 (8-ounce) cans sliced water chestnuts, drained
3 pounds mushrooms, sliced
3 bunches green onions, cut into 1-inch slices
3 cloves garlic
crêpe shells
butter

Combine wine and next 5 ingredients to make a marinade. Add venison and pork and refrigerate overnight. To make a sauce, boil reserved pork bone and trimmed fat in water. Season with salt and pepper. Thicken with cornstarch dissolved in water. When ready to make crêpes, drain meat and stir-fry until crispy. Add water chestnuts and next 3 ingredients and sauté briefly. Sauté crêpe shells in butter to warm. Spoon in meat mixture and roll up. Serve with sauce.

Yield: 10 to 12 servings

Sergio Rodriguez
Executive Chef
Catering by Don Strange
San Antonio, Texas

GLAZED VENISON ROAST

1 (2 to 3-pound) venison roast, boned
olive oil
salt and pepper to taste

4-6 cloves garlic, sliced lengthwise
4-6 strips bacon
2 tablespoons honey
¼ cup Heinz 57 steak sauce

Coat roast with oil, salt, and pepper. Tie roast together. Cut slashes into top of roast. Slice garlic into slivers and insert in slashes on roast. Place bacon strips across top. Place meat in a roasting pan. Bake at 325° for 2 hours, 30 minutes to 3 hours for medium rare. Combine honey and steak sauce. Use honey mixture to baste roast 3 to 4 times while cooking.

Nancy Boultinghouse

MEDAILLONS DE VENAISSON AU POIVRE VERT
VENISON MEDALLIONS WITH GREEN PEPPERCORN SAUCE

3 pounds whole venison backstrap	2 tablespoons butter
	salt to taste
3 tablespoons canned green peppercorns	¼ cup brandy
	1 cup whipping cream
2 tablespoons vegetable oil	

Trim venison of any fat, tendons, or connective tissue. Place in a glass baking dish. Rinse peppercorns in cold water. If firm, roughly crush in a mortar and pestle. Press peppercorns onto entire surface of venison. Cover with plastic wrap and refrigerate several hours. Heat oil and butter over high heat in a large skillet. Leaving peppercorns on meat, sauté venison quickly on all sides until just browned. Do not overcook. Reduce to medium-high heat and discard excess fat. Season with salt. Pour brandy over meat and deglaze skillet, gently scraping bottom of pan. Carefully ignite brandy with a long match. Allow flame to subside. Transfer meat to a warm dish. Cover loosely with foil and place in a 225° oven to keep warm. Pour cream into skillet. Bring to a boil. Lower heat and simmer until reduced by at least half. Sauce should be golden and the consistency of thin gravy. Adjust seasoning as needed. Cut venison into ¼-inch slices. Place 3 overlapping slices on each plate. Pour sauce over medallions and serve immediately.

Yield: 6 servings

Note: If desired, use the backstrap of other game such as nilgai or wild pig.

Monica Burdette
The Inn at El Canelo
Raymondville, Texas

VENISON LONDON BROIL

¼ cup vegetable oil	1 clove garlic, chopped
¼ cup tomato juice	red wine (optional)
¼ cup soy sauce	meat tenderizer
¼ cup packed brown sugar	venison backstrap

Combine oil and next 5 ingredients to make a marinade. Sprinkle meat tenderizer over venison. Add venison to marinade and refrigerate 8 to 10 hours. Cook venison on a grill 10 to 20 minutes on each side.

Yield: 4 servings

Note: If using meat from an older deer, soak meat in milk or water for 4 to 5 hours before adding tenderizer. This reduces the gamy flavor. If using water, change water twice.

Melinda Wright

VENISON ROLL-UPS

8 (¼-inch) venison round steaks	1 stick butter
salt and pepper	fresh sliced mushrooms
1 (7-ounce) package stuffing mix	¼ cup all-purpose flour
diced onion to taste(optional)	2 cups cold water
diced celery to taste (optional)	¼ cup Worcestershire sauce

Pound out steaks and season lightly with salt and pepper. Prepare stuffing according to package directions, adding onion and celery. Spoon stuffing onto steaks and roll up. Secure with a toothpick, if necessary. Roll-ups should be about 2 inches in diameter. Place roll-ups, seam-side down, in a lightly greased baking dish or Dutch oven. Bake at 350° for 30 minutes. Meanwhile, prepare a gravy by melting butter in a skillet. Add mushrooms and sauté. Mix together flour and water until smooth. Stir into skillet. Add Worcestershire sauce. Bring to a boil. Cook and stir until thickened. Pour over roll-ups and cover. Bake 30 minutes longer.

Yield: 6 to 8 servings

James Lopez

Venison Chili

5 cups canned tomatoes
1½ pound onions, chopped,
   plus extra for browning meat
1 pound bell peppers, chopped
2 cloves garlic, chopped, plus
   extra for browning meat
½ cup chopped fresh parsley
1 pound ground pork
2½ pounds ground venison

½ cup chili powder or to taste
2 (15-ounce) cans red kidney
   beans, undrained
2 teaspoons salt
1½ teaspoons black pepper
2 tablespoons Worcestershire
   sauce
½ cup red wine

Simmer tomatoes 5 minutes in a Dutch oven. Add onion and bell pepper and cook until tender. Add garlic and parsley. In a skillet, brown pork and venison with onion and garlic. Drain and add to tomato mixture. Stir in chili powder and next 4 ingredients. Add water to desired consistency. Simmer, covered, for 60 minutes. Uncover and cook 30 minutes. Add wine just before serving.

Yield: 8 servings

Melinda Wright

Doves in Sherry Sauce

12-15 dove breasts, boned
¼ cup seasoned flour
4 tablespoons butter
1 small onion, minced
¾-1 cup sherry, divided
1 (14½-ounce) can tomatoes

1 (4-ounce) jar marinated
   mushrooms, undrained
1 tablespoon dry chicken
   bouillon
1 tablespoon Worcestershire
   sauce
1 cup water

Dredge dove in flour. Melt butter over medium-high heat in a large saucepan or Dutch oven. Add dove and sauté. Remove dove and add onion to saucepan. Sauté until softened. Return dove to pan. Add ¾ cup sherry and remaining 5 ingredients. Bring to a boil. Reduce heat and simmer 60 minutes or until meat is tender. If desired, add remaining ¼ cup sherry and cook 15 minutes longer. Serve with rice or noodles.

Note: If desired, make your own marinated mushrooms (recipe on page 50).

**Monica Burdette
The Inn at El Canelo
Raymondville, Texas**

NILGAI STEW

Nilgai, a member of the antelope family, was imported by the King Ranch several decades ago. They have so flourished in this area that the population is now greater in South Texas than in India where they originated! Although the meat is very dark red, it is quite mild tasting.

1 tablespoon olive oil	1 teaspoon black peppercorns
1 nilgai backstrap, cut into	1 cup dry red wine
1-inch cubes	1 cup water
1 cup sliced onion	4 serrano chili peppers, seeded
1 cup sliced celery	and chopped
1 cup sliced mushrooms	1½ cups chopped fresh parsley
3 tomatoes	1 beef bouillon cube
3 cloves garlic	½ cup all-purpose flour
1 teaspoon cumin seed	1½ cups hot water

Spray a skillet with nonstick cooking spray. Add oil and nilgai and cook until well browned. Remove meat and add onion, celery, and mushrooms to skillet and sauté until browned. Meanwhile, dip tomatoes briefly in boiling water and remove skin. Grind garlic, cumin, and peppercorns in a molcajete or spice grinder. Add to tomatoes and puree. Return meat to skillet and add tomato mixture. Add wine and next 4 ingredients. Cover and simmer at least 60 minutes. Mix together flour and water until smooth. Slowly stir into stew to thicken. Serve with noodles or wild rice.

Frances McAllen
McAllen Ranch

NILGAI BURGER

4 pounds nilgai	1 teaspoon salt
4 green onions	1 teaspoon black pepper
handful of fresh cilantro	½ teaspoon garlic powder
2 bell peppers	½ teaspoon BBQ spice
¼ cup olive oil, plus extra for cooking	1 (10¾-ounce) can condensed cream of mushroom soup

Put nilgai through a grinder. Without cleaning grinder, grind onions, cilantro, and bell peppers. Mix ground meat and vegetables by hand. Add oil and next 4 ingredients and mix well. Form into 8 patties. Rub a large skillet with olive oil and slowly brown patties on both sides. Reduce to low heat. Pour soup over patties. Cover skillet and cook until centers are pink. Serve on toast.

Yield: 8 servings

Variation: Venison and elk also work great in this recipe.

Nancy Boultinghouse

JAY'S GRILLED QUAIL

2 cups white wine vinegar	1 tablespoon vermouth
1 cup olive oil	1 teaspoon hot pepper sauce
¼ cup lime juice	1 teaspoon onion salt
zest of 4 limes	black pepper to taste
4 cloves garlic, chopped	10-12 quail
2 bay leaves	10-12 slices bacon
1 tablespoon soy sauce	

Combine vinegar and next 10 ingredients to make a marinade. Add quail and refrigerate at least 8 hours. Remove quail, reserving marinade. Wrap each quail with a slice of bacon and secure with a toothpick. Grill over low coals for about 30 minutes, basting often with marinade. Do not overcook.

Yield: 4 to 6 servings

Jay Ellison

PHEASANT

1 pheasant, cut into pieces	1 cup plus 1 tablespoon
2 cups buttermilk	vegetable oil, divided
1 cup all-purpose flour	¼ teaspoon ground allspice
salt and pepper to taste	½ cup water

Soak pheasant in buttermilk for 2 hours. Drain and dredge pheasant in flour. Season with salt and pepper. Fry in 1 cup oil until golden brown. In a skillet, combine remaining 1 tablespoon oil, allspice, and water. Bring to a boil over high heat. Reduce to low heat and place pheasant legs and thighs in bottom of skillet. Put breasts on top. Steam about 30 minutes. Meat will almost fall off the bone and melt in your mouth. Use pan drippings for gravy.

Nancy Boultinghouse

🏠 BAKED RATTLESNAKE

For our most adventurous outdoor cooks...

THIN CREAM SAUCE

1 tablespoon butter	⅛ teaspoon black pepper
1 tablespoon all-purpose flour	1 cup milk
¼ teaspoon salt	

ENTREE

1 rattlesnake, skinned, dressed, and washed	2 fresh limes, thinly sliced
1 recipe Thin Cream Sauce	1 teaspoon white pepper
4 ounces fresh mushrooms, sliced	1 teaspoon dried basil
	1 teaspoon dried rosemary

Melt butter in a saucepan over low heat. Blend in flour, salt, and pepper. Cook over low heat until mixture is smooth and bubbly. Remove from heat and stir in milk. Heat and stir until boiling. Boil, stirring constantly, for 1 minute. To prepare entree, cut snake into 3-inch sections and place in a large baking dish. Cover with cream sauce and remaining 5 ingredients. Bake at 300° for 60 minutes or until tender.

Faye Carter

Vegetables
& side dishes

Working The Land

Working The Land

An area rich in history and culture, the Rio Grande Valley was also a land rich in soil and climate. Prior to the 20th century, this area saw relatively little agricultural development. Made up of mostly hot, dry chaparral, Valley land was thought to be of little use other than cattle ranching. But, with the advent of irrigation, everything changed. Massive pump houses on the banks of the mighty Rio Grande gushed water into an extensive canal system, giving life to the dormant soil.

Speculators bought up vast tracts of former Spanish land grants, cut them into smaller parcels, and sold them to Midwesterners and foreign investors who responded to newspaper ads touting the Valley as a new Eden. Between 1910 and 1930, the Valley experienced a mass influx of tens of thousands of out-of-state farmers and adventurers eager to purchase and till the cheap land. Almost daily, land parties arrived

Above:
Early ad enticing Valley "settlers."
Cover page: *His building was his billboard: Jas. N. Kilgore of Harlingen claimed "RGV lands especially adapted for growing California grapes, oranges, lemons, alfalfa, sugar cane... see for yourself."*
At left: *Rumored to be the first citrus trees planted in the Valley, this 1920s (?) photo shows tall orange trees located on the Laguna Seca Ranch near San Manuel / Linn. Their current fate is unknown.*
Below right: *This crop wheel was used as propaganda to show prospective farmers that the Valley's bounty lasted all year long.*

> **DID YOU KNOW?**
>
> JOHN SHARY, OFTEN CALLED "THE FATHER OF VALLEY CITRUS" DIED THINKING HIS CITRUS INDUSTRY WAS INVINCIBLE. HE GREW CITRUS FOR A NOW-UNHEARD-OF THIRTY-FIVE YEARS WITHOUT A DAMAGING FREEZE. SINCE HIS DEATH IN 1947, FOUR MAJOR FREEZES HAVE HEAVILY DAMAGED THE CITRUS INDUSTRY IN 1950, 1967, 1983 AND 1989. THE MULTI-MILLION DOLLAR INDUSTRY HAS REBOUNDED EACH TIME.

by train, pulling past palm tree-lined tracks into communities that weren't much more than a few houses and maybe a church. Bumping down dirt roads, the wide-eyed land-seekers were shown around by enthusiastic salesmen ready to sell them a chunk of paradise. The promise of an "endless" water supply, virtually rock-free soil and an extended warm growing

season proved too much to resist.

Though rough and lacking in some necessities, the Valley offered optimum possibilities for the farmers. Most grew traditional vegetables and other cash crops—sugar cane, cotton and corn—with varying degrees of success. Local farmers also began experimenting with citrus trees. Those first trees quickly developed into a thriving citrus industry. Orchards and packing sheds sprang up to

Above: Land party excursions appealed to those looking for one last American frontier.
Left: The inside of a pump house was a mass of roaring steam pipes and rattling valves.
Below: Early Hidalgo, Texas with a pump house at right. Circa 1920. The pump house still stands today, as does the two-story building in the foreground. Photo taken from the 1886 Courthouse which lost its second story in a fire in the late 1920s.

accommodate the growing demand. Grapefruit was king, and green groves spread over the landscape like a blanket. For decades, citrus has remained an important

part of the Valley economy, weathering hard times and freezing cold, but always proving resilient.

In the 1920s, Texas A&M University established a research station in Weslaco for the sole purpose of developing and improving local agricultural products such as the Ruby Red and Star Ruby grapefruits. Intensely sweet and red, Valley grapefruit has become the favorite of gourmets everywhere, and is an especially popular gift at Christmas time. The 1015 Onion—a large, sweet, easy-to-grow, shelf-hardy variety —was another by-product of the research station. It is marketed across the U.S. and enjoys favorable reviews.

Today, the Valley continues to expand its agricultural horizons. All kinds of exotic vegetables grow next to fields of

Above: Whistle while you work...1950's-era grapefruit workers sort and pack the Valley's exotic export.
Above inset: Among the various products hawked by grove owners was grapefruit wine (in the 70's) and "pop-style" Rio Rey juice, marketed by John Shary as "pure, unadulterated juice from Lower Rio Grande Valley grapefruit."

melons, sorghum, and sugar cane. New industries like tree and grass farms, flower crops for pharmaceuticals, aloe vera, and even shrimp farming along the coast attest to the versatility of the land, and the people, of this place we call Mesquite Country.

Above: Among the Valley's most enduring crops is cotton. Large gins, like this early McAllen establishment, processed tons of the white, fluffy stuff during the height of the season. With the advent of high-tech ginning processes and selective farming techniques, the number of cotton gins has dwindled from its peak in the late 50s and early 60s to a handful today.

RED CURRANT CABBAGE

1 medium to large head red
cabbage, cut into lengthwise
strips
1 (14½-ounce) can chicken
broth, or 2 cups homemade

3 cloves garlic, chopped, or to
taste
1 cup Parmesan cheese
3 tablespoons red currant jelly
½ cup pine nuts

Combine cabbage and chicken broth in a large saucepan. Steam 10 minutes or until tender. Drain well. Return cabbage to saucepan. Stir in garlic, cheese, and jelly. Add pine nuts and cover. Simmer 7 to 10 minutes. Toss gently and serve.

Yield: 8 servings

Note: This dish is best made just before serving so cabbage does not over-cook. Wonderful with venison or other wild game.

Elizabeth McAllen Roberts

COPPER PENNY CARROTS

Since it's served chilled, this vegetable side dish is refreshingly different.

1 medium onion, finely chopped
1 (10¾-ounce) can tomato soup
½ cup salad oil
1 cup sugar
¾ cup cider vinegar

1 teaspoon prepared mustard
1 teaspoon Worcestershire sauce
1 teaspoon garlic salt
2 pounds carrots, sliced and
cooked

Combine onion and next 7 ingredients. Pour over carrot slices. Marinate in refrigerator for 24 hours.

Yield: 8 servings

JoAnna Vernetti Troppy

EASY BAKED CORN

1 egg, beaten
1 cup sour cream
1 (8- to 12-ounce) package
   cornbread mix
½ teaspoon salt

¼ teaspoon black pepper
1 tablespoon sugar
2 (16-ounce) cans corn, drained
1 stick margarine, melted

Combine egg and sour cream. Stir in cornbread mix and next 3 ingredients. Add corn and mix well. Add margarine. Pour into a greased 9X13 inch baking dish. Bake at 350° for 30 to 40 minutes.

Yield: 6 to 8 servings

Priscilla Hawkins

SCALLOPED CORN AND TOMATOES

Perked-up way to serve corn!

2½ cups corn
4 medium tomatoes, chopped
½ cup chopped bell pepper
1 medium onion, grated
2 tablespoons sugar

1 teaspoon salt
⅛ teaspoon black pepper
⅓ cup breadcrumbs
3 tablespoons butter, melted

Spread corn in a greased 2-quart casserole dish. Top with a layer of tomato, and then a layer of bell pepper and onion. Sprinkle with sugar, salt, and black pepper. Combine breadcrumbs and butter and sprinkle over top. Cover and bake at 350° for 45 to 55 minutes.

Yield: 6 to 8 servings

Nancy Boultinghouse

GREEN BEAN BUNDLES

Everyone will want seconds!

1-1½ pounds fresh green beans, trimmed
3-4 slices bacon, halved
⅓ cup packed brown sugar

5 tablespoons butter, melted
½ teaspoon garlic salt
½ teaspoon dried basil

Steam beans for 8 to 10 minutes. Divide beans into individual servings. Wrap each serving with a half slice of bacon. Secure with a toothpick. Place in a baking dish. Combine sugar and remaining 3 ingredients. Pour mixture over beans. Bake at 350° for 30 minutes. Do not overcook.

Yield: 6 to 8 servings

Kathryn Kaplan

TEXAS JALAPEÑO ONION RINGS

1 cup buttermilk
9 fresh jalapeño peppers, chopped
3 large Texas 1015 onions, or other sweet onions, cut into ¼-inch rings

2 quarts peanut oil
4 cups all-purpose flour
salt to taste

Combine buttermilk and jalapeño pepper in a blender. Blend until only small flecks of pepper remain. Pour into a large bowl. Add onion rings and toss well. Cover and let stand at room temperature 4 to 5 hours. Heat oil to 325° in a deep fryer. Drain onion rings in a colander, shaking to remove excess liquid. Dredge rings thoroughly in flour. Do not shake off excess. Fry in oil, in batches, for 3 minutes or until golden brown. Drain on several layers of paper towels. Season with salt.

Yield: 12 appetizer servings or garnishes

Paula Fouchek
Texas Fresh Promotional Board

1015 GLAZED ONION RINGS

Texas 1015 onions, developed in the Rio Grande Valley, are known for their SUPER-sweetness. They are available at grocery stores and road-side stands in the spring. If not available in your area, look for Vidalia or other sweet onions (not as good, of course).

2 tablespoons butter
4 large Texas 1015 onions, or other sweet onions, thinly sliced into rings
2 tablespoons vinegar
2 tablespoons packed brown sugar

1¼ teaspoons curry powder
1½ tablespoons chopped parsley
salt and pepper to taste
paprika to taste
sliced red chili pepper for garnish

Heat butter in a large skillet. Add onion rings and toss for a few minutes. Do not brown. Stir in vinegar, sugar, and curry powder. Add parsley. Cover and cook 5 minutes or until onions are almost crisp-tender. Uncover and cook 2 to 3 minutes longer or until glazed. Season with salt, pepper, and paprika, and garnish with chili pepper. Serve hot as a side dish, or cold as an appetizer. Reheat, if necessary, with extra butter.

Yield: 4 servings

Mary F. Lary

ONION PATTIES

Wonderful with BBQ or fajitas. For a change, try for breakfast instead of hash browns.

¾ cup all-purpose flour
1 tablespoon sugar
2 teaspoons baking powder
1 tablespoon cornmeal (optional)

1 teaspoon salt
milk
2½ cups chopped onion
vegetable oil for frying

Combine flour and next 4 ingredients. Add enough milk to make a very thick batter. Add onion. Drop by heaping tablespoonfuls into hot oil, flattening slightly when in oil. Fry until browned.

Yield: 24 patties

Joyce Obst
Obst Family Farms
Alamo, Texas

STUFFED TEXAS ONIONS TOLUCA

Very much a South Texas taste!

4 medium Texas Spring Sweet or
  1015 onions
¼ pound Mexican chorizo,
  casings removed
¼ pound lean ground beef
½ teaspoon freshly ground black
  pepper
¼ teaspoon salt

4 thick slices Muenster, Gruyère,
  or Mexican goat cheese
½ tablespoon chopped fresh
  cilantro
4 flour tortillas, heated
picante sauce
guacamole

Slice off top of onions so they will sit flat. Starting at the root end, hollow out about half the center of each onion. Steam 20 minutes or until translucent, but not too soft. Cool. Sauté chorizo and next 3 ingredients over medium heat for about 12 minutes. Divide mixture among onion cavities. Place stuffed onions in an ovenproof dish. Top each with a slice of cheese. Bake, uncovered, at 350° for about 10 minutes. Broil until cheese melts and browns slightly. Sprinkle with cilantro. Place each in the center of a tortilla and serve immediately with picante sauce and guacamole.

Yield: 4 servings

Paula Fouchek
Texas Fresh Promotional Board

ONION CASSEROLE

Great way to use up lots of onions when a farmer friend gives you a 25 pound bag!

6-8 medium onions, sliced
1 cup chopped celery
5 tablespoons butter, divided
1 (2¼-ounce) can sliced black olives
1 (2-ounce) jar pimiento
3 tablespoons all-purpose flour

1 teaspoon salt
½ teaspoon black pepper
1 cup half-and-half
½ cup cream
1 cup chopped or whole pecans
¾ cup Parmesan cheese
paprika

Cook onion in boiling water until tender. Drain. Sauté celery in 2 tablespoons butter until tender. Arrange onion, celery, olives, and pimiento in a greased 9X13 inch dish. Melt remaining 3 tablespoons butter in a saucepan. Stir in flour, salt, and pepper. Gradually pour in half-and-half and cream. Cook and stir until sauce thickens. Pour sauce over vegetables. Top with pecans and cheese. Sprinkle with paprika. Bake at 350° for 25 to 35 minutes.
Yield: 6 to 8 servings

Bob Goodrich

ONION-GLAZED ROASTED NEW POTATOES

2 pounds small new potatoes, unpeeled
2 tablespoons olive oil
1 teaspoon dried rosemary
1 teaspoon salt

¼ teaspoon black pepper
1 large red onion, coarsely chopped
¾ cup chicken broth
2 tablespoons chopped parsley

Place potatoes in a roasting pan and drizzle with oil. Sprinkle rosemary, salt, and pepper over potatoes. Bake at 425° for 20 minutes. Sprinkle onion over top and drizzle evenly with broth. Bake 60 minutes or until onions caramelize, shaking and turning the pan every 10 to 15 minutes. Transfer to a serving bowl and sprinkle with parsley.
Yield: 6 to 8 servings

Kathryn Kaplan

GARLIC AND HERB ROASTED NEW POTATOES

Very tasty and easy - looks like it was a lot of work.

¼ cup olive oil
8 large cloves garlic, mashed
20 new potatoes, halved
1 tablespoon chopped fresh
  rosemary, or 1 teaspoon dried

1½ teaspoons chopped fresh
  thyme, or ¾ teaspoon dried
salt and pepper to taste

Combine oil and garlic. Place potatoes in a baking dish. Sprinkle with rosemary, thyme, salt, and pepper. Pour oil mixture over top and toss well. Bake, stirring occasionally, at 400° for 45 minutes or until tender and crusty. Serve hot.

Yield: 4 to 6 servings

Mary Vance Jones

BAKED POTATO CHEESE CASSEROLE

8 potatoes, baked, peeled, and
  diced
1 pound processed cheese loaf,
  diced
½ pound Teleme or sharp
  cheddar cheese, diced
½ cup chopped green onions

1 cup mayonnaise
¼ cup chopped celery
¼ cup chopped bell pepper
½ pound bacon, chopped and
  partially cooked
¼ cup sliced black olives
¼ cup sliced green olives

Combine potato and next 6 ingredients and toss. Place in a greased oblong or round baking dish. Top with bacon and olives. Bake at 325° for 60 minutes.

Yield: 10 to 12 servings

Diane McVeigh

SCALLOPED POTATO CASSEROLE

You can put this together on Saturday and heat just before dinner on Sunday.

1½ cups coarsely grated cheddar cheese, divided
1 cup sour cream
1 (10¾-ounce) can condensed cream of mushroom soup
4 tablespoons butter or margarine, melted

⅓ cup sliced green onions
3 pounds potatoes, peeled, cubed, and boiled
½ teaspoon salt
⅛ teaspoon black pepper
½ cup cracker crumbs or homemade dried breadcrumbs

Combine 1 cup cheese and next 4 ingredients in a lightly greased, deep 3-quart casserole dish. Gently stir in potato, salt, and pepper. Top with remaining ½ cup cheese and crumbs. Bake at 350° for 30 minutes, or longer if refrigerated.

Yield: 8 to 10 servings

Nancy Boultinghouse

TIA EVA'S SWEET POTATO CASSEROLE

Sure to become a favorite at holiday family dinner gatherings.

2 teaspoons vanilla, divided
6-8 sweet potatoes, cooked and mashed
1 cup packed brown sugar
1 teaspoon pumpkin pie spice

pecans to taste
large white or colored marshmallows
4 egg whites
3 tablespoons granulated sugar

Combine 1 teaspoon vanilla and next 4 ingredients in a large saucepan. Cook over low heat for about 5 minutes. Cool. Pour into a greased 9X13 inch baking dish. Decorate with marshmallows, placing them about 1 inch apart. Beat egg whites until soft peaks form. Blend in granulated sugar and remaining 1 teaspoon vanilla. Pour over marshmallows to cover. Bake at 350° for 10 minutes or until golden brown.

Yield: 8 to 10 servings

Norma L. Cardona

PEPPER-JACK SPINACH

Even "non-spinach lovers" go for this elegant dish.

4 (10-ounce) packages frozen
  chopped spinach
1 stick butter
1 small onion, finely chopped
¼ cup all-purpose flour
1 cup evaporated milk
1 teaspoon black pepper
dash of cayenne pepper
2 teaspoons celery salt

2 teaspoons garlic salt
1 teaspoon salt
¾ pound Monterey Jack Pepper
  cheese
2 teaspoons Worcestershire
  sauce
2 tablespoons lemon juice
buttered breadcrumbs

Cook spinach. Drain, reserving 1 cup cooking liquid. Melt butter in a skillet. Add onion and sauté until tender. Mix in flour until smooth. Slowly stir in reserved cooking liquid and milk until smooth. Cook until thickened. Add black pepper and next 7 ingredients. Stir until melted. Mix in spinach and place in a 9½X13 inch casserole dish. Top with breadcrumbs and refrigerate overnight or freeze. When ready to serve, bake at 350° for 20 minutes or until bubbly.

Yield: 10 to 12 servings

Variations: Use this mixture as a stuffing for large mushroom caps. Bake at 350° for 10 to 15 minutes. Recipe may be halved and a smaller dish used.

Varner Bell and Mary Vance Jones

BAKED CHAYOTE

A member of the squash family, it was called chayotli by the Aztecs, and is known as chocho in South America, and mirliton in Creole cookery. It is a chartreuse-colored, pear-shaped fruit which often becomes quite wrinkled and grows on a cucumber-like vine. The seed has a slight almond flavor and is delicious. Young, tender chayotes may be sliced and served raw in salads. You can use them in soufflés or cook them au gratin, but be sure they are tender.

chayotes, ½ each per serving
butter or vegetable oil

salt and pepper to taste

Cut chayotes in half, lengthwise. Spread with butter. Place, cut-side down, on a baking sheet. Bake at 350° until tender. Season with salt and pepper and serve hot.

Variation: To make stuffed chayotes, scoop out seed of halved chayotes. Stuff with dressing of choice, enriched with chopped, cooked pork, chicken, or sausage. Bake at 350° until tender.

YELLOW SQUASH CASSEROLE

4 tablespoons butter or
margarine
2 cups chopped yellow squash
1 (6-ounce) package cornbread
stuffing mix
1 (10¾-ounce) can condensed
cream of chicken soup

1 (8-ounce) can water chestnuts,
chopped
2 cups sour cream
1 medium onion, chopped
1 cup yellow cheese (optional)

Melt butter in a 9X13 inch casserole dish. Cook squash in boiling water in a saucepan and drain, reserving liquid. Prepare stuffing mix, using reserved cooking liquid instead of water. Combine squash, stuffing, soup, and next 3 ingredients. Place in casserole dish. Top with cheese. Bake at 350° for 30 minutes.

Yield: 8 servings

Karen Valdez

SPICY TOMATO SQUASH

Spicy side dish, good with game.

4 small calabaza or yellow
squash, cut into bite-size
pieces

1 (10-ounce) can tomatoes with
green chiles, drained
2 (8-ounce) cans tomato sauce
lemon pepper to taste

Cook squash and drain. Add tomatoes with green chiles, tomato sauce, and lemon pepper. Bring to a boil. Simmer to desired tenderness.

Yield: 4 servings

Rene De La Garza

ZUCCHINI MAISON

4 cups sliced zucchini
(6 medium)
2 ripe tomatoes, peeled and
thinly sliced
¼ cup thinly sliced onion

¼ cup olive oil
2 tablespoons chopped parsley
salt and pepper to taste
Parmesan cheese

Parboil or microwave zucchini until soft. Place in a casserole dish and top with tomato. Sauté onion in oil. Stir in parsley and spread over tomatoes. Sprinkle with salt, pepper, and Parmesan cheese. Bake at 375° for 15 minutes or until cheese melts.

Yield: 6 servings

Carla Cozad

SAUTÉED GRATED ZUCCHINI

1½ pounds zucchini, trimmed
1 teaspoon salt
1 tablespoon unsalted butter
1 tablespoon olive oil
1 tablespoon sliced green
　onions with tops

black pepper to taste
Italian seasoning to taste
　(optional)
1 clove garlic, mashed and
　minced (optional)

Grate zucchini in a food processor fitted with a grating disk, or grate by hand. Transfer to a colander and sprinkle with salt. Toss and let drain 25 minutes, or place on paper towels and press to squeeze out moisture. Heat butter and oil in a 10-inch skillet over medium heat. When foam subsides, add green onions and sauté 2 minutes or until tender. If draining in colander, press zucchini with the back of a spoon to extract excess liquid. Stir into skillet. Season with pepper, Italian seasoning, and garlic. Sauté 3 minutes or until zucchini is crisp-tender.

Yield: 4 servings

Barbara Steidinger
Texas Agri-Women, Inc.

VEGETABLE ZUCCHINI CASSEROLE

2-3 pounds zucchini, sliced
½ cup chopped onion
1 (10¾-ounce) can condensed
　cream of chicken soup
1 cup sour cream

2 cups grated carrot
1 (8-ounce) package herb-
　seasoned stuffing mix
1 stick margarine, melted

Cook zucchini and onion in boiling salted water for 15 minutes. Drain. Combine soup and sour cream. Stir in carrot. Add soup mixture to zucchini and onion. Combine stuffing mix and margarine. Spread half of stuffing mixture in a greased 9X13 inch baking dish. Spoon soup mixture over top. Sprinkle with remaining stuffing mixture. Bake at 350° for 25 to 30 minutes.

Yield: 8 to 10 servings

Nancy Boultinghouse

STUFFED ZUCCHINI WITH TOMATO SAUCE

Great with Italian food.

ZUCCHINI

4 zucchini
1 tablespoon olive oil
¼ cup chopped onion
1 large clove garlic, minced

¼ cup chopped prosciutto or
   Canadian bacon
¼ cup Parmesan cheese
3 tablespoons minced fresh basil
2 tablespoons breadcrumbs

TOMATO SAUCE

1 tablespoon olive oil
½ cup minced onion
2 pounds plum tomatoes,
   chopped

¼ cup minced fresh basil
salt and pepper to taste

Parboil zucchini for about 5 minutes and drain. Cool and cut lengthwise. Scoop out and finely dice pulp. Heat oil in a skillet. Add onion and garlic and sauté 2 minutes. Add zucchini pulp and cook until liquid evaporates. Remove from heat and stir in prosciutto and next 3 ingredients. Stuff zucchini shells with pulp mixture and place in a baking dish. Add ¼-inch water to dish. Cover with foil and bake at 350° for 15 minutes. Uncover and bake 15 minutes longer. Serve with heated tomato sauce. To make sauce, heat oil in a medium saucepan. Add onion and sauté 5 minutes. Stir in tomatoes, basil, salt, and pepper. Cook until sauce thickens.

Yield: 6 servings

Note: Use leftover sauce over pasta.

Laura Martinez Ilgun

BROILED VEGETABLES WITH HERB VINAIGRETTE DRESSING

VEGETABLES

2 leeks, quartered

2 red bell peppers, quartered

2 yellow squash, halved

2 zucchini, halved

HERB VINAIGRETTE DRESSING

2 teaspoons chopped fresh chives

1 tablespoon chopped fresh parsley

½ cup apple cider vinegar

2 teaspoons prepared mustard

1 cup extra virgin olive oil

1 tablespoon fresh lemon juice

1 teaspoon salt

½ teaspoon freshly ground black pepper

½ cup water

Broil or grill vegetables for 3 to 5 minutes, being careful not to burn. Arrange on a serving plate. Combine all dressing ingredients and pour over vegetables.

Yield: 2 servings

Note: Reserve leftover dressing for salads.

Diane Myers

WILD RICE AND MUSHROOM DRESSING

4 strips bacon
1 medium onion, chopped
2 cups cooked wild rice
2 cups cooked white rice
½ teaspoon dried thyme

1 bay leaf
1 (8-ounce) can sliced
  mushrooms, undrained
¼-½ cup chicken broth
salt and pepper to taste

Cook bacon in a skillet until crisp. Transfer bacon to paper towels and crumble. Add onion to bacon drippings in skillet. Sauté until softened. Combine bacon, onion, and rices in a greased 2-quart casserole dish. Mix in thyme, bay leaf, and mushrooms. Add enough broth to moisten dressing. Season with salt and pepper and mix thoroughly. Bake at 325° for 30 minutes.

Yield: 8 servings

Claudia Medina

TORTILLA CHIP DRESSING

My mother made this up in 1940. Her original recipe says "use a 15 cent bag of chips".

1 (10-ounce) bag tortilla chips,
  crumbled
1 (16-ounce) can cream-style
  corn
2 slices bread
1 cup milk

2 eggs, beaten
1 large onion, chopped
1 large bell pepper, chopped
leaves of 6 stalks celery
2 tablespoons vegetable oil

Place chips in a bowl. Cover with corn and next 3 ingredients. Sauté onion, pepper, and celery leaves in oil. Add to chip mixture and mash with a potato masher until just coarsely blended. Stuff into a turkey. Place remaining dressing in a casserole dish. Bake, uncovered, at 350° for 60 minutes.

Yield: 8 servings

Note: Serve with jalapeño jelly instead of traditional cranberry sauce.

Hilda Lewin

EASY CHEESY RICE

1 tablespoon vegetable oil
1 cup uncooked rice
2 tablespoons chopped onion
dash ground cumin
dash garlic powder
1½ teaspoons instant chicken
   bouillon
dash black pepper

2 cups cold water
1 (4-ounce) can chopped green
   chilies
4 ounces colby cheese, cubed
4 ounces Monterey Jack cheese,
   cubed
1 (8-ounce) container sour
   cream

Heat oil in a saucepan over medium heat. Add rice and onion. Sauté gently, stirring occasionally, until mixture just starts to brown. Blend in cumin and next 3 ingredients. Add water and chilies. Bring to a boil over high heat. Cover pan tightly with a lid and reduce heat to low. Cook 20 minutes or until all water is absorbed. Remove from heat and place lid on saucepan at an angle. Let stand about 10 minutes. Stir in cheeses and sour cream. Place in a greased casserole dish. Bake at 350° for 20 minutes or until cheese melts.

Yield: 8 servings

Monica Burdette
The Inn at El Canelo
Raymondville, Texas

HOPPIN' JOHN SQUARES

½ cup chopped bell pepper
1 tablespoon finely chopped
   onion
2 tablespoons margarine or
   butter
2 tablespoons all-purpose flour
¾ teaspoon chili powder
¼ teaspoon ground cumin

1¼ cups milk
1 cup grated cheddar cheese,
   divided
1 (15-ounce) can black-eyed
   peas, drained
1 cup cooked brown rice
¾ cup diced ham
2 eggs, beaten

Sauté pepper and onion in margarine until tender. Mix in flour, chili powder, and cumin. Stir in milk and cook and stir until bubbly. Remove from heat. Stir in ¾ cup cheese and remaining 4 ingredients. Place in a well-greased 8X8X2 inch baking dish. Bake at 350° for 30 minutes or until set. Top with remaining ¼ cup cheese. Let stand 5 minutes before cutting.

Yield: 6 servings

Nancy Boultinghouse

GREEN CHILI GRITS

1½ cups quick grits
1 (7-ounce) can chopped green
chilies
3 eggs, beaten
1 stick butter
1 pound grated cheddar cheese

1 tablespoon seasoned salt
1 tablespoon Worcestershire
sauce
Tabasco sauce to taste
paprika

Prepare grits according to package directions. Stir in chilies and next 6 ingredients. Place in a 9X13 inch pan. Sprinkle with paprika. Bake at 325° for 60 minutes. Cut into squares.

Yield: 12 servings

Note: This recipe can be prepared ahead. Serve with BBQ or as a change from rice or potatoes.

Hilda Lewin

MEXICAN STUFFING

"This recipe of my grandmother's is better than good - MUY BUENO!"

3 pounds lean ground beef
1 pound mild pork sausage
1 cup chopped sweet pickles
1 cup chopped olives
1 cup chopped onion
1 cup chopped bell pepper
1 cup chopped celery

3 (7-ounce) packages herbed
croutons
chicken broth
1 large Delicious apple, peeled
and chopped
½ cup raisins

Combine beef and sausage in a large pan or deep skillet. Brown over low heat. Mix in pickles and next 4 ingredients and sauté briefly. Add croutons and enough chicken broth to make a juicy stuffing. Mix in apple and raisins. Stuff into a bird or divide mixture among large baking pans. Bake at 350° for 45 minutes.

Yield: 20 servings

Armando Ramirez

TURKISH RICE PILAF

This is a rich and flavorful rice dish.

3 tablespoons butter, divided
¼ cup pine nuts
salt and pepper to taste
¼ cup black currants
2½ cups chicken broth

1½ uncooked cups long-grain rice
1 bunch green onions, white only, finely chopped
¼ cup fresh dill, finely chopped

Melt 2 tablespoons butter in a saucepan. Add nuts and sauté until golden brown. Add remaining 1 tablespoon butter, salt, pepper, currants, and broth. Bring to a boil. Add rice and stir once. Cover and cook on high heat for 5 minutes. Reduce heat and cook 15 minutes or until all liquid is absorbed. Fold in green onions and dill. Remove from heat. Take off cover, place a napkin over the saucepan, and replace the cover. Let stand up to 30 minutes. Gently transfer to a serving dish.

Yield: 8 servings

Note: Goes great with grilled or roasted beef or lamb.

Laura Martinez Ilgun

Traditional regional cooking

¡Viva La
Tradición!

Above: Elephants and camels marching down Main Street Mission in this 1909 circus parade must have been a strange and thrilling sight.

Cover page: Regardless of family economic conditions, special occasions like first communions and weddings are often spared no expense, and are revered as extremely important dates in the lives of many Hispanic families.

Below: A Sunday picnic or pachanga (here with members of the Baker family and friends at Sal del Rey, c.1910) has long been a favorite weekend family pastime.

¡Viva La Tradición!

Life in the Rio Grande Valley is a delicious blend of customs and traditions. Indeed, to live in the Valley is to live in a cultural every man's land, where boundaries are, at best, fuzzy, and it is difficult to tell where one influence begins and another ends. Even the predominant Mexican culture is rooted in a blend of many other cultures. There is no mistaking the influences of the ancient Indian way of life and the strong religious and cultural influences of the Spanish colonization. But not so obvious are the influences of the Moors and Jews who came to the New World after their expulsion from Spain in the late 15th century, and the European culinary and social influences of Imperial France as it tried, in vain, to make Mexico its own province in the mid-1800s. It is this surprising cultural chemistry that gives the Valley its unique flavor.

And nowhere is that blend of cultures more evident than on holiday tables and in family kitchens. At Christmastime, Valley dinner tables commonly boast platters of steaming *tamales*, along with other dishes like turkey and dressing or glazed ham, that are indicative of the English, German, Polish, Swedish and other cultural influences introduced to this area by settlers from the north. New Year's Day is always made sweeter by delicate *buñuelos*, a deep-fried sugary treat that is a Mexican tradition this time of year. Another delicious New Year's Day tradition is *menudo*, a salty tripe soup that is said to be the best remedy for an overly joyous New Year's Eve!

Family celebrations in the Valley are a feast for the senses. Weddings are the most elaborate, often lasting until dawn.

Above & Left: The faces change, but the ritual stays the same. Young Valley lovers have tied the knot many different ways—rather formally in the style of the 1920s, and surrounded by friends in the 1960s.

The celebration of marriage is, quite literally, a community affair, as it is customary for family members and friends to provide everything from invitations to food

and, in return, be named as *padrinos*, or godparents, to the bride and groom. One beautiful wedding custom involves encircling the bride and groom with a ceremo-

nial *lazo*, or rope, to symbolize the sacred bond of marriage. And no wedding reception would be complete without the delicate sugar-coated wedding cookies called *pan de polvo*, or literally translated, powder bread.

The *quinceañera*, the Spanish term for a girl's 15th birthday, is another important family milestone.

This is a young woman's introduction to the adult world, both spiritually and socially. It is a coming out party of sorts, and is often as elaborate as a wedding celebration, with girls donning beautiful white gowns of silk, satin, or lace.

First Communion is also a beautiful spectacle, as little girls in tiny veils and white dresses, and restless boys in their Sunday best experience this holy rite of passage.

Above: Little boys and girls in their Sunday best prepare for a First Communion.
Below: Cities have their own festivals and traditions like Charro Days in Brownsville, the Candlelight Posada at Christmastime in McAllen, and the Texas Citrus Fiesta in Mission. John Shary, known as the father of Texas grapefruit, and Mrs. A. Y. Baker were crowned the Fiesta's first King and Queen in 1935.

Even casual family gatherings smack of regional flavor. Virtually every birthday party in the Rio Grande Valley features a brightly colored *piñata*, a tradition brought to the region by Spanish settlers. Barbecues, often called *pachangas*, are settings for everything from family reunions to political fundraisers. These feature aromatic and savory meats like *barbacoa*, made from the tender meat of the cow's head, *cabrito*, or goat, which is believed to have been brought to the region by Spanish Jews, and *fajitas*, the savory beef skirt favorite that originated in South Texas. Music has a long tradition in the

Valley, and family celebrations are often accompanied by the festive brass sounds of *mariachi*, the more romantic string sounds of a strolling trio, or the popular accordion-based, polka-style music known as *Tejano*.

Community events and festivals sparkle with color, local customs, and music. One of the oldest—Mission's

Texas Citrus Fiesta—pays tribute to the important role agriculture has played in the success of the Valley.

Perhaps the largest and best known of the regional festivals is Charro Days in Brownsville. Each February, Brownsville celebrates a valuable friendship with its sister city of Matamoros with several days of community events and activities. The centerpiece of the celebration is a grand parade in which school children, dressed in splendid Mexican costumes, do traditional dances in the street. The three-hour spectacle is the Rio Grande Valley's very own version of the Macy's parade!

These beautiful customs, unique celebrations, and exotic flavors are the products of a diverse blend of cultures, and they are what makes living in the Rio Grande Valley so special. Visitors are charmed and surprised by the many poignant moments they experience here. And once they get a taste of the intoxicating potion that is the culture of Mesquite Country, many find it hard to leave.

¡HEY, COMPADRE!

A FUN CUSTOM

IN THE LATE 19TH CENTURY, ONE OF THE NEW YEAR'S OBSERVANCES ON SOUTH TEXAS RANCHES WAS THE *rifa*, OR DRAWING. THE NAME OF EVERY MAN AND WOMAN—OLD, YOUNG, SINGLE, OR MARRIED—WAS WRITTEN ON A STRIP OF PAPER. MEN'S NAMES WERE PUT INTO ONE GLASS, WOMEN'S NAMES INTO ANOTHER. THEN, ONE BY ONE, NAMES WERE DRAWN FROM THE MEN'S GLASS AND PAIRED WITH NAMES FROM THE WOMEN'S GLASS. THE RESULTING PAIRS BECAME *compadres* AND *comadres*, OR PALS. THESE FRIENDSHIPS HAD NO ROMANTIC SIGNIFICANCE, BUT AT PARTIES, THE PAIRS WOULD DANCE TOGETHER AND BRING EACH OTHER SPECIAL GIFTS.

¡HEY, COMADRE!

Above left: From weddings, to parties, to an evening out for dinner, no Valley function is quite complete without the requisite sounds of a mariachi band or strolling trio.

PURE AND SIMPLE AUTHENTIC GUACAMOLE

3 ripe avocados
juice of ½ lime

salt and pepper to taste

Cut avocados in half and scoop pulp into a large bowl. Mash with a fork, leaving it a little chunky for an appealing look. Add lime juice, salt, and pepper. Serve with tortilla chips, or as a garnish on tacos.

Yield: 6 servings

Note: Never buy very dark, mushy avocados that easily "cave in" when gently pressed. A fool-proof way to ripen them is to buy firm avocados, 3 to 4 days before ready to use. Place in a brown paper bag, close top, and leave on the counter. Check daily for ripeness. When ripe, remove from bag and refrigerate until ready to use.

Monica Burdette
The Inn at El Canelo
Raymondville, Texas

CHILE CON QUESO

1 (2-pound) loaf processed
cheese, cut into chunks
1½ (4-ounce) cans chopped
green chiles
1 (14½-ounce) can tomatoes,
chopped

½ small onion, finely chopped
1 clove garlic, finely chopped
2 tablespoons whipping cream
salt to taste

Combine all ingredients in a double boiler. Cook until melted. Serve hot with tortilla chips or a vegetable platter.

Yield: 10 to 15 servings

Note: If desired, substitute two (10-ounce) cans tomatoes and green chiles for the chopped green chiles and the chopped tomatoes.

Hilda Lewin

NACHOS

This is a very easy appetizer to fix, with countless variations. Start with tortilla chips from a package, or make your own. Lay them in a single layer on a baking sheet. Sprinkle grated cheese over them and add whatever toppings you choose.

NACHOS
tortilla chips   grated cheddar cheese

OPTIONAL INGREDIENTS
sliced canned jalapeño peppers   refried beans
taco meat   guacamole, added after baking
chopped onion   cilantro, added after baking
chopped tomato

Spread chips on a baking sheet. Sprinkle with cheese. Top with optional ingredients. Bake at 425° on the highest oven rack until cheese melts.

Note: A lot of people are microwaving their nachos these days, but I prefer the taste and texture when they are baked.

Monica Burdette
The Inn at El Canelo
Raymondville, Texas

QUESO FLAMEADO
"FLAMED" CHEESE

1 pound *Queso Asadero* (stringy   1 pound Mexican *chorizo*
Mexican cheese) or mozzarella
cheese

Cut cheese into chunks and place in a broiler-proof serving pan. Fry chorizo in a skillet, crumbling into chunks, until well cooked. Drain fat and transfer to paper towels to further absorb excess fat. Spread chorizo over cheese. Broil until cheese is bubbly. Serve immediately with tortilla chips or hot, soft corn tortillas.

Monica Burdette
The Inn at El Canelo
Raymondville, Texas

AGUAS FRESCAS
FRESH WATER

Similar to making lemonade - keep tasting 'til you get it right! Very popular soda alternative in Mexico.

1-2 pounds fresh fruit of choice   **sugar to taste**
1-2 cups water

Peel and seed fruit. Puree in blender. Pour fruit into a pitcher. Add water until mixture reaches a liquid consistency. Stir in sugar.
Yield: About 10 to 12 servings

Note: Use fruit such as cantaloupe, honeydew melon, watermelon, pineapple, or peaches.

Melissa McAllen Guerra
Santillana Ranch
Linn, Texas

AGUA DE TAMARINDO
TAMARIND WATER

1 pound tamarind   **sugar to taste**
1½ quarts or more water

Crack peels off tamarind pods. Peel as thoroughly as possible and remove veins. Cook tamarind in boiling water until softened. Drain, reserving liquid. Press tamarind through a strainer, removing seeds and remaining veins. Add fruit to a 2-quart pitcher. Stir in reserved liquid. Fill pitcher with water. Mix in sugar. Stir before serving.
Yield: 2 quarts

Melissa McAllen Guerra
Santillana Ranch
Linn, Texas

TÉ DE NARANJA
ORANGE LEAF TEA

6 leaves from an orange tree, washed   **sugar, honey, or sugar substitute to taste**
2 cups water

Boil leaves in water. Strain liquid and sweeten with sugar.
Yield: 2 servings

Teresa Alamia

AGUA DE JAMAICA
HIBISCUS FLOWER TEA

This makes a very pretty, bright red drink. But don't use the hibiscus out of your yard! Buy it in the vegetable section of South Texas supermarkets. The dried flowers are expensive, but you only use a small amount at a time.

1-1½ cups dried Flor de Jamaica	**1½ quarts water**
(Hibiscus blossoms)	**sugar to taste**

Combine *Flor de Jamaica* and water in a saucepan and bring to a boil. Cook until water is bright red and flowers are wilted and faded. Strain liquid, discarding flowers. Strain liquid through a coffee filter to remove any sediment. Place in a 2-quart pitcher. Fill pitcher with water and add sugar.

Yield: 2 quarts

Note: This is just like making regular iced tea - strengthen or weaken the flavor as desired.

> Melissa McAllen Guerra
> Santillana Ranch
> Linn, Texas

OLD MEXICO HOT CHOCOLATE

Different brands of the special chocolate used in this recipe are found everywhere in Mexico and in the Mexican food section of South Texas supermarkets. It is delicious - already sweet and cinnamony. Use either "Oso" brand from Saltillo, or "Polar" from Monterrey.

2 squares Mexican chocolate	**pinch of salt**
½ cup boiling water	**pinch of nutmeg**
1½ cups milk	**pinch of cinnamon**
½ cup sugar	**1 egg white**

Melt chocolate in boiling water in a saucepan. Add milk and next 4 ingredients. Heat to just below boiling, constantly beating with an egg beater or *molinillo*. When ready to serve, beat egg white until very stiff. Fold into hot mixture and serve. Drink should be very thick and sweet.

Yield: 2 servings

> Margaret Looney McAllen

CORN TORTILLAS

Masa harina is available in most grocery stores in the U.S. - I even got some in Frederick, Maryland!

2 cups masa harina, loosely packed   **1 cup warm water**

Follow package directions to mix masa (dough), using a little more water than called for on the package. Slit the sides of a plain plastic food storage bag to make a long rectangle. Do not use plastic wrap as this will cling to dough too much. Divide dough into 14 to 16 pieces and roll into balls. One at a time, place a ball in the center of half of the plastic. Fold other half of plastic over to cover. Using a tortilla press or a flat-bottom glass pie pan, press until ball is flattened to about ⅛-inch thick. Carefully peel top layer of plastic off. Turn tortilla onto palm of hand, and carefully peel off remaining plastic. Proceed as follows:

FOR PLAIN 'OLE FLAT TORTILLAS: Cook on a lightly greased hot griddle for 1 minute on each side or until brown spots appear and tortilla is still soft.

FOR CRISPY TORTILLAS: Fry in about 1 inch of very hot oil for about 30 seconds. Turn with tongs and fry 30 to 60 seconds or until well browned. Turn over again, if needed.

FOR CRISPY TACO SHELLS: Fry in about 1 inch of very hot oil for about 10 seconds. Place the edge of a pancake turner in the center of the tortilla. Using tongs or a long, 2-pronged fork, fold tortilla in half. Fry about 30 seconds. Turn over and fry 30 to 60 seconds or until well browned.

FOR PUFFY TORTILLAS: Fry in 2 to 3 inches of very hot oil in a Dutch oven. Immediately begin to scoop hot oil over tortilla with a long spoon or pancake turner. It should puff in a few seconds. Cook 30 seconds and turn. Continue to scoop with oil until well browned.

FOR PUFFY TACO SHELLS: Fry in 2 to 3 inches of very hot oil in a Dutch oven. Immediately begin to scoop hot oil over tortilla with a long spoon or pancake turner. When tortilla puffs up, place the edge of a pancake turner in the center of the tortilla. Using tongs or a long, 2-pronged fork, fold tortilla in half. Continue to scoop oil over tortilla for 30 seconds. Turn and fry until browned.

FOR TOSTADAS (tortilla chips): After pressing masa flat, peel off one side of plastic. Using the blunt edge of a table knife, gently cut into quarters. Holding tortilla flat in palm, carefully peel off other layer of plastic. Proceed as

above for crispy or puffy tortillas.
Yield: 14 to 16 tortillas

Variation: For variety, try adding spices, such as chili powder, cayenne pepper, or cumin, with masa harina and water when mixing.

**Monica Burdette
The Inn at El Canelo
Raymondville, Texas**

FLOUR TORTILLAS

Flour tortillas are the Tex-Mex equivalent of plain white bread. Use as an accompaniment to Mexican food or fold and fill for tacos (Tex-Mex sandwich!).

5 cups all-purpose flour	**¾ - 1 cup vegetable shortening**
2 teaspoons salt	**1¾ cups hot water**

Combine flour and salt in a bowl. Cut in shortening with a pastry blender until well blended. Add water and mix well until a dough forms. Knead by hand and form into little balls (*testales*). Roll out with a rolling pin into 5- to 6-inch circles. Cook tortillas on one side on a medium to medium-high griddle for 1 minute. Turn and cook. Flip back to first side to finish cooking.
Yield: 25 to 30 tortillas

Note: If desired, roll out and stack tortillas in a tightly sealed container, placing wax paper between tortillas. Refrigerate up to 1 week and cook as needed.

Yolanda Ramirez

 TORTILLAS DE MANTECA

masa for 2 dozen corn tortillas	**salt to taste**
¾ cup vegetable shortening	

Combine all ingredients. Divide into 12 pieces and form into shapes like big biscuits, about ½-inch thick. Cook over very low heat on a griddle. Turn about 4 times, taking enough time between turns to get middle done. Serve with butter and choice of sweet or savory filling.
Yield: 12 servings

Teresa Alamia

PAN DE CAMPO
CAMP BREAD

This traditional "cowboy bread" was created out on the range. Looks like a cross between a flour tortilla and a biscuit. Can be used as bread with any meal - especially good for sopping up soups, stews, or chili.

10 cups all-purpose flour   **1½ tablespoons salt**
3½ tablespoons baking powder   **1 cup vegetable shortening**

Sift together flour, baking powder, and salt in a large bowl. Make a well in the center. Cut shortening into dry ingredients until mealy. Add warm water, a little at a time, until dough sticks together. Knead and let rest 10 minutes. Form into balls about 4 to 5 inches in diameter. Let rest 10 minutes. Roll out dough into circles about ¼-inch thick. Prick with a fork and place on a baking sheet. Bake at 400° for about 25 minutes.

Yield: 8 "loaves"

Note: For crustier bread, use warm milk instead of warm water.

Variation: Campfire Method: Make dough as instructed above. Do not place on baking sheet. Build a fire using mesquite deadfall. When fire has cooked down to bright red coals, place lid of a cast iron Dutch oven (the kind with a 1-inch rim sticking up around the perimeter) on the coals to heat. On a sheet of thick aluminum foil, put about 2 shovelfuls of coals. Place bottom of Dutch oven on these coals to heat. Dutch oven is ready when a small piece of dough in bottom of Dutch oven turns brown. Discard the small piece of dough. Put first rolled out "loaf" of camp bread in bottom of Dutch oven. Put hot lid on top. Place about 2 shovelfuls of coals on lid. Check bread for doneness in about 15 minutes. When done, remove lid and place on hot coals to keep hot for next "loaf". Remove bread from Dutch oven and serve immediately, or place in a box lined with clean kitchen towels until ready to serve. Repeat process until all "loaves" are cooked. This is usually a good campfire assignment for one person while the rest of the group is out working cattle or hunting.

Evelyn East
Santa Fe Ranch

🏛 SEMITA
MEXICAN YEAST BREAD

CINNAMON TEA

peelings of 3 potatoes
3 quarts water

1 (1-ounce) package whole
  cinnamon

SEMITA

½ package dry yeast
5 cups sugar, divided
cinnamon tea, divided

11½ cups all-purpose flour,
  divided
3 eggs
1 cup vegetable shortening

Combine all tea ingredients in a saucepan. Simmer 10 to 15 minutes. Strain tea and keep warm. To prepare *semita*, dissolve yeast in 1 cup sugar and 1 cup warm tea. Stir in 2¼ cups flour. Knead about 20 minutes. Let rise 2 hours, 30 minutes to 3 hours. Add 2 ¼ cups flour and eggs to dough. Knead about 20 minutes, mixing in 1 cup tea while kneading. Let rise 2 hours, 30 minutes to 3 hours. Mix in remaining 4 cups sugar, remaining 7 cups flour, and shortening. Knead with greased hands, adding tea when necessary, until all flour is incorporated and dough is soft and smooth. Let rise again. Knead dough and form into round balls. Let stand on counter to dry for a short time. Roll out with a rolling pin. Spread by hand into greased, round baking dishes or pie pans. Cut 4 or 5 slits around the edge of the dough. Allow to rise 2 hours, 30 minutes to 3 hours. Bake at 325° to 350° for 35 to 45 minutes.

Yield: 6 to 8 (nine-inch) loaves

Carmen Guerra

 CHAMPURRADO
BREAKFAST PORRIDGE

3 cups water, divided
1 stick cinnamon
1 (12-ounce) can evaporated
  milk

1 cup sugar
⅔ cup masa harina
1 tablespoon cocoa powder

Boil 2½ cups water and cinnamon stick until water turns caramel colored. Remove cinnamon stick and add milk and sugar. Use remaining ½ cup water to rinse out milk can and pour into a bowl. Add masa harina and cocoa. Mix well and slowly stir into milk mixture. Cook, stirring constantly, until mixture thickens and comes to a soft boil.

Variation: This atole, also called Atole de Masa, can be made without the cocoa.

Jovita Villarreal

BREAKFAST TACOS

6 flour tortillas (use recipe on
  page 233, or purchase ready-
  made)
pan or link sausage (optional)
diced potato (optional)
bacon (optional)

chorizo (optional)
3 eggs, lightly beaten
salt and pepper to taste
grated cheese
picante sauce

Cook or heat tortillas on a hot griddle. In a medium skillet, cook sausage, potato, bacon, or chorizo. Drain fat. Add egg and cook until set. Season with salt and pepper. Fold hot tortilla in half and fill with egg mixture. Top with cheese and picante sauce.

Yield: 6 servings

MIGAS CON HUEVO
FRIED TORTILLAS WITH EGG

2 eggs
1 tablespoon milk
1 corn tortilla, cut into bite-size
  squares

1-2 tablespoons vegetable oil
salt and pepper to taste

Beat eggs and milk in a bowl. Fry tortilla in oil in a skillet until crunchy and golden brown. Reduce heat and add egg mixture. Cook until egg sets. Season with salt and pepper.

Yield: 1 serving

Josefina Guerra

MACHACADO CON HUEVO
DRIED MEAT WITH EGG

½ cup lightly packed shredded
  carne seca
oil or lard for frying
2 tablespoons chopped onion
2-3 peppercorns

1 clove garlic
2 tablespoons chopped canned
  or fresh tomato
3 eggs, lightly beaten
salt (optional)

Fry shredded *carne seca* in a small amount of oil. Add onion and cook slightly. Grind peppercorns and garlic in a *molcajete*. Stir tomato into meat mixture and cook briefly. Add egg and peppercorn mixture. Cook until egg sets. Season with salt if necessary, but with care, as the meat is usually rather salty.

Yield: 2 servings

BUÑUELOS
FRIED DOUGH FRITTER

My mother always put a silver quarter in the skillet to keep the oil from burning. She says she would leave the quarter in the skillet every New Year's Eve to cool off and take out the next morning, but to this day, she never found out how it disappeared, for she never found the quarter the next morning! I wonder which of her 13 children was the culprit!

15 green leaves from a Mexican green tomato plant (optional)
3 cups water, divided
1 teaspoon anise seed
4 cups all-purpose flour
4 egg yolks
pinch of sugar
pinch of salt
1½ tablespoons baking powder
2 tablespoons vegetable shortening
1 cup sherry
1 cup sugar
2 teaspoons cinnamon
vegetable oil for frying

Boil leaves in 2 cups water and cool. Boil anise in remaining 1 cup water and cool. Strain liquids and combine. In a bowl, combine flour and next 5 ingredients. Add sherry and just enough of strained liquid to form the dough into a ball. Knead dough until smooth and elastic. Let rest 2 hours. Combine sugar and cinnamon and set aside. Form dough into small balls. Roll out balls as thin as possible. Beginning with the *buñuelos* rolled out first, gently pull each one to thin the dough. Fry in oil in a deep skillet, pricking quickly with a fork. When golden, turn and fry briefly on other side. Transfer to paper towels to drain. Sprinkle with sugar mixture.

Note: Roll out all buñuelos before beginning to fry. Start frying with the buñuelos rolled out first, as they are drier and will not absorb as much oil.

Celia Arredondo

CAJETA
MEXICAN CARAMEL

1 quart milk	1 teaspoon baking soda
1¼ cups sugar	¼ cup water

Combine milk and sugar in a large, deep saucepan. Bring to a boil over low heat, stirring constantly. Dissolve baking soda in water. Slowly add only the liquid from the baking soda mixture, discarding any solids. Be prepared to lift pan off the stove; the mixture will rise considerably and quickly. After it subsides, return pan to low heat. Continue to simmer, stirring constantly, for 1 hour, 30 minutes or until mixture turns thick and brown and the bottom of the pan can be seen in the wake of the spoon.

Note: Great on ice cream or fresh bananas. Store in the refrigerator for up to 2 weeks.

Victoria Shawn Stephen

CAPIROTADA
MEXICAN BREAD PUDDING

This is a traditional Easter dish, but is delicious year round!

2 cups water	1 cup raisins
6 ounces *piloncillo* (Mexican brown sugar)	1 loaf French bread, sliced ½-inch thick
2 (2-inch) sticks cinnamon	1½ cups cheddar cheese
1 teaspoon anise seed	1 cup pecans

Combine water and next 3 ingredients in a saucepan. Bring to a boil, stirring until *piloncillo* dissolves. Strain liquid and return to pan. Add raisins and bring to a boil until raisins plump. Do not boil too long or too much liquid will evaporate. Remove raisins from liquid. To assemble, place a single, tightly packed layer of bread slices in an 8X8 inch glass or metal pan. Sprinkle with cheese, pecans, and raisins. Pour a third of cooking liquid over top. Repeat process twice, ending with a topping of cheese, pecans, and raisins. Cover with foil and bake at 350° for 20 minutes.

Yield: 9 servings

Blanca Shawn

EMPANADAS DULCE DE CALABAZA
PUMPKIN MINI-PIES

FILLING

1 medium-size ripe, yellow
 pumpkin, halved
sugar to taste

cinnamon to taste
ground cloves to taste

CRUST

5 cups all-purpose flour
1 teaspoon salt
6 tablespoons sugar, plus extra
 for topping

2 teaspoons baking powder
1½ cups vegetable shortening
8-10 tablespoons cold water

Place pumpkin halves, cut-side down, on a baking sheet. Bake at 350° until softened. Separate peel and pulp, placing pulp in a large saucepan. Mash well with a potato masher. Add sugar, cinnamon, and cloves. Heat until flavors blend. To prepare crust, combine flour and next 3 ingredients in a bowl. Cut in shortening until particles are the size of small peas. Add enough water for mixture to leave sides of bowl and form a ball. Roll out dough and cut into (3- to 4-inch) circles. Prick with a fork. Place a spoonful of pumpkin mixture on each circle and fold over, crimping edges with a fork. Sprinkle with sugar. Bake at 350° for 20 to 25 minutes or until nicely browned.

Luz Jimenez and Margaret H. McAllen
McAllen Ranch

FLAN
MEXICAN CARAMEL CUSTARD

½ cup plus 2 tablespoons sugar	1 (12-ounce) can evaporated
4 eggs	milk
1 (14-ounce) can sweetened	1 tablespoon vanilla
condensed milk	

Place sugar in a 9X13 inch glass pan. Bake at 350° until sugar melts and turns a tawny color. Tilt pan to coat sides of dish with caramelized sugar. Cool. Place eggs in a bowl. Beat lightly with an electric mixer. Mix in milks and vanilla. Pour mixture into pan. Set in a hot-water bath with water halfway up the sides of pan. Bake, on the lowest rack in the oven, at 350° for 60 minutes or until a knife inserted in the center comes out clean. Cool 30 minutes. Invert dish onto a serving plate with a small ridge so that caramel will not spill.

Yield: 8 servings

Amelia Murray

DULCE DE FRIJOL
PINTO BEAN CANDY

This recipe came from a dear aunt, Teodorita Vela Cardenas. She used to cook this candy at Christmas-time and give it to friends and family. I wanted to learn how to make this delicious candy, so I took time with her on one occasion and measured the ingredients that it contained.

4-5 cups dried pinto beans	2 sticks cinnamon
3 quarts milk	3½ cups sugar

Soak beans overnight and cook in water. Rinse and drain well. Measure to equal 12 cups of beans. Combine beans and milk in a blender in batches. Pass blended mixture through a strainer and pour into a large pot. Add cinnamon and sugar. Stir until sugar dissolves. Bring to a boil, stirring constantly. Reduce heat and simmer 2 hours, 30 minutes to 3 hours or until candy thickens. Pour into jars and refrigerate. Eat by itself or with saltine crackers.

Carmen A. Guerra

🏠 GASNATES

About once a week, China Treviño and I would drive to Linn, about 13 miles away, to pick up the mail, visit the Guerra General Store, perhaps make a purchase or two, then visit with Doña Leonor Guerra. Often, she would offer us a plate of her delicious gasnates with coffee or a refreshing drink. These were so good and so unusual that I begged her for the recipe.

½ teaspoon salt
1 tablespoon water
8 egg yolks
2-3 tablespoons whiskey
all-purpose flour

1 tablespoon vegetable
  shortening
powdered sugar
cinnamon
oil for frying

Combine salt and water. Mix in egg yolks and whiskey. Work in as much flour as possible with hands. Add shortening and work in well. Roll out paper thin. Cut into strips and form into rings. Combine sugar and cinnamon in a shallow bowl. Fry dough rings in very hot oil until lightly browned. Dip in sugar mixture.

Carmen Guerra

🏛 GORDITAS DE QUESO

When I was a little girl, I recall my mother making these delicious, round, fat cookies made with Mexican cheese. We would all help grind the corn so she could make them. But before we had any gorditas, she first had to make the delicious Mexican cheese. Of course, in order to really be good, we used our cows' fresh milk with all the cream. In my mind, I can still see her on the floor, grinding the "cuajada" or curdled milk and the piloncillo on the metate. Since I can't do all these things like mother used to do, I finally worked out my own recipe. My family likes these so much that I make a big batch and freeze the gorditas, or the recipe can be halved.

1 (24-ounce) carton small curd cottage cheese
1 cup corn oil
2 sticks corn oil margarine
4 eggs
1 cup packed brown sugar
2 teaspoons cinnamon
1 cup dark corn syrup

1 cup chopped nuts (optional)
4 cups masa harina
2½ cups all-purpose flour
2 tablespoons baking powder
1 cup sugar
1¾ cup milk
½ cup honey
1 cup grated white cheese

Cream cottage cheese and next 4 ingredients. Add cinnamon and next 8 ingredients. Mix well. Stir in cheese until well mixed. Using a soup spoon, drop mounds of dough onto a greased baking sheet. Bake at 350° for about 30 minutes.

Yield: about 10 dozen cookies

Celia Arredondo

PAN DE POLVO
MEXICAN WEDDING COOKIES

COOKIES

1 stick cinnamon	5 cups all-purpose flour
1 cup water	3 teaspoons cinnamon
2¾ cups vegetable shortening	1½ teaspoons baking powder
1¼ cups sugar	

TOPPING

4 (1-ounce) packages whole cinnamon	1 cup sugar, or to taste

Prepare a cinnamon tea by simmering cinnamon stick in water. Measure tea to equal ¾ cup. Cream shortening and sugar in a bowl. In a separate bowl, combine flour, cinnamon, and baking powder. Mix measured tea and dry ingredients, alternately, into shortening mixture. Roll out to about ½-inch thick or less. Cut into shapes with cookie cutters. Bake at 350° for 15 minutes or until lightly browned. Meanwhile, prepare topping by grinding whole cinnamon. Mix with sugar. Dust baked cookies with topping while still warm. Cool and cover tightly. Will keep several days in a tightly covered container, several months frozen.

Yield: 9 dozen cookies

Estella Lane

ALBÓNDIGAS OAXAQUEÑAS
MEATBALLS FROM OAXACA

2 pounds ground beef
1 teaspoon dry chicken bouillon
½ cup dry rice
2 eggs
½ cup breadcrumbs
3 hard-cooked eggs, quartered
3 tablespoons vegetable oil

1 onion, sliced
2 tomatoes
2 canned chipotle chili peppers,
  or to taste
2 teaspoons or 2 cubes tomato
  concentrate
2 cups water

Combine beef and next 4 ingredients in a bowl. Divide mixture into 12 equal portions. Roll into balls, placing a piece of egg in the center of each. In a medium saucepan, heat oil. Add onion and sauté until golden. Puree tomatoes in a blender. Add tomato and chili peppers to saucepan. Cook over medium heat for a few minutes. Add tomato concentrate and water. Bring to a boil. Add meatballs and cook over medium heat until meat is done. Serve hot.

Yield: 6 to 8 servings

Note: Serve over steamed white rice; accompany with refried black beans.

Tracey L. Garrido

CHALUPAS SUPREMISIMOS

This low fat chalupa recipe makes a fun night at our house — everyone builds their own — the combinations are endless!!

CHICKEN IN SALSA

3 chicken breasts
1 (14½-ounce) can chicken broth
2 cups water
1 medium onion, diced
2 cloves garlic, minced

1 teaspoon vegetable oil
1 (10-ounce) can tomatoes and green chiles
1 (14½-ounce) can whole tomatoes

TORTILLAS AND TOPPINGS

2 (15-ounce) cans black beans
12 corn tortillas

1 head red leaf lettuce, grated

OPTIONAL INGREDIENTS

½ pound cheddar cheese, grated
8 Roma tomatoes, chopped
¼ head red cabbage, grated

1 (6-ounce) can black olives, sliced
½ cup sliced green olives
2 avocados, sliced or diced

Combine chicken, broth, and water in a saucepan. Cook until chicken is tender. Meanwhile, sauté onion and garlic in oil until softened. Add tomatoes and chiles and whole tomatoes. Crush tomatoes and simmer 15 to 20 minutes or until liquid reduces. Shred cooked chicken and add to tomato mixture. Cover and keep warm. To prepare beans, warm in a medium skillet and mash with a potato masher. Cook, stirring often, 10 to 15 minutes or until beans are of a spreading consistency. While beans cook, toast tortillas by placing them directly on a rack in a 400° oven. Cook 4 to 5 minutes, flip and cook a few minutes longer. To assemble, spread beans or chicken or both over tortillas. Top with lettuce and optional ingredients.

Yield: 4 to 6 servings

Note: Serve with sweet iced tea or Tamarind Water (page 230), plenty of hot sauce, and Capirotada (page 239) for dessert.

Victoria Shawn Stephen

GREEN ENCHILADAS

GREEN ENCHILADA SAUCE

½ (10-ounce) package frozen chopped spinach
2 (10¾-ounce) cans condensed cream of mushroom soup
1 (4-ounce) can green chilies, drained, washed, and seeded

1 large onion, chopped
⅛ teaspoon garlic powder
½ teaspoon salt
1 (14½-ounce) can chicken broth

ENCHILADAS

1 (3-pound) chicken
½ pound Monterey Jack cheese, grated
½ pound cheddar cheese, grated
¼ cup minced onion
2 tablespoons chopped jalapeño peppers, or to taste

¼ cup crushed corn chips
1 teaspoon salt
25 corn tortillas
vegetable oil
Green Enchilada Sauce
⅔ cup sour cream
paprika

Puree spinach and next 3 ingredients in a blender. Add garlic powder and salt and blend. Bring broth to a boil in a large saucepan. Reduce heat and add spinach mixture. Simmer 15 to 20 minutes. To make enchiladas, boil chicken until tender. Skin and debone, and dice meat. Combine chicken meat, Monterey Jack cheese, and next 5 ingredients. Soften tortillas in hot oil, 5 seconds per side. Drain tortillas on paper towels. Divide chicken mixture among tortillas. Roll and place, seam-side down, in a 9X13 inch ovenproof dish. Pour sauce over top and cover with foil. Bake at 350° for 30 minutes or until bubbly. Top with sour cream and sprinkle with paprika.

Yield: 8 to 10 servings

Note: Be careful not to heat tortillas in oil too long when softening, as they will get too crispy to roll up.

Lica Pinkston
Santa Fe Ranch

PUFFY BEEF TACOS

This recipe is a little time-consuming, but very well worth the effort. The picadillo can be used in a variety of ways, including as a main dish, accompanied by rice and beans as side dishes.

PICADILLO
1 pound lean ground beef	⅓ cup tomato sauce
1 tablespoon vegetable oil	¼ cup water
⅓ cup chopped onion	1 teaspoon dry beef bouillon
⅓ cup chopped bell pepper	¼ teaspoon salt
2 cloves garlic, minced	¼ teaspoon black pepper

TACO SHELLS
2 cups masa harina	vegetable oil
1 cup warm water	

TOPPINGS
shredded lettuce	grated colby cheese
chopped tomato	picante sauce
finely chopped onion	

Brown beef in oil in a skillet over medium-high heat. Drain. Add onion, bell pepper, and garlic. Sauté 5 minutes or until vegetables are tender. Add tomato sauce and next 4 ingredients. Bring to a boil. Reduce heat and simmer about 20 minutes. To prepare taco shells, follow directions for Corn Tortillas for Puffy Taco Shells (page 232). Transfer each to a paper towel-lined baking sheet and keep warm. Repeat with other tortillas, beginning with flattening the masa into a tortilla. To serve, spoon about 2 tablespoons of picadillo into a taco shell. Add toppings as desired.

Yield: 14 to 16 tacos

Monica Burdette
The Inn at El Canelo
Raymondville, Texas

Espinaca Tacos
SPINACH TACOS

"Espinaca Tacos" is a recipe that I concocted in a moment of desperation. I was entertaining friends in Caracas, Venezuela one Sunday and they were having such a great time that they stayed and stayed and stayed! I noticed that my happy friends were getting hungry, and I was in a spot as a hostess. I decided to give the Venezuelans a treat, tortillas. Tortillas are unknown in Venezuela where they use corn for their famous "Arepas". Needless to say, my friends were delighted with the strange but tasty food. I served the tacos with refried beans on the side.

2 tablespoons vegetable oil
1 small onion, chopped
½ medium bell pepper, chopped
salt and pepper to taste
1 large ripe tomato, chopped
1-2 fresh serrano chili peppers, chopped (optional)

pinch of ground cumin
1 (14-ounce) can spinach, drained, or 1 pound fresh, chopped
6 eggs, beaten
12 white corn tortillas

Heat oil in a skillet. Add onion and bell pepper and sauté until onion is transparent. Add salt, pepper, and next 3 ingredients. Reduce heat and simmer 3 to 5 minutes. If tomato is not juicy and sauce seems dry, add 1 tablespoon tomato juice. Add spinach and cook and stir 3 minutes if canned, 6 minutes if fresh. Fold in egg and cook until set. Heat tortillas and fill with spinach mixture.

Yield: 4 to 6 servings

Ana Bergh

TACOS CHULETA AL TOCINO HOLANDES
HOLLAND TACOS WITH PORK AND BACON

Ramon says he calls these "Holland Tacos" because of the mozzarella cheese - not because tacos have migrated to Holland!

1 pound pork tenderloin, diced
5-6 slices bacon, diced
½ medium onion, chopped

1 cup grated mozzarella cheese
12 corn or flour tortillas

Sauté pork and bacon over medium heat until pork is done medium well. Add onion and cook until transparent. Sprinkle cheese over meat mixture and cover 3 minutes or until cheese melts. Spoon mixture into tortillas. Fold tortillas to make tacos. Serve with rice and beans.

Yield: 4 to 6 servings

Ramon Garcia
Maria Bonita Restaurant
McAllen, Texas

ARROZ CON POLLO
RICE WITH CHICKEN

olive oil
6 pieces chicken
1 teaspoon salt
1 cup dry long-grain white rice
1 medium onion, chopped
1 large clove garlic, minced

4 canned tomatoes, chopped,
  juice reserved
1 teaspoon ground cumin
4 peppercorns, crushed
¼ bell pepper, chopped
¼ red bell pepper, chopped

Cover bottom of a skillet with oil. Season chicken with salt and sauté in oil until very brown. Drain off excess oil and remove chicken. Add rice to skillet and cook until browned. Add onion and garlic and sauté. Stir in tomatoes and remaining 4 ingredients. Add water to reserved tomato juice to equal 2 cups. Add juice mixture and chicken to skillet and cover. Reduce heat to low and cook 20 minutes or until liquid is absorbed. Do not stir.

Yield: 6 servings

Hilda Lewin

CALABAZA CON POLLO
SQUASH WITH CHICKEN

Calabaza, also called Mexican Squash or tatuma squash, are small- to medium-sized and oval-shaped. Some are larger with a crooked neck. These are very good if you can find them. Zucchini (Italian Squash) is not a good substitute as it becomes too soft and watery.

1 frying chicken, cut into pieces
vegetable oil for frying
1 small onion, chopped
1¼ teaspoons black
  peppercorns
1 heaping teaspoon cumin seed
6 cloves garlic or to taste

2-3 tomatoes, chopped
1 large or 4 small calabaza,
  peeled, seeded, and cubed
2-3 ears corn, kernels removed,
  or 1 (12-ounce) can corn,
  drained
salt to taste

Brown chicken in oil in a large skillet or Dutch oven. Remove chicken and drain most of oil. Add onion to skillet and sauté. Crush peppercorns, cumin, and garlic in a *molcajete* or spice grinder and add to skillet. Add tomato and sauté briefly. Add *calabaza* and cook briefly. Add chicken and corn kernels. Cover and simmer 45 minutes or until chicken is tender.

Yield: 6 to 8 servings

Note: If using canned corn, do not add until chicken is almost done.

Variation: Substitute lean pork for chicken, if desired. The calabaza can also be cooked as above without adding any meat.

Luz Jimenez and Margaret H. McAllen
McAllen Ranch

CARNE GUISADA

Like picadillo, carne guisada can be served as a main dish or as a filling for tacos.

2-3 pounds round steak, cubed
vegetable oil
1 tablespoon all-purpose flour
2 tablespoons chopped bell
    pepper
2 tablespoons chopped onion
2 tablespoons chopped tomato

1-2 cloves garlic, chopped
¼ - ½ teaspoon ground cumin
⅛ teaspoon black pepper
½ cup tomato sauce
½ (14½-ounce) can tomatoes
salt to taste
¼ cup water

Brown steak in a small amount of oil. Sprinkle flour over steak and stir to coat. Add bell pepper and remaining 9 ingredients. Cook 30 to 45 minutes or until meat is done and sauce is thick. For use in tacos, cook sauce longer to further thicken.

Marilyn Putz

PORK CHOPS IN *TOMATILLO* SAUCE

10 tomatillos, husks removed
1 serrano chili pepper
½ medium onion, chopped
3 cloves garlic, minced

1 tablespoon butter or vegetable
    oil
salt and pepper to taste
4-6 thick pork chops

Broil or toast tomatillos and chili pepper on a griddle. Peel tomatillos and pepper, removing any burned spots. Place tomatillos and chili pepper in a blender and puree. Sauté chopped onion and garlic in butter. Add tomatillo mixture, salt, and black pepper. Cook well. Brown pork chops in a skillet, removing excess grease from pan. Place chops in a casserole dish. Pour tomatillo mixture over top. Bake at 350° until chops are well cooked and tender. If desired, cover with foil to prevent drying.

Yield: 4 to 6 servings

Note: Tomatillo sauce is also good for enchiladas.

Margaret H. McAllen
McAllen Ranch

ASADO RANCHERO

This is a "stewy" variation of the "Pork Chops in Tomatillo Sauce".

4 pounds pork, cubed	3 cloves garlic
1 cup chopped onion	¼ teaspoon black pepper
salt to taste	¼ teaspoon ground cumin
1½ pounds tomatillos	1 teaspoon dried oregano

Fry pork until cooked. Add onion and salt and sauté. Boil tomatillos until softened. Drain and place in a blender. Add garlic and remaining 3 ingredients and liquefy. Pour tomatillo liquid over meat mixture and let stand 15 minutes. Return to heat and simmer 15 minutes.

Yield: 8 servings

Amparo Garcia

POZOLE

2 pig's feet, quartered	5 large tomatoes, peeled
2 pounds pork loin	1 tablespoon dry chicken
3 chicken breasts	bouillon
salt to taste	pinch of powdered oregano
1 head plus 2 cloves garlic,	2 (14½-ounce) cans hominy,
divided	drained
1½ onions, divided	

GARNISHES

1 large head lettuce, chopped	ground chili piquin
2 large bunches radishes,	oregano
chopped	10 small limes, halved
3 large onions, finely chopped	

Cook pig's feet, pork loin, and chicken in a large pot or *cazuela* filled with water. Add salt, 1 head garlic, and 1 whole onion. When meat is cooked, remove from broth and shred. Reserve broth and discard garlic and onion. Peel tomatoes and remaining 2 cloves garlic. Slice remaining ½ onion. Combine tomatoes, garlic, and onion in a blender and puree. Heat a greased skillet. Strain tomato sauce into skillet and cook about 10 minutes. Add tomato sauce, shredded meats, bouillon, oregano, and hominy to broth. Cook over low heat until flavors blend. Serve in soup bowls. Place each garnish in a separate serving bowl. Each person can garnish *pozole* as desired.

Yield: 15 to 20 servings

Note: Refrigerate leftover pozole up to 1 day, or freeze.

Mildred Chapa

MENUDO

A very hearty tripe soup which is said to be good for hang-overs!! Menudo is traditionally cooked in an earthenware pot - a very large bean pot can be substituted.

1 (1 to 1½ pound) calf foot, quartered
2 pounds honeycomb tripe, well washed and cut into small squares
1 large onion, chopped
3 cloves garlic
6 peppercorns
2 tablespoons salt or to taste

4 quarts water
3 large chile ancho, toasted
1 large poblano chili pepper, roasted, peeled, seeded, and deveined
canned green chiles, peeled
1½ cups canned hominy, drained
1 scant teaspoon dried oregano

Combine calf foot and next 6 ingredients in a large pot. Bring to a boil. Reduce heat and simmer, uncovered, until the tripe and foot are just tender, but not too soft. Cut chilis, poblano pepper, and green chiles into strips and add to meat mixture while cooking. Remove calf foot from pot and cool. Strip off fleshy parts, coarsely chop, and return to pot. Add hominy. Cook slowly, uncovered, for 2 hours. Season with salt to taste and oregano.

Yield: 7 or 8 servings

Note: Serve in large, deep bowls with hot tortillas and small dishes of chopped onion and serrano chili peppers, wedges of lime, and salsa de tomate verde cruda for each person to help themselves. The flavor of menudo is greatly enhanced with freshly prepared hominy.The menudo should be a bit picante. After all, it is to shake you up a bit after the night before. If it is not hot enough, toast and grind some of the chili seeds and add them to the menudo.

Fran Alger

CABRITO EN SANGRE
KID GOAT IN BLOOD SAUCE

1 young goat, blood reserved
when butchered

shortening for frying

SAUCE

reserved blood
3 cloves garlic
2 bay leaves
2 sprigs thyme
sweet marjoram
salt and pepper
1 sprig mint
2 tablespoons vegetable
shortening

4 cumin seeds
2 whole cloves
½ teaspoon dried oregano
1 sprig sweet marjoram
2 chili pequins, ground, or
Habanero chili peppers to
taste
2 cups reserved broth
dried oregano

Cut goat into small pieces, including the bones. Place goat in a large stock pot and cover with water. Boil meat 1 hour, 30 minutes or until tender. Remove goat, reserving broth. Fry goat in shortening and add the sauce. To make sauce, combine blood and next 4 ingredients in a pan. Add water, season with salt and pepper, and cook. In a separate pan, heat shortening. Remove and crumble cooked blood and add to shortening. Stir in cumin seeds and remaining 5 ingredients. Add sauce to fried goat and let cook slowly until sauce thickens. Serve in bowls sprinkled lightly with oregano.

Celia Arredondo

CABRITO GUISADO
KID GOAT STEW

1 small *cabrito* (kid goat)
1½ tablespoons vegetable oil
2 tablespoons all-purpose flour
1½ teaspoons lemon pepper

½ teaspoon ground cumin
½ teaspoon minced garlic
1 (8-ounce) can tomato sauce
¾ teaspoon salt

Cut meat into bite-size pieces. Brown meat in oil in a saucepan. Add flour and stir until browned. Cook and stir 2 minutes longer. Add lemon pepper and next 3 ingredients. Add water to cover meat. Stir in salt and cover. Simmer 35 to 45 minutes or until tender. Uncover and simmer 5 minutes. Add water as needed to prevent scorching.

Robert dela Garza

MOLLEJAS CON CHAMPIÑONES
SWEETBREADS WITH MUSHROOM SAUCE

1 pound sweetbreads, washed
and drained
salt and pepper
all-purpose flour for dredging
1 stick margarine, divided
½ medium bell pepper, finely
chopped
1 small onion or 4 green onions,
finely chopped

1 clove garlic, finely chopped
3 chili piquins, finely chopped
chopped celery or celery leaves
(optional)
chopped parsley (optional)
2 cups hot water
1 (10¾-ounce) can condensed
cream of mushroom soup

Remove any excess fatty tissue or skin from sweetbreads. Season with salt and pepper and dredge in flour. Melt ½ stick margarine in a skillet. Add sweetbreads and sauté 10 minutes or until thoroughly browned on both sides. Add remaining ½ stick margarine. Scatter bell pepper and next 5 ingredients over sweetbreads. Add hot water and bring to a boil. Reduce heat and cover. Simmer 60 minutes, checking occasionally to be sure sweetbreads are not sticking and that there is enough water. Uncover and cook 30 minutes or until almost all water is gone and sweetbreads are tender. Place soup in a bowl and whip with a fork until smooth. Gradually stir soup into sweetbreads mixture. If too thick, thin with extra hot water. Serve over hot biscuits or in pastry shells.

Yield: 4 to 6 servings

Note: If serving a large group, cut sweetbreads into bite-size pieces before serving.

Variation: Substitute ½ large jalapeño pepper or 1 to 2 serrano peppers, both seeded and finely chopped for the chili piquins, if desired.

Margaret B. Smith

CHORIZO
MEXICAN SAUSAGE

This is a very general recipe, with amounts totally up to the cook! This recipe is definitely for experienced or adventurous cooks. A safer route is to look for "Chorizo Spice Mix" in the Mexican spice section of the grocery store.

5 pounds ground pork   **black peppercorns**
salt   **cumin seed**
1 cup vinegar   **sage**
oregano   **bay leaves**
garlic   **chili powder**

Combine all ingredients.

Yield: 5 pounds sausage

Note: Use in Breakfast Tacos (page 236) or Queso Flameado (page 229).

Freezes extremely well. Divide into freezer storage bags.

Fedora Guerra

TAMALES A LAS MACALENAS

Tamale making is an ancient Mexican and South Texas ritual. To learn to make the perfect tamale is a right of passage for any lover of truly indigenous Mexican dishes. As you learn, you can develop your own native variations and special secrets for your own version of this delicious tradition. The process requires at least 2 days, depending on the amount you wish to make. This recipe will produce about 40 dozen tamales, but the recipe can easily be halved. Properly stored and frozen, tamales will last for up to a year. A "tamalada" (tamale-making session) is the perfect occasion for gathering friends and family members, since you really should have at least 3 people for the different tasks involved. During the first stage, you need 1 person to make the meat filling, 1 to make the masa, and 1 to prepare the corn shucks. Later you'll need 1 person to spread masa on the shucks, 1 to spread the filling, and 1 to roll up and fold the tamales. The products of a joint effort such as this are usually shared by the people who shared in the work!

MEAT FILLING

9 pounds lean beef rump roast, trimmed
15 pounds Boston butt pork roast, trimmed and fat rendered
8 pounds venison rump roast, trimmed
30 dried *chili colorado* pods (red "chile ancho"), or to taste

9 heads garlic, peeled
6 tablespoons cumin, crushed
5 tablespoons black peppercorns, ground
5 tablespoons dried oregano (optional)
1 cup lard or rendered fat
masa harina

MASA (DOUGH)

40 pounds prepared ground yellow corn masa (see note)
5 pounds lard or manteca

1 (16-ounce) package chili powder, or "chile ancho"
3 cups salt

CORN SHUCKS
3 pounds corn shucks

Cut beef, pork, and venison into chunks. Cook beef and pork in 2 separate pans of boiling water until well cooked. Remove beef from pan, reserving broth. Add venison to broth and cook until done. Reserve both broths. Cut all meat into small chunks. Shred meat or put through a meat grinder on a medium coarse setting.

Sort and remove stems from chili pods. Split into halves and remove seeds. Wash thoroughly and allow to soak in hot water for 20 minutes or until softened. Place chili pods and a small amount of soaking liquid in a blender and puree. Strain puree. Puree garlic in same blender. Add garlic, cumin, peppercorns, and oregano to chili puree. Melt lard in a large saucepan over medium high heat. Add pureed mixture. Cook and stir well. Allow to cool 30 minutes. Thicken with masa harina or flour. Stir until smooth. Sauce should be the consistency of spaghetti sauce. Adjust spices as desired. Combine ground meats in a large tub or mixing bowl. Add sauce and blend until completely saturated. Refrigerate overnight, or continue.

To make masa, place prepared masa in a large tub or bowl. Add lard and knead with hands or a paddle. Add chili powder (or use leftover chile ancho used in meat) and salt. If desired, add enough water to loosen masa. Continue to knead until well blended and smooth.

To prepare shucks, clean to remove dirt and silks and then soak shucks in a large pan or sink. Select shucks by color, strength, and size. A perfect shuck is about 6 inches wide and 8 inches long. Small brown patches are acceptable, but trim off large rips or major imperfections. Shucks that are about 9 to 12 inches wide should be split vertically in 2. Shucks between 6 to 9 inches should be trimmed down for only 1. Separate shucks chosen for use and place into a second bath until needed. Reserve all unused shucks and trimmed pieces for use in steaming process.

To assemble, set up work table to accommodate 3 people, 1 to spread masa onto shuck, 1 to fill meat and 1 to roll. Prepare deep pan or pot for steaming tamales and place beside work table. Cover bottom of pan with reserved shuck leaves and pieces.

Place a rack, 1 to 1½ inches high, over shucks in pan. Fill pan with reserved broths or water to just below rack. Roll masa into 2-inch balls. Place a ball on each shuck. Cover with plastic from a storage bag. Spread masa with fingers or the back of a spoon into a 6-inch square at the bottom edge of the shuck, leaving about 1½ inches of bare shuck at the top. Layer meat vertically on masa at right or left edge of shuck. Meat should be layered in a 1-inch wide strip from the bottom edge to the top of masa square. Do not layer meat onto bare shuck. Starting with the meat edge, roll shuck around meat. If bare shuck edge is ragged or discolored, trim neatly with scissors. Fold remaining inch of bare shuck flap over to cover seam of the edge of the roll. Place, seam-side down, on rack in pan. Arrange tamales in rows to fill first layer in pan. For the second layer, place perpendicularly to tamales on layer below, to create a layer going 1 way, the next going another. Repeat until tamales are within 2 inches of rim. Cover with a lightweight, wet cotton towel. Cover tightly with a lid and bring to a boil. Steam tamales for 45 minutes or until masa no longer sticks to shuck when unrolled. Add broth or water to keep from boiling dry.

Yield: about 40 dozen tamales, 2 to 3 tamales per serving

Note: Use beef, pork, and venison as called for, or any combination thereof.

Prepared masa can be purchased at a tortilla factory. If desired, prepare your own masa from a mix. (See directions on bag of Masa Harina.)

To store, cool tamales in refrigerator and then seal in freezer storage bags, 12 per bag. Freeze up to 1 year. Reheat by steaming for 15 minutes. If desired, assemble tamales and freeze without cooking. When ready to serve, cook as above.

The perfect tamales have a good proportion of meat and masa and the masa will separate from the surrounding shuck with ease.

Luz Jimenez and Margaret H. McAllen
McAllen Ranch

TAMALES DE ELOTE FRESCO
FRESH CORN TAMALES

Here is another traditional method for a different kind of tamales - much less time-consuming than the previous recipe.

12-14 ears corn, shucks reserved **½ cup lard or vegetable**
2 tablespoons salt **shortening**
3½ cups water, boiling

Remove corn kernels to measure 8 cups. Place kernels in a blender or food processor and grind. Combine corn, salt, and lard. Blend well. Place 2 tablespoons corn mixture on the widest end of the corn shuck, covering three-fourths of the shuck. Roll in jelly-roll fashion. Fold the narrow end of the shuck. Place a mortar or *molcajete* upside-down in the center of a pot. Place some of remaining shucks around the mortar to prevent tamales from scorching. Place tamales, folded-end down, on the shucks. Pour boiling water into pot. Cook 45 to 60 minutes. Add water as needed to prevent scorching.

Yield: 4 to 5 dozen tamales

Gilda dela Garza

MCALLEN RANCH *BARBACOA*

Since Spanish rule in 1745 until the present, it is assumed that the method of preparing Barbacoa (a head of beef) has undergone little change, if any. The following procedure is presently used at the McAllen Ranch when we periodically butcher beef for distribution among our employees.

Preparation of the head: The head is delivered fresh to the cow camp where preparation begins. First, the head is thoroughly washed and rinsed throughout and the horns are removed close to the head as they now serve no purpose.

The Pit (which it is!): An easy pit is constructed by placing a 55-gallon barrel, free of noxious materials, in an upright position below ground level with drain holes at the bottom. This should be sitting on a small bed of gravel. A good metal lid to be placed over the barrel is also essential. This now is your permanent *barbacoa* pit.

The Cooking Container: You will need a large tin can which can usually be purchased at your local hardware store. It should be large enough to hold your cow's head, but it should fit easily into the barrel.

The Cooking Fire: Fill your 55-gallon barrel with mesquite logs which will provide the fire you will use. Light it and allow it to burn down 2 to 3 hours. Now the barrel has about 24 inches of coals. Remove half of these and save to place on the lid. The pit should be close to red hot. Now add about 1¼ to 1½ quarts water to the cooking container, then add the head. Then place the container, with the head enclosed and the lid secured, in the pit. Place the metal barrel lid on top of the barrel and put the remainder of the coals on top of the barrel lid.

Cooking Duration (6 to 7 hours): The traditional *barbacoa* is eaten only in the early hours of the morning. So with this in mind, the head should be laid to rest in the late afternoon and should be removed only when your guests have arrived the following morning. *Barbacoa* has a tendency to cool very fast and no time should be lost between removing it from your pit and enjoying the efforts of your cooking.

James A. McAllen
McAllen Ranch

MOUNTAIN OYSTERS
A SUPERB DELICACY

When your guest exclaims, "This is so good, what is it?", just answer as any slightly untruthful diplomat would do and say "Sweetbreads". If your guest persists in wanting to know more, you will have to explain that the item being served is really "mountain oysters" or "calf fries" and they are often known by other names. They are only available at round-up time on a ranch when calves are branded and ear-marked and the owner and caporal decide that it is time to make steers out of some of the bull calves. These particular bull calves are not considered worth keeping for breeding purposes so they will be fattened and sent to market. During a round-up, the vaqueros (cow-hands) like to toss these oysters onto the mesquite-burning fire that is heating the branding irons. Soon there is a delicious aroma in the corrals and the camp cook is ready with a big pot of hot coffee. The men cannot resist taking a break with a cup of coffee, a fresh tortilla, and an oyster or two. The men will collect quite a few of the oysters to take to the "big house", as the owner's home is always known. Friends of the owner or manager will be eagerly awaiting an invitation to partake of the promised feast of oysters. They were a great favorite with Teddy Roosevelt, Will Rogers, Gary Cooper, and many other notables. If you have a few or a lot of this fine delicacy, there are many ways of preparing them. Experiment and surprise your family with a new dish.

Method 1: Place oysters in a saucepan and cover with boiling water. Add 1 teaspoon vinegar and ½ teaspoon salt. Simmer 15 minutes or until tender. Drain, plunge into cold water, drain again, and remove tough outer covering. Slice oysters lengthwise or crosswise. Sprinkle lightly with paprika and salt. Dust in flour and sauté slowly in butter and olive oil until golden brown on both sides. Add dry white wine or dry sherry to remaining butter and oil and reduce slightly. Spoon wine sauce over oysters. Serve on thin slices of Canadian bacon or ham, or on slices of toast.

Method 2: Skin and wash oysters, split in half, and dredge lightly in flour. Fry gently in butter and olive oil. Add finely chopped shallot and parsley during final 5 minutes of cooking. Add a dash of each of the following: sherry, salt, black pepper, and steak sauce. Thicken with 1 tablespoon cornstarch mixed in cold water. There will not be much gravy, but it will be rich and full of flavor.

Yield: at least 2 oysters per person

Margaret H. McAllen
McAllen Ranch

SOPA DE FIDEO
VERMICELLI

3 tablespoons vegetable oil
1 (5-ounce) package dry *fideo* (vermicelli)
½ cup chopped onion
2 cloves garlic, minced

⅛ teaspoon ground cumin
1½ teaspoons salt
2 large tomatoes
1 bell pepper, finely chopped
3-4 cups chicken broth

Heat oil in a large skillet. Add *fideo* and sauté, stirring occasionally, until golden brown. Add onion and sauté 2 minutes. Remove from heat. In a blender, liquefy garlic and next 3 ingredients. Return skillet to heat. Add liquefied mixture and bell pepper. Simmer 5 minutes. Stir in broth. Cover and simmer 20 minutes or until *fideo* is cooked. Add water, as needed, if sauce gets too dry.

Yield: 4 to 6 servings

Josefina Guerra

ARROZ CON GARBANZOS
MEXICAN RICE WITH CHICKPEAS

3 tablespoons vegetable oil
½ medium onion, finely chopped
½ medium tomato, finely chopped
2 cloves garlic, chopped

⅔ cup dry long-grain white rice
½ cup chopped carrot
1 ⅓ cups chicken broth
1½ tablespoons tomato sauce
1 (16-ounce) can garbanzo beans (chickpeas)

Heat oil in a skillet. Add onion and next 3 ingredients. Sauté until rice is lightly browned. Add carrot, broth, and tomato sauce. Cover and simmer 15 minutes. Remove skin from each garbanzo bean and add to skillet. Simmer 10 minutes.

Yield: 6 servings

Karen Valdez

ARROZ A LA MEXICANA
MEXICAN RICE

Soaking the rice is a little bit of trouble and takes a little time, but both are worth it - it comes out perfectly every time!

1½ cups dry long-grain white rice

6 tablespoons peanut or safflower oil

1 large tomato (about ½ pound), peeled, seeded, and chopped, or ⅔ cup canned

⅓ medium onion

1 clove garlic

3½ cups well-salted chicken broth, or water containing 1½ teaspoons salt

Pour hot water over rice and let stand about 25 minutes. Drain into a sieve and rinse well in cold water. Shake sieve and let drain for a while. Heat oil in a skillet. Stir in rice, making sure grains are well coated. Sauté rice, stirring occasionally, for 10 minutes or until a pale golden color. Drain off excess oil. Puree tomato, onion, and garlic in a blender or food processor. Add to rice and cook on high heat, stirring constantly, for 3 minutes or until almost dry. Stir in broth and then do not stir again until done cooking. Reduce to medium heat and cook, uncovered, for 10 minutes or until most of liquid is absorbed. Cover and cook over low heat for 5 minutes. Remove from heat and let stand, covered, for 30 minutes.

Yield: 10 servings

Note: Prepare ahead, if desired. When ready to serve, reheat at 300° for 40 minutes or until heated through.

Rice freezes very well.

Marilyn Putz

ELOTE DESGRANADO
MEXICAN CART CORN

8 large ears corn, kernels
removed, or 2 (16-ounce)
packages frozen
3 tablespoons butter or
margarine
⅓ cup mayonnaise

1 (12-ounce) package white
Panela cheese, grated
salt to taste
cayenne pepper or chili powder
to taste

Cook corn and drain. Combine corn, butter, and mayonnaise in a saucepan. Fold in cheese and heat until cheese melts. Serve with salt and cayenne pepper or chili powder at the table.

Yield: 6 servings

Karen Valdez

FRIJOLES A LA CHARRA
MEXICAN RANCH BEANS

This is your basic boiled pinto bean recipe. Use leftovers to make refried beans by heating in frying pan, then mashing with a potato masher.

1 (2-pound) bag pinto beans
6 tomatoes, diced
1 (1-pound) package bacon,
diced

1 bunch green onions, diced
1 bunch cilantro, chopped
1-2 jalapeño peppers, chopped
4 teaspoons salt

Inspect beans, discarding rocks and imperfect beans. Rinse beans and place in a pot. Cover with water 2 inches above beans. Bring to boil. Reduce heat and simmer, covered, for 1 hour, 30 minutes. Add water if needed. Add tomato and remaining 5 ingredients. Simmer about 1 hour, 30 minutes.

Uvaldo Olivarez

¡GRACIAS, GRACIAS, GRACIAS!
(THANKS, THANKS, THANKS!)

TESTERS

Sandra Thomas,
Co-Chairman
Jennifer Wright,
Co-Chairman
Maricruz Abbott
Cynthia Alperin
Lettie Arguelles
Susan Barbee
Lynne Beeching
Myles Beeching
Carolyn Bell
Nancy Boultinghouse
Monica Burdette
Lucy Canales
Lynn Carter
Kristi Clark
Todd Clark
Carla Cozad
Celine Cozad
Jane Cozad
Monica Cozad
Joanna Crane
Dalia de la Viña
Gilda de la Garza
Martina Duran
Alice East
Martha Ellison

Julie Flores
Sharon Flores
Amy Frase
Sharon Friedrichs
Tracy Girault
Jane Gordon
Cody Gregg
Susanne Gregg
Rachel Guzman
Gay Hargis
Susie Harkness
Kathy Haynes
Irma Hernandez
Chris Hollister
Colleen Hook
Kathy Hook
Cheryl A. Jones
Kathryn Kaplan
Julie Kittleman
Sara Kuehn
Andrea Lacy
Melissa Lackey
Jennifer La Mantia
Mary Lary
Hilda Lewin
Sharon McGhee
Madelaine McLelland

Norma Miller
Lori Montañez
Page Moore
Jacque Morse
Yvonne Notzen
Sue Peterson
Jennifer Pollett
Noelia Ramirez
Shan Rankin
Nancy Reyes
Donna Rodriguez
Sylvia Ruiz
Beth Sawyer
Mary Cozad-Schach
Sandi Sparrow
Victoria Stephen
Jerry Talbott
Karen Valdez
Billie Vanderveer
Edna Villarreal
Curtis Whatley
Jane Williams
Kita Wreden
Melinda Wright
Enedelia Zuniga
Leslie Yzaguirre

The Hidalgo County Historical Museum wishes to thank everyone who helped this project by contributing recipes, time, ingredients (for testing), and creativity.

Maricruz Abbott
Anne Addington
Gloria Agado
Betty Aguirre
Teresa Alamia
Rosita Alcorn
Fran Alger
Cynthia Alperin
Lettie Arguelles
Anne Armstrong
Celia Arredondo
Mary R. Ashley
Marilyn Atkins
Shirley Bair
Analee Baker
Gillespie Baker
Elizabeth Ballard
Susan Barbee
Anne Barton
Maria Baxter
Lynne Beeching
Myles Beeching
Carolyn Bell
Varner Bell
Doris Bentley
Ana Bergh
Betty Bergh
Skeets Betts
Helene Bleibdry
Nancy Boultinghouse
JoAnne Braun
Linda Browder
Billie P. Brown
Bonnie Brown
Shannon Brown

Dora Brown
James Bull
Monica Burdette
Kathryn S. Cain
Lucy Canales
Chon Cantu
Norma Cardenas
Norma L. Cardona
Faye Carter
Lynn Carter
Sandra Catlett
Mildred Chapa
Patricia G. Chapa
Kristi Clark
Todd Clark
Illa Clement
Peggy Cloninger
Marion Conlin
Doris T. Cook
Lucha Coyula
Carla Cozad
Celine Cozad
Jane Cozad
John Cozad
Monica Cozad
Joanna Crane
Gilda de la Garza
Lucille de la Garza
Rene de la Garza
Robert de la Garza
Sylvia de la Garza
The Honorable Kika
  de la Garza
Dalia de la Viña
Patty O. Dickerson

Doug Dillard
Mark Dizdar
Dora Dovalina
Betty Driscoll
Allen Dreyer
Martina Duran
Debby Dyer
Alice East
Evelyn East
Lupita Echazarreta
Joe Edmonson
Jay Ellison
Martha Ellison
Kathy Escamilla
Mike Fain
First Nat'l. Bank-Edinburg
Cris Flores
Cristina R. Flores
Julie Flores
Sharon Flores
Tom Fort
Paula Fouchek
Oliver Franklin
Amy Frase
Sharon Friedrichs
W. H. Gaines
Kathy Gannaway
Amparo Garcia
Aurora Garcia
Christina M. Garcia
Crystal M. Garcia
Diana Rodriguez de Garcia
Jose Luis Garcia
Jose Refugio Garcia
Lucio Garcia

Ramon Garcia
The Reverend Ernesto L. Garcia
Tracey L. Garrido
Juanita Garza
Becky Gerling
Evelyn K. Gillum
Tracy Girault
Jana Lee Jones Gondran
Gloria Gonzalez
Maria Gonzalez
Bob Goodrich
Jane Gordon
Macaria G. Gorena
Mariella Gorena
Virginia Graham
Cody Gregg
Susanne Gregg
Helen K. Groves
Arcadio Guerra
Carmen (Mrs. Rafael A.) Guerra
Carmen (Mrs. D. V.) Guerra
Enrique "Kiko" Guerra
Evangelina G. Guerra
Fedora Guerra
Josefina Guerra
Judith Fernandez de Guerra
Maria Maldonado de Guerra
Maxine R. Guerra
Melissa McAllen Guerra
Carlota M. Gutierrez
Cecilia Gutierrez
Rachel Guzman

Isabel Haggar
Gay Hargis
Susie Harkness
Lisa Harms
Priscilla Hawkins
Carla Conley Haynes
Catherine Haynes
Kathy Haynes
Irma Hernandez
Shirley Herres
Beverly Hershberger
Debbie Hilton
Maria E. Hinojosa
Ruben Hinojosa
Audrey Hodek
Carl Hoffmeyer
Mara Lessa Holand
Ivy Holzem
Chris Hollister
Colleen Curran Hook
Kathy Hook
Carol Hudsonpillar
Judy Hunt
Phyllis Hutchins
Laura Martinez Ilgun
Luz Jiminez
Eileen Johnson
Cheryl A. Jones
Jackie Jones
Jill Jones
Joan Jones
Mary Vance Jones
Joy Judin
Kathryn Kaplan
Geraldine Kapluck
Lois Keefe
Alice Keller

Elena S. Kenedy
Martha Kirkendall
Julie Kittleman
Mary Kittleman
Coylie Koelle
L. H. Krautkremmer
Ruby de la Garza Krautkremmer
Sara Kuehn
Melissa Lackey
Andrea Lacy
Jennifer LaMantia
Estella Lane
Mary Lary
Irma Valdez-Laurel
Tonii Leadbetter
Hilda Lewin
Carmela Longoria
Juan Luis Longoria
Carol Lynn Looney
Margaret Looney
James Lopez
Nawona Lyssy
Dorothy Martin
Zoila Martinez
Mary E. May
Frances McAllen
James A. McAllen
Margaret McAllen
Margaret Rohde McAllen
Mrs. Robert A. McAllen
Maxine McClendon
Loreita A. McCormick
Sharon McGhee
Madelaine McLelland
Dianne McVeigh
Ana Medina

Aurora V. Medina
Claudia Medina
Mary Lou Medina
Sandra Medina
Mary Lil Melden
Fran Michael
Giovanna Milano
Norma Miller
Caren B. Mims
Marilyn Moffitt
Joan Moldt
Ida Laura Monroe
Lori Montanez
Page Moore
Mary Morris
Jacque Morse
Amelia Murray
David Mycue
Diane Myers
Myra Navarro
Jackie Nirenberger
Vi Norton
Yvonne Notzen
Joyce Obst
William Ogilvie
Uvaldo Olivarez
Lynn Wright Parker
Nada Pell
Ruth Penn
Weneslado Perez
Robb Peterson
Sue Peterson
Billie Pickard
Lica Pinkston
Jennifer Pollett
Margie Haley Pollock
Mary Alice Ponce

Marilyn Putz
Armando Ramirez
Noelia Ramirez
Yolanda Ramirez
Shan Rankin
Susan Rankin
Leslie Stephen Renzie
Nancy Reyes
Rosanna Robalino
Elizabeth McAllen Roberts
Anne Marie Robertson
Chonita Rodriguez
Donna Rodriguez
Sergio Rodriguez
David Ross
Emma Ross
Marcia Ross
Sylvia Ruiz
Martha Russell
Barbara Savage
Beth Sawyer
Mary Cozad-Schach
Norma Schach
Ray Schaleben
Kenneth Schauer
Erren Seale
Blanca Shawn
Diane Shea
Lena Showers
Ellen Sigrist
Margaret B. Smith
Neva Smith
Sandi Sparrow
Mary F. Speier
Ron Speier
Pokey Spence
Sandra Perez Spencer

Carol Campbell Steer
Barbara Steidinger
Leslie Stephen
Victoria Shawn Stephen
Josephine Stone
Mrs. Don Stone
Ann Sumers
Cathy Conley Swofford
Jerry Talbott
Sandra Thomas
Linda Y. Thompson
Benito Treviño
Jesusa Treviño
Toni Treviño
Inez Troppy
JoAnna Vernetti Troppy
Karen Valdez
Valley DocuServ
Billie Vanderveer
Beatrice G. Vela
Tina Villanueva
Edna Villarreal
Jovita Villarreal
Skip Welty
Curtis Whatley
Jane Williams
Sue Wilson
Jennifer Wiltsie
Joyce Wood
Kita Wreden
Jennifer Wright
Mary Jo Wright
Melinda Wright
Bessie Yeary
Leslie Yzaguirre
Katherine Zeigler
Enedelia Zuniga

GRINGO GLOSSARY

AGUA Water.

ALBONDIGA Meatball.

ALCACHOFA Artichoke.

ARROZ Rice.

ASADO Roasted.

ATOLE Porridge.

BARBACOA Cow head cooked in underground pit.

BOTANA Appetizer.

BUÑUELO Thin crispy fried bread, sprinkled with sugar.

CABRITO Young kid goat.

CAJETA Caramel sauce sold in jars.

CALABAZA Squash; in most Mexican cooking, indicates "tatuma" squash.

CAMARON Shrimp.

CARNE SECA Dried meat.

CEVICHE Raw fish marinated in lime juice with hot peppers and spices.

CHALUPAS Fried corn tortilla topped with beans, vegetable garnish.

CHILE PEQUIN Tiny, very hot pepper.

CHORIZO Sausage; in most Mexican cooking, indicates "Mexican" sausage.

CHULETA Chop (usually pork).

CILANTRO Aromatic fresh herb often used in Mexican cooking.

COMAL Cast iron griddle, usually used to cook tortillas.

ELOTE Corn.

EMPANADA Filled pie, can be sweet or savory.

ENCHILADA Corn tortilla rolled and filled with meat or cheese, cooked in a sauce.

ESPINACA Spinach.

FIDEO Vermicelli.

FLAUTA Corn tortilla filled with meat or cheese, rolled very tightly, then fried.

GRAPEFRUIT Valley specialty; include Texas Rio Red, Texas Ruby Red, Pink.

GUISADO Stewed.

HONGOS Mushrooms.

JALAPEÑO PEPPER Very hot medium sized pepper. Can be purchased fresh or canned.

JAVELINA Small game animal, similar in size to a pig. Only small ones are suitable for cooking.

JÍCAMA Root type vegetable. Peel brown skin before eating.

LEMON, VALLEY Valley specialty; larger, less tart than regular lemon

LIME, MEXICAN Smaller, juicier than regular lime. Similar to key lime.

LOMO Loin.

MACHACADO Shredded dried meat. Used as breakfast dish mixed with eggs.

MASA Dough.

MASA HARINA Dry mix used to make corn tortillas.

METATE Flat stone "pan" used to grind corn.

MOLCAJETE Round stone "bowl" used to grind spices. Similar to "mortar and pestle."

MOLINILLO Carved wooden utensil with wooden rings used to make Mexican hot chocolate.

MOLLEJAS Sweetbreads (gland).

MOUNTAIN OYSTERS Whimsical name given to testicles removed from castrated bulls.

NILGAI Large game animal. Type of antelope.

NOPALITO Small, tender pad from prickly pear cactus.

ONION, 1015 Valley specialty; sweet onion.

ONION, TEXAS SPRING SWEET Valley specialty; sweet onion.

PICANTE Spicy; usually a sauce.

PICO DE GALLO Chunky salsa made from tomatoes, onions, peppers, lime juice; usually served with tacos and meats.

PILONCILLO Cone-shaped Mexican brown sugar.

PIÑATA Decorated paper container filled with candy or other goodies. It is suspended, then struck with decorated stick to break open and spill its contents for guests to enjoy.

POLLO Chicken.

PUERCO Pork.

QUESADILLA Corn tortilla filled with cheese, then grilled or fried.

QUESO Cheese.

SALSA Sauce.

SERRANO PEPPER Very hot small to medium sized pepper. Usually purchased fresh; often used in making pico de gallo.

SOPA Soup.

TACOS Corn or flour tortilla folded in half and filled with meat, garnished with fresh vegetables.

TAMALES Cigar-shaped little "pies" filled with spicy meat mixture, cooked in corn shucks.

TOMATILLO Small green vegetables, similar to tomatoes. Discard dry outer husk before cooking.

TORTILLA Thin, round corn or flour bread cooked on a griddle. Looks like a thin pancake.

INDEX

A

O

MESQUITE COUNTRY *Tastes & Traditions* from the *Tip of Texas*

Please send me ____ copy(ies) of **Mesquite Country** at $19.95 plus $3.50 shipping & handling per book. Texas residents please add $1.64 sales tax per book. To open a wholesale account, please contact HCHM at (210) 383-6911.

Also available from HCHM, **The Heritage Sampler** by Margaret McAllen, a collection of anecdotes and vignettes about Rio Grande Valley history. Please send me ____ copy(ies) of **The Heritage Sampler** at $13.95 plus $3.50 shipping & handling per book. Texas residents please add $1.15 sales tax per book.

☐ Visa ☐ MasterCard Exp. Date _____

Card number _____

Signature _____

NAME _____

ADDRESS _____

CITY _____ STATE _____ ZIP CODE _____

Please make checks payable to the Hidalgo County Historical Museum,
121 East McIntyre, Edinburg, TX 78539.
Proceeds from the sale of this cookbook will benefit HCHM.

- -

MESQUITE COUNTRY *Tastes & Traditions* from the *Tip of Texas*

Please send me ____ copy(ies) of **Mesquite Country** at $19.95 plus $3.50 shipping & handling per book. Texas residents please add $1.64 sales tax per book. To open a wholesale account, please contact HCHM at (210) 383-6911.

Also available from HCHM, **The Heritage Sampler** by Margaret McAllen, a collection of anecdotes and vignettes about Rio Grande Valley history. Please send me ____ copy(ies) of **The Heritage Sampler** at $13.95 plus $3.50 shipping & handling per book. Texas residents please add $1.15 sales tax per book.

☐ Visa ☐ MasterCard Exp. Date _____

Card number _____

Signature _____

NAME _____

ADDRESS _____

CITY _____ STATE _____ ZIP CODE _____

Please make checks payable to the Hidalgo County Historical Museum,
121 East McIntyre, Edinburg, TX 78539.
Proceeds from the sale of this cookbook will benefit HCHM.